GOOD FOOD
FOOD

GREAT
BUSINESS

HOW TO TAKE YOUR
ARTISAN
FOOD IDEA
FROM CONCEPT TO
MARKETPLACE

susie wyshak

CHRONICLE BOOKS
SAN FRANCISCO

Library of Congress Cataloging-in-Publication
Data available.
ISBN 978-1-4521-0708-0

Manufactured in China

Designed by Sara Schneider
Typesetting by DC Typography, Inc.

10 9 8 7 6 5 4 3 2 1

Chronicle Books LLC
680 Second Street
San Francisco, California 94107
www.chroniclebooks.com

contents

Introduction 11

STEP

1

BONE UP ON THE SPECIALTY FOOD BUSINESS   13

CHAPTER

1

Learn About the Food Industry 14

BURNING QUESTION: *Am I Ready for Entrepreneurship?* 14
About the *Good* in Good Food 14
12 Good Reasons to Start a Food Business 15
3 Reasons Not to Get into Food 18
5 Perils and Paradoxes of Specialty Food 19
Learn the "5 Staples" for a Good Food Marketing Mix 20
   *Inside Scoop: BOLA Granola Uses the 5 Staples to Grow
   by Small Batches* 21
   Takeaways 23
Great Business Action Plan 23

CHAPTER

2

Prepare for Greatness 24

BURNING QUESTION: *What if I Only Want to Run a Part-Time
   Business?* 24
The Art of Connecting the Dots 24
Set S.M.A.R.T. Goals 25
Prioritize Your Goals 27
Investigate Your Options 27
Make Good Decisions 30
Take Action to Connect the Dots 31
   Inside Scoop: Mama Baretta Reaches Out for Success 32
Mind Your Mind, Squash Your Fears 33
   *Inside Scoop: Punk Rawk Labs Connects the Dots
   for Success* 34
   Takeaways 35
Great Business Action Plan 36

STEP

COOK UP YOUR BUSINESS IDEA   37

CHAPTER

Create Your Mission, Realize Your Vision 38

BURNING QUESTION: *Must My Food Really Serve a Lofty Goal?*
(It's Just Food!) 38
State Your Mission: Why Are You Doing This? 38
Compare and Contrast: Transforming Business Ideas into
   Dream Lifestyles 40
Learn the ABCs of How You Can Make Food 41
   Inside Scoop: Tessemae's All Natural Becomes an
   Accidental Manufacturer 45
Write Your Vision Statement: Where Do You Want to Go
   with This? 46
   Inside Scoop: Askinosie Chocolate, Stone-Buhr Flour, and
   Lotus Foods Draw Inspiration from What's Right in
   Front of Them 49
Outline Your Guiding Principles: Your Rules of the Road 50
   Takeaways 51
Great Business Action Plan 52

CHAPTER

Find Your Niche 53

BURNING QUESTION: *Do I Really Need a Business Plan*
   Before I Start? 53
3 Little Big Questions: Who, What, How? 53
Picture Your Customers 53
How to Fulfill Your Customers' Deepest Needs 57
There's a Business for Every Customer Need 58
Discover Your Competition 59
Plot Your Company and Product Strategies 60
   Inside Scoop: Justin's Nut Butter Connects the Dots
   Between Craving and Business 63
   Inside Scoop: Ocho Candy Grows on Four Key Pillars 68
Prove Your Idea: Your Tasting-Party Shoot-Out 70
   Takeaways 71
Great Business Action Plan 72

CHAPTER

Brand Your Business 73

BURNING QUESTION: *I've Got a Computer. Can I DIY My Brand?* ... 73
What Branding Is and Why It's Important 73
Inside Scoop: Droga Confections Brands Strategically for
Great Food Gifts 74
Draft a Branding Strategy 75
Name and Tagline Your Company and Products 77
Write Your Authentic Story 81
Takeaways 83
Great Business Action Plan 84

STEP

MAKE YOUR FOOD PRODUCTS REAL   85

CHAPTER

Package Your Product 86

BURNING QUESTION: *When Do I Start Working on Packaging?* 86
The Point of Packaging 86
Inside Scoop: Sweet Revolution Makes a Big Impact with
a Small Footprint 87
Define Your Packaging Elements 88
Inside Scoop: Poco Dolce Packs for the Occasion 91
Balance Packaging Sustainability and Function 91
Plan and Write Your Packaging Information 93
Test Your Packaging 97
Produce Your Packaging 98
Takeaways 100
Great Business Action Plan 101

CHAPTER

⑦

Find the Best Ingredients 102

BURNING QUESTION: *When Do I Finalize My Ingredient*
Sources? 102
The Goals: Traceability, Trust, and Transparency 102
Identify Product Certifications That Support Your Promise 104
How to Source Good Ingredients 106
Takeaways 110
Great Business Action Plan 111

CHAPTER

Get into Production 112

BURNING QUESTION: *Where Is the Best Place to Start My
Food Business?* 112
Things All Food Entrepreneurs Go Through 112
   *Inside Scoop: Neo Cocoa Envisions Local Chocolaty
Goodness* 115
Choose Your Production Method and Reality Check the Plan 116
   Inside Scoop: Rustic Bakery Evolves Organically 119
   *Inside Scoop: Peas of Mind Realizes Its Vision for
Healthful Kids' Meals* 122
Test Your Products 129
Analyze Nutrient Profiles and Shelf Stability 130
   Takeaways 131
Great Business Action Plan 132

STEP

GET YOUR FOOD PRODUCTS TO MARKET   133

CHAPTER

Where Will You Sell? 134

BURNING QUESTION: *Do I Really Need to Sell in Stores?* 134
Plot Your Sales and Distribution Phases 134
   *Inside Scoop: Maitelates Alfajores Mixes the Perfect
Cookie Business* 135
Phase 1: Selling Direct—Higher Profits, Closer Connections 135
   *Inside Scoop: Terra Verde Farms Builds a Business
Around a Lifestyle* 141
Pick Your Places: Distribution Options at a Glance 141
Phase 2: Selling Wholesale—Higher Volume, Lower Profits,
Greater Impact 142
   Inside Scoop: Lusty Monk Spreads Itself 146
   *Inside Scoop: Red Boat Fish Sauce Targets Several
Channels for Sales Success* 150
Phase 3: Going International—Massive Reach and Volume 156
   Takeaways 159
Great Business Action Plan 159

CHAPTER

10

Price Your Products 160

BURNING QUESTION: *Can't I Just Make Up Good Prices?* 160

Don Your Pointy-Headed Accounting Hat 160

How to Project Sales Without Any Sales History 160

Determine How Much You Can Charge 161

A Few More Pricing Tips and Costing Tricks 167

Takeaways 168

Great Business Action Plan 168

CHAPTER

11

Promote Your Products 169

BURNING QUESTION: *How Do I Get the Buzz Started?* 169

Understand Marketing: Learn Your AIDAEs 169

Plan Your Marketing Strategy 170

Phase 1: Get Online—Plan. Shoot. Build 172

Inside Scoop: Back to the Roots Sprouts DIY Success 180

Phase 2: Launch and Ride the Word-of-Mouth Wave 181

Phase 3: Keep the Buzz Alive with Promotions and Marketing
Support 185

*Inside Scoop: Amella Caramels Remixes for Marketing
Success* 187

Takeaways 190

Great Business Action Plan 191

STEP

5

MAKE IT REAL! 192

CHAPTER

12

Now You're Cookin': Sell and Engage Post-Launch 193

BURNING QUESTION: *What Is "Engagement" Anyway?* 193

Cultivate a Service Culture 193

Your Number-One Selling Tool: Samples 194

Master Order Fulfillment 197

Sell Wholesale and Get Repeat Orders 198

Meet Wholesale Buyers at Trade Shows 200

Win Awards 202

Manage Your Time and Measure Your Results 203

Takeaways 204

Great Business Action Plan 205

CHAPTER

Set Up Your Business 206

BURNING QUESTION: *How Much Money Do I Need?* 206

Understand the Importance of Structure 206

Set Up Your Back-Office Systems 206

Build Your Support System: Commune, Contract, and Hire 209

    Inside Scoop: Rooibee Red Tea Builds on Connections 218

Decide on Your Business Structure 219

    Inside Scoop: Runa Guayusa Organizes to

    Maximize Good 221

Fund Your Food Company 222

    Inside Scoop: SchoolHouse Kitchen Learns the Hard Way

    about Structuring a Business 228

    Takeaways 229

Great Business Action Plan 230

CHAPTER

So You Really Want to Start a Food Business? 231

BURNING QUESTION: *Is It That Complicated?* 231

From Pie in the Sky to Reality 231

    Inside Scoop: Squarebar Charts a Good Food Business

    Playbook 232

Sketch Out Your Business Plan 234

Rethinking? Re-Imagine the Idea of Good Food 237

Time to Connect the Dots 239

    Food Business Glossary 240

    10 Easy First Steps and Further Reading 245

    Acknowledgments and Many Thanks 248

    Index 251

    About the Author 256

INTRODUCTION

On January 2, 2011, I marched into Foodzie's San Francisco office, declaring "I want to write a book about how to start a food business." (It wasn't like a home-invasion kind of thing; I was the food scout for this online artisan-food marketplace.) Along with snow flurries that December, a storm of bacon jam and maple caramels and cheese-cakes in jars had descended on epicurious foodies around the country. National magazines had brought more visibility to some of the unique specialty food products we'd been selling on Foodzie, and during the busy holiday season, the nuances of food production, packaging, shipping, and assuaging distraught customers became real-time, make-or-break lessons in do's and don'ts.

For months, small artisan food crafters around the country had confided their challenges to me. Stories of success and misadventures jammed up in my brain like candy on an unattended production line. I wondered why running a food-product business was just so confusing, and decided to seek the answer firsthand. It was finally time to develop my own food products—something I'd talked myself out of since the '80s (yes, I'm old) when I first bought Stephen Hall's *From Kitchen to Market*. Within months after diving into business as The Nutless Pro-fessor, the clouds parted, and it all became so clear: For every rule in the playbook, there was an exception. This was why—despite tapping into incubator programs, books, seminars, and consultants—many food entrepreneurs had no choice but to learn from those in the trenches.

I dropped my own business plans to ponder how I could get these hard-knock lessons into the hands of future entrepreneurs. Sometimes your dreams need to simmer until the time is right. And after some serious synchronicity, the time came, and the book was under way.

WHAT CAN THIS BOOK DO FOR YOU?

My quest is to share ideas and tips for starting and running a great specialty food business that I got from actual businesses, from the masters to tiny artisans, who took the plunge and learned the hard way. To make this happen, I canvassed the country and interviewed business owners for insights. This book collects the business wisdom from more than seventy-five food industry experts, specialty food buyers, and entrepreneurs (listed on page 248) with an inside look at their successes, struggles, and strategies—so you can learn the easy way (or easier, anyway). Reading these pages, you will:

- Learn personal habits and business fundamentals that will help you in every walk of life.

- Learn how to choose the business idea or ideas that best fit you and your personality.

- Learn how to determine the viability of those ideas.

- Learn the concrete steps you need to take to make your business a reality.

In each chapter, **Inside Scoops** share food business stories from seasoned and well-funded companies as well as scrappy and small start-ups. In addition, **Good Ideas** spark creative thinking, while **Take 5s** offer five quick tips about a particular topic.

At the end of every chapter, **Takeaways** summarize what you've learned, and a **Great Business Action Plan** gives you a checklist of things to think about and do to make progress. By the time you've digested this book, you'll be a master in what I call "connecting the dots," with a knack for piecing answers together to get what you want. You'll very likely have refined your business and product ideas. Then, in the last chapter, it's time to put your business plan together, step by step, for a real shot at success. Or, after crunching the numbers and reflecting on the realities, you may decide that getting into the food business isn't for you. Either way, you'll have learned how to fearlessly pursue your dreams—and that's a recipe for a great life.

Speaking of life, what of that Nutless Professor? In 2013, the California Homemade Food Act went into law, and I once again began dabbling, at least for my local fan base, with selling snacks made in my home kitchen. The rest is TBD, although I'm pretty sure that after decades of resisting, my calling is more supporter and writer than crafter. And now, on to discovering your calling. . . .

STEP
1

BONE UP ON THE SPECIALTY FOOD BUSINESS

LEARN ABOUT THE FOOD INDUSTRY

BURNING QUESTION: AM I READY FOR ENTREPRENEURSHIP?

Are you hunkered down at your job, clandestinely reading, champing to start your own thing? You're not alone. The majority of food entrepreneurs seem to be career changers from nonfood industries, driven to start their own ventures and often with the nest eggs to fund them. So much of taking the plunge revolves around over-coming fear: fear of the unknown, of making the wrong decisions, of giving up security. While your fears can melt away with smart planning and decision-making, entrepreneurship isn't for everyone. Read on and track your reactions so you can answer this very important question for yourself.

ABOUT THE *GOOD* IN GOOD FOOD

What exactly does *Good Food* mean? A quick Google search on the phrase turns up events, organizations, consultants, products, grocery stores, and the ever-so-useful Good Food Jobs site. It's a bona fide buzz phrase, but for a good reason. We're a world on the brink of bad food threatening our collective future. Overly processed ingredients and pesticide-laden produce abound. By recent counts, 90 percent of our corn is genetically modified. The people out there making Good Food are fighting that tide, and changing the world for the better in the process.

When you think about what food might deserve the lofty title of Good Food, consider these three qualities the Good Food Awards identified after much deliberation:

- TASTY: the product is delicious, and it makes those who eat it happy.

- AUTHENTIC: the product contains high-quality ingredients, including local and seasonal goods, and nothing artificial (including no genetically modified organisms [GMOs] or synthetic pesti-cides); ideally, the company embraces cultural traditions.

- RESPONSIBLE: when making the product, the company considers the well-being of its workers, its consumers, and the planet. Trust, traceable ingredients, and transparency into how the company does business are paramount.

What makes Good Food different from so-called "specialty foods," the prettily packaged foods you find in fancy gourmet shops? Specialty products have their own trade group, the Specialty Food Association, which puts on the twice-yearly Fancy Food Show, North America's largest specialty food trade show. The association identifies specialty products as having:

- quality, innovation, and style in their category

- originality and authenticity

- a commitment to specific processing rules or traditions, superior ingredients, limited supply, or extraordinary packaging

While specialty foods may not fall under the Good Food definition, due to their ingredients or sourcing practices, many Good Food products are also specialty products, thanks to artful crafting and amazing package design.

On to the elephant in the room: Are food products "bad" if they use genetically modified (GMO) corn or conventionally grown produce? Not necessarily, says your candy-corn-eating author. Yet there's no arguing that natural is more likely healthier for our bodies and planet. Small food producers across the country are banding together with this in mind, fighting for more transparency and positive change in our food supply. The hope is that, with greater demand, clean ingredients will become more readily available, and staples such as organic butter and non-GMO corn syrup will become more affordable.

12 GOOD REASONS TO START A FOOD BUSINESS

The rewards of your own business are fulfilling in themselves. The joy of feeding people only multiplies that fulfillment. Every business starts with a motivation. As you read about other food entrepreneurs' motivations, ponder what your own might be:

1 **Share a Family Recipe.** Food deeply reflects culture, which may be why "an old family recipe" is behind so many businesses. Lauryn Chun decided to bottle kimchi, using the recipe from her mom's Southern

California restaurant, Jang Mo Gip (which means "mother-in-law's house" in Korean). She got licensed, created her brand, and started selling at a small market in Manhattan. After mastering shipping—no small feat for fermented food in glass bottles—Lauryn set up a website and joined some online marketplaces, and soon Mother-in-Law's Kimchi was gracing the pages of *O, The Oprah Magazine* on the cusp of the fermented-foods trend.

2 **Spark the Local Economy.** Bob and Lora La Mar needed a new vocation after a government ban of sportfishing went into effect, making their former business obsolete. They taught themselves to make sea salt and slowly grew a business turning Northern California seawater into finishing salts. Their big-picture goal for Mendocino Sea Salt & Seasoning was to help make California's Mendocino County an agri-tourism destination and create much-needed jobs. (In late 2012, a family matter led the La Mars to, at least temporarily, cease operations and turn their attention elsewhere. Their path exemplifies the types of choices and changes you very well may face as an entrepreneur.)

3 **Work at Home.** "Cottage food" or "homesteading" laws allow the use of a home kitchen for small food businesses in many states (for more, see "Good Idea: Start as a Home-Based Business," page 41). Lisa Cierello channeled her desire to be a work-at-home parent into Lisa's Cookie Shop in Warwick, New York, transforming her detached garage into a commercial kitchen. Not only can Lisa stay at home to take care of her daughter, but she can also earn a decent living selling to local shops and online nationwide. Plus, her house smells like cookies all the time!

4 **Connect with Community.** Many entrepreneurs describe the overflowing joy they feel as customers enjoy their food. Selling food from mobile carts, at farmers' markets, and directly to retailers all provide this in-person connection. At P.O.P. Candy in Santa Monica, California, Bill Waiste works full time cooking up candy, while his wife, Rachel Flores, helps out nights and weekends—in addition to working full time. Farmers' market customers and collaborations with other producers (such as a granola maker) fulfill the couple emotionally and financially.

5 **Innovate Packaging for Good Eating.** In the past, travelers lived on preserved and dried foods such as salt cod, flat breads, and beef jerky. Now, canned, frozen, and aseptically packaged innovations such as juice boxes solve our modern-convenience desires. Small changes in the way a food is packaged can create major markets. Peeled Snacks re-imagined dried fruit—a 10,000-year-old category—into a healthful snack with bright, kid-friendly portable packs and singsongy names. Cyrilla Suwarsa and her sister work directly with small Indonesian cashew farmers to make and package their flavored Nuts Plus Nuts in metallic pouches swanky enough for upscale hotel minibars.

6. **Create a Market for Small Farmers.** From domestic produce and meats to fairly traded coffee and cacao beans, each food start-up that sources responsibly from small producers makes a positive difference. Both Gelateria Naia, maker of gelato on a stick, and St. George Spirits, famed for its fruit-based spirits, name the small family farms supplying their fruit. The artisans at Grace & I transform local fruits into gorgeous fruit-and-nut loaves, a simple and giftable concept.

7. **Preserve a Tradition.** Even before the Slow Food movement brought local foods and recipes to the forefront, many food companies shaped themselves around regional food traditions. The rarer an item, the more it attracts interest from foodies and the press. A quest to revitalize a dying food tradition infuses even more meaning into your work. Red Boat Fish Sauce created a market in the United States for a high-grade, centuries-old Vietnamese ingredient (see "Inside Scoop: Red Boat Fish Sauce Targets Several Channels for Sales Success," page 150). The story of Saratoga Sweets shows how revitalizing a holiday tradition can pay off. The company revitalized the Victorian "peppermint pig," a hot-pink mint candy (no, not a natural food) you smash with a mallet. Little did this candy shop expect it would eventually churn out hundreds of thousands of crunchy pigs annually.

8. **Cater to Restricted Diets.** Kosher, gluten-free, and nut-free foods are all growing categories with an increasing demand from consumers. And they are now sold in mainstream stores. Divvies, located outside New York City, carved out its niche by catering to kids with allergies, making treats that are free of eggs, nuts, and dairy products. Similarly, Attune Foods' business plan was to grow its probiotic bar business while broadening its brand into other digestive-health solutions, which led it to successfully acquire several established, healthful cereal brands.

9. **Re-create a Popular Food in a "Better for You" Way.** Free-range, "minimally processed" beef jerky capitalizes on the desire for familiar tastes without the bad-food factor. Did you know that Snickers is the best-selling candy in the United States? Perhaps that explains why Ocho

Candy, Justin's Nut Butter, and Brooklyn artisans Liddabit Sweets found similar success with their own twists on a peanut-caramel-nougat bar.

10 **Make a Fulfilling Living.** Pati Grady connected the dots between her desire to start a cookie company and the profit potential inspired by her hometown's claim to fame: baseball. In October 2004, The Cooperstown Cookie Company launched its baseball-shaped shortbread cookies at the World Series Gala. Pati then licensed the use of Major League Baseball team names to sell customized cookie packs at stadiums.

11 **Fill a Local Hunger.** Beyond the foodie gulches, many places need better food options. Good People Popcorn emerged for the love and want of great, locally made popcorn. Two sisters and a cousin started this thriving Detroit business with a vision of making Good Food using sugar and butter produced in Michigan. They sell in local retail stores and at their charming shop.

12 **Simply Because You've Always Wanted to Start a Food Business.** You've saved up a bunch of cash. You could buy a car, go back to school, or travel the world for a year. Or you could use some of that nest egg to school yourself and develop a line of Good Food products (which, incidentally, will likely take you on travels and lead you to buy an oh-so-practical car for deliveries).

3 REASONS NOT TO GET INTO FOOD

Let's get the tough love over with. The food business is difficult. Many food artisans I worked with at Foodzie (including some interviewed for this book) have shuttered their businesses, some because they burned out, some because they simply couldn't make a living. (Meanwhile, Foodzie got acquired and is now a fond memory.) Take a good look at a few reasons *not* to start a food business:

1 **Everyone Says You Should.** Your own passion and determination need to drive your foray into entrepreneurship . . . even if it's just a part-time business. Everyone might be saying you should sell your (insert your food product here), but do *you* want to? Will they pay for those killer brownies you now give out at no charge?

2 **You Want to Work Less.** Depending on your product, sixty- to eighty-hour weeks are not uncommon when launching a food business. Justin

Gold labored for five years, working lots of part-time jobs to pay the bills, before Justin's Nut Butter finally hit its stride. The only way you'll work less than that is if you're just dabbling in entrepreneurship and don't necessarily need to live off the business (or make a profit). Or if you're currently working 90 hours a week.

③ You Think You Can Get Rich Quick: You can set up an online store and start selling your food in days. Making a living is another proposition. Many of the food companies on *Inc. Magazine*'s "Top 500: The Top Fastest Growing Companies" list got started 10 or more years earlier. The simpler and more mainstream your idea, the easier it is to get sales rolling and profit—although you'll also have more competition. Vosges Haut-Chocolat sold about $25 million of chocolate in 2012, an impressive bite out of that year's $2 billion-plus premium U.S. chocolate market. Drooling over these numbers (or the idea of chocolate)? Well, remember that sales numbers do not reflect profitability or how much the owner is taking home.

5 PERILS AND PARADOXES OF SPECIALTY FOOD

Running a food business is a lot more complicated than selling an iPhone app or knitted hats. Consider this perspective from Liz Gutman, after she and Jen King had run Liddabit Sweets for a couple of years: "We joke that it's hard for us not to tell advice seekers 'Just don't do it!' You can read all the books you want, take courses, write a plan, and be super-prepared, but there's absolutely nothing you can do to really prepare for running a small business."

Part of what the Liddabit gals are referring to are a few issues that confront many food entrepreneurs:

① High Production Costs. In the early days of your business, you may have just a few customers, each buying small quantities of your product. Lower purchase volumes mean higher packaging, ingredient, and transportation costs, all of which may add up to an end product that is too expensive to make and ship.

This may lead to:

② Responsible Spender's Dilemma. You've spent your life savings building your business, and now you find yourself unable to get outside funding to continue.

If you do manage to procure funding, you may run into:

3 **The Artisan's Dilemma.** You're so dedicated to making a great product yourself that you have no time to sell it.

If you do find the time to both make and sell your product, look out for:

4 **Pricing Problems.** Once you're successful and need to sell your product through distributors or at wholesale, it's easy to lose money if you don't price properly.

And finally, if you are able to maintain your cash flow while working with distributors, the following may occur:

5 **The Scarcity Paradox.** As your brand becomes better known and your distribution increases, the small independent stores that supported you at the beginning may not be able to carry your product anymore—they need exclusive products to attract shoppers.

Keep reading to increase your chance of avoiding these oh-so-common pitfalls.

LEARN THE "5 STAPLES" FOR A GOOD FOOD MARKETING MIX

What's a pantry without a few essential cooking staples? (Mine are flour, sugar, butter, and chocolate.) With the right staples, you can create dozens of recipes with minor proportion changes, cooking methods, or tiny temperature tweaks. The same goes for businesses. Every Good Food business blends what I call the "5 Staples," and knowing them will help you overcome the five perils and paradoxes you just read about.

In 1960, professor E. Jerome McCarthy proposed the first four staples—what he called "the 4 Ps"—as the key to every company's marketing, no matter the industry. These are product, price, place, and promotion. I have added a fifth P to the mix—***promise***. This P represents the promise of goodness, which underlies all that you do.

Here's an introduction to the 5 Staples and how they relate to one another:

- PRODUCT. Your product(s) must appeal to and delight the people you hope will become your customers.

- PRICE. Your price should be acceptable to the retail customer as well as any partners and distributors who help you reach that customer, and enable you to make a profit.

- PLACE. Your target customers need to be able to find your products in places they like to shop. These places should also sync with your brand, or if they do not, you should have a good reason for selling there. (For example, if you get an offer to sell in a discount clothing store, you will have to weigh the potential revenue against the potential negative effect—also called "pitchfork effect"—on your brand's value.)

- PROMOTION. You need to tell consumers about your product in a way that compels them to buy it, engage with it, and spread the word about it.

- PROMISE. This promise reflects your commitment to creating sustainable good for people involved with your company while caring for the planet throughout your business practices.

Each decision you make about one of the Ps impacts the overall "recipe" of your product. Though this may seem like a complicated concept, consider that as a consumer, you are already familiar with the 5 Staples mix. For example, let's say you hear about a rare truffled sea salt (Product) from a friend. It interests you, so you Google the salt to find out how much it costs (Price) and where it's sold (Place). On the product's website, you read rave reviews and see a photo of the very pig that ferreted out the truffles (Promotion). You also read about the company's commitment to donate part of its profits to help preserve forests in France (Promise). The Product must deliver the value that the Promotion and Promise imply. The Price must be acceptable, and you must be able to find it at an easily accessible Place. No matter the story, the food itself must meet (and ideally exceed) all expectations.

INSIDE SCOOP:
BOLA GRANOLA USES THE 5 STAPLES TO GROW BY SMALL BATCHES

Michele Miller needed to make a living. So in 2008, with no written plan, she combined a recipe she had perfected over decades with a "small is beautiful" ethos to create BOLA Granola. Her vision was to be a premier regional company in the Northeast and to make a granola that would be consumed within weeks of coming out of the oven.

CONTINUE ▶

She got started sharing a space with a local ice cream company. Customers loved the granola, but the conflict between hot ovens and cold ice cream soon became apparent. So Michele located a dedicated 1,400-square-foot room and raised enough financing to install gas lines, plumbing, and a couple of ovens. Michele's handmade approach is simplicity itself—she doesn't even use a mixer. "It's very low tech," she notes. "The fanciest thing we have is a weigh-and-fill machine" for packing bags. With her own kitchen, Michele can easily develop new products to add to the mix. See how she blended the 5 Staples into a thriving small business:

- **PRODUCT.** The BOLA team mixes and bakes each 36-pound batch of granola by hand. This process generates almost no crumbs, which Michele sees as a differentiator from machine-mixed granolas. To ensure freshness, she opts to send stores smaller shipments, versus one big one. Smaller shipments mean faster turnover and fresher granola.

- **PRICE.** Ingredients are 65 percent organic, rather than 100 percent, which keeps the price accessible. Despite BOLA's small size, the price is still lower than some mass-produced national brands. The business is profitable and growing, because customers can afford to eat the granola daily. (Products consumed daily are a recipe for revenue!)

- **PLACE.** BOLA granola was first sold locally at small stores in the Berkshire hills of western Massachusetts, a vacation area. Michele then started selling on her website as well as through Foodzie. Online sales raised her visibility among eaters new to the brand and helped vacationers keep ordering granola once they returned home. Soon, Dean & DeLuca put BOLA in its catalog. "It took off from there," says Michele. She decided to limit distribution to ensure freshness. Early on, Michele had sold at farmers' markets, but she found them difficult to staff. So she put that "place" on the back burner.

- **PROMOTION.** In-store sampling has been key to promoting BOLA Granola. Just about every weekend, Michele takes to the road for demos, during which she asks, "Have you had a BOLA granola today?" That opens the door to chat with customers. An early rave from Epicurious.com's food blog brought the company national visibility, and today Michele uses Facebook to share her excitement about company developments.

- **PROMISE.** Michele values and rewards her employees, acknowledging that without their care and attention, she couldn't do her job. Most have been with Michele since the beginning or are related to someone who worked with her before.

Michele sums it up: "The number-one thing is, I like the way we're doing it. It's a good time to be a small producer."

TAKEAWAYS

- Good Food is a unique blend of food products that are tasty, authentic, and responsible.
- Making food products may require more time, money, and commitment than you can imagine. The rewards and fulfillment you gain can be worth it, however.
- The motivation to start a food business needs to be your own. You shouldn't go into business just because someone else thinks it's a great idea.
- Just like the perfect recipes, a business needs to identify and follow a delicate balance of 5 Staples: product, price, placement, promotion, and a promise that appeal to the target customer.

GREAT BUSINESS ACTION PLAN

☐ Nail down the 5 Staples concept.

☐ Think about your three favorite food brands' mix, including how, why, and when you buy them.

☐ Think about how you might apply the 5 Staples to your own product or products.

ON *GOODFOODGREATBUSINESS.COM*

Learn more about the specialty food industry and find links to useful research resources.

PREPARE FOR GREATNESS

BURNING QUESTION:
WHAT IF I ONLY WANT TO RUN A PART-TIME BUSINESS?

Do it. You'll join the ranks of many who either get their start making small batches of foods or partner with contract manufacturers, called co-packers, to make their food. You might even start as a seasonal business—like crab cakes or a less fruity fruit cake—to test the waters. Just know that half time usually does not mean half the cost or half the sweat.

THE ART OF CONNECTING THE DOTS

Have you ever learned about a certain make and model of car, and then suddenly see it everywhere? Was it there before and you didn't notice, or is it suddenly more popular? Did seeing the car lead you to make or change a decision, or seek out new information? This is what I call "connecting the dots," piecing together life's puzzle, the intersection of goals, knowledge, decisions, actions, and awareness.

Steve Jobs famously said that you can look back and connect the dots to see how things happened. Well, imagine connecting dots forward, to anticipate problems and create opportunities. Perhaps because entrepreneurs feel as if they are following their destiny, unexplainable synchronicity and serendipity often play into the opportunities that direct a company's future. For example, say you really, really want to read this book. And you want to exercise more. Connect those goals to make it work, perhaps exercycling as you read. Or start a book group to read this book, perhaps connecting you with possible partners.

Connecting the dots is similar to the law of attraction, but more tangible and action oriented. The methodology is truly simple, and it can apply to pretty much every area of life:

1 Set S.M.A.R.T. goals to define exactly what it is you want.

2 Investigate your options through detective-style research and talking to people; stay aware as opportunities arise.

(3) Make good decisions by understanding the little and big opportunities that will fulfill your goals. Really "own" your decisions.

(4) Take action to connect the dots by noticing relationships between ideas ("That lime-green car paint would look great for our café walls!"), following up, and again deciding what to pursue in pursuit of your goals.

Make connecting the dots part of your DNA, and I think you'll be surprised with how quickly you get what you want and how good your progress feels. As you connect, synchronicity (those happy accidents and coincidences) will become an everyday occurrence. I know some of you brilliant introverts may be shuddering, "Leave me alone! I just want to craft!" Set that feeling aside for now, and plan to pat yourself on the back with every connection you make.

Now, let's dig in to some dot-connecting practices, which will become more and more familiar as you read how people just like you created their great businesses.

SET S.M.A.R.T. GOALS

When it's time to make your pie-in-the-sky dreams a reality, setting goals will move you forward. While goal setting seems straightforward (after all, we do it daily), we can easily phrase goals in an ineffective way. Vague or overly ambitious goals lead to less than desirable results or no results at all. In 1981, a fellow named George T. Doran came up with a "S.M.A.R.T." goal-setting methodology that's become standard in corporate America and beyond. This technique keeps you on track and accountable, especially when you're being pulled in myriad directions. Oh yes, your goals will change. Or go away. Your timeline will triple. Partners you counted on will disappear. Still, starting with goals is key to focusing your time and energy in the right ways.

S.M.A.R.T. stands for Specific, Measurable, Attainable, Relevant, and Time-bound. Let's illustrate S.M.A.R.T. goal setting with the example of finding a commercial kitchen in which you might want to produce your foods:

> "On Sunday, August 10, I will ask ten farmers' market vendors if they know of a commercial kitchen within five miles of my home that costs less than $20 per hour and includes a commercial Hobart mixer and dry goods storage."

Here's how that goal breaks down:

- SPECIFIC. Exactly what do you want in an ideal commercial kitchen? Where would it be? What features would it have? How much would it cost per month?

- MEASURABLE. "Asking around" for leads on kitchens is not a measurable goal. "Ask 10 people at the farmers' market" is.

- ATTAINABLE. Is your goal doable, or is it unrealistic? For example, finding a rent-free kitchen steps from your home might be ideal, but it's unlikely.

- RELEVANT. Be sure your goal actually contributes to your bigger-picture goals and isn't a distraction. Printing cute aprons with your logo isn't relevant, unless they're part of your brand and customers see you wearing them.

- TIME-BOUND. Set a specific target date for accomplishing each goal. The date might slip by, but picking a deadline will keep you focused and help you prioritize. Set realistic dates; everything does not need to be done "today" (or even worse, "yesterday").

No matter how fly-by-the-seat-of-your-pants you consider yourself, try the S.M.A.R.T. technique. Yes, your goals will change. Yes, everything will take twice as long as you expect. Now that we've got that out of the way, make it a goal to set goals.

When writing your goals, try not to use "don't," "stop," or other negative words. Negatives can subconsciously bring you down. Use positive phrases instead.

Note the negative words (in italics) in the following examples:

- *Stop* working in my *cramped* kitchen by December 31.

- *Get over* my *fear* of public speaking by January 31.

The following goals accomplish the same aim, in much more positive language:

- Find a kitchen at $25/hr or less by December 31 that is large enough to accommodate production of ten thousand products a month and provides refrigerated storage.

- Develop a love of and confidence in public speaking by joining Toastmasters by January 31.

PRIORITIZE YOUR GOALS

Your business is a project, and projects revolve around setting goals, creating tasks to accomplish those goals, and assigning people and due dates to those tasks. If you've remodeled a house, planted a garden, or raised a child, you've had to think about "before Y can happen, X needs to happen." In her book *Wishcraft*, Barbara Sher puts forth the idea of reverse flowcharts, a visual concept to help with your S.M.A.R.T. goal setting. Think in terms of "dependencies." What does each step depend on to get done?

Combine Goals and Set Your Life on Fire

While guiding people through goal setting, I like to "maximize" to accomplish multiple goals at once. If you want to learn Italian and to start a business importing Italian olive oils, a fact-finding trip to Italy is a chance to prep with Italian lessons, meet some producers to understand how olives grow, and master tasting subtle differences between oils. While on the trip, you might come up with branding or other food product ideas, and have that fling that's been on your bucket list so long. Plus, your business trip will likely be tax deductible. Your business isn't putting your personal life on hold. It's making your life happen!

Or, say a friend suggests visiting that new goat-cheese farm. You could look at the invitation as a distraction. Or you might see the farm as the connection between your hunt for new cheeses and your desire to build farm-direct relationships. Oh! Oh! And your chance to learn about licensing, cheesemaking, and funding, and even discover little food shops along the way that could potentially sell your products.

INVESTIGATE YOUR OPTIONS

Starting a business means endless research. Fear not—you're born to research. Have you ever gone shopping for a new car? Hunted for somewhere to live? Used an online dating site or asked friends to find someone for you? You'll use the same techniques to research your food business. "Market research" simply means learning about the market, or people, you might wish to serve. These future customers are called your "target market." Every product you see is targeted to a certain market: craft beer to discerning imbibers, cookie mixes to parents short on time, and flavored bulk olive oils to high-end restaurant chefs.

As with your car shopping or dating research, you'll use two kinds of research techniques. *Primary research* relies on firsthand investigation, such as conducting a survey, chatting with other food manufacturers, talking to shoppers at stores, or speaking with retail staff. Once engaged in conversation with subjects, a limitless font of information may flow. Nudge yourself into making a call rather than sending an e-mail. What's the worst answer you could hear? "Sorry," or "no," or "Let's set up another time"? Introduce yourself by saying, "I have a goal to start a food business, and I would love a bit of your time to learn..." After you've gotten acquainted, put your detective or journalist hat on, and really dig, asking question after question. Be sensitive to the person's responses, respecting their time and choice not to share certain facts. Never share what you learn about someone else's business with others unless you have permission.

Enhance this firsthand investigation by staying aware of what's around you and developing a willingness to connect with strangers. If random people pique your interest for whatever reason, engage them in conversation. Politely say, "I couldn't help but overhear..." or "I noticed that you..." You might end up with valuable new information. Or you might learn nothing, but you'll definitely miss out on some possibilities if you don't engage. Be mindful of body language: If someone keeps turning away, take the hint.

The next type of fact finding is *secondary research*, in which you tap into existing information, such as the stellar State of the Specialty Food Industry report from the Specialty Food Industry or data culled from articles and websites specific to your area of interest. For example, a study from Mintel/Specialty Food Association after the 2008 financial crash revealed a shift to eating at home. This trend explained the high growth of kitchen staples such as dairy (up 108 percent), soup (up 86 percent), savory spreads (up 83 percent), and sauces and seasonings (up 58 percent). Add statistics such as those to the fact that affluent professionals are too busy to cook, and you've got a good case for locally sourced ready-to-eat meals.

A Little Research Can Answer "What Should I Make?"

Portland, Oregon, chef Kris Pennella wanted to get into the specialty food business but wasn't sure what she wanted to make. She began with primary research, visiting local grocery stores to seek out opportunities in the marketplace. Her only guideline was that it be a "gourmet grab-and-go" item that she could make herself (versus hiring someone else to make). She asked the store staff what they thought customers would like to buy. Based on their feedback, Kris settled on the idea of savory tarts with fillings made of local, seasonal ingredients. Little Pots & Pans developed a loyal local following and, in 2012, Kris accepted an offer to buy out her company and recipes.

New York food entrepreneur Jeff Santos, owner of Brazilian Specialty Foods, also had a niche to fill. But rather than serve consumers, he wanted to create a food that high-volume restaurants would use daily. (Note: high volume + daily = dollars!) He hit the streets and, through many conversations, found that *churrascarias* (Brazilian steakhouses) in New York bemoaned not having Brazilian sausages, which were unavailable due to meat-import bans. Jeff decided to fulfill this need. He imported special Brazilian seasoning to New York and began to make the sausages. He first supplied local restaurants. Then he moved on to distribute his products nationwide. Today, the company sells thousands of pounds of sausage weekly. Jeff used no technology. He went out, connected with people, listened, strategized, capitalized on the imported-meat ban, and grew his business.

TAKE 5:
RESEARCH TIPS

Get your research off to a swift start by trying out these tips:

1. Analyze how businesses you admire "did it." Read their press releases. Look for articles. Follow them on social media. Better yet, find their founders' contact information and ask them directly.

2. Listen. Make "good eavesdropping" a practice. Hear what customers ask farmers' market vendors and what customers are saying to one another. Engage in conversations using open-ended questions that don't have "yes" or "no" answers.

3. Ask. It's never too early to get feedback on your idea. Talk to your friends (and strangers) about what you're thinking, ask for introductions, and reach out to old colleagues. Soak it all in with the wide-eyed curiosity of a child. Buddhists call this "beginner's mind." You can sort out the good from bad advice

CONTINUE ▶

---

later, and decide who might be jealous or maybe projecting their fears. (Your secondary research will balance out these opinions too.)

(4) Observe trends, being mindful if your products fall into a trend that's on the downswing. What's featured at the ends of store aisles? What are magazines and blogs featuring and writing about? Tap into local artisan food fairs and online marketplaces to see what's new and what's overdone.

(5) Put your detective hat on when speaking to possible suppliers or partners. Dig for details, asking who, what, why, when, and how with genuine interest. These folks work with lots of companies, so they may have a broad view of what's new, needed, and hot. Piece together the answers and connections.

MAKE GOOD DECISIONS

Once armed with some research, you'll need to begin making thoughtful decisions about your next steps. This will be more difficult than it sounds—your temptation may be to procrastinate, overthink to death, or rely on intuition at the expense of analysis. But as an entrepreneur, you will need to make hundreds, if not thousands, of decisions, so get yourself started on the right foot by instilling these proven decision-making techniques into your DNA:

1 Reduce your options to three, which allows you to focus your time and energy. Having fewer options helps you research more efficiently.

2 Project ahead to envision your desired outcome—and any possible pitfalls. What's the best thing that could happen if you make a certain decision? What's the worst? Be ready for all outcomes.

3 To avoid becoming paralyzed by indecision, accept "good enough." Life and career coach Susan Whipple points out that a decision is rarely purely right or purely wrong. Your vision of "perfection" may be leading you to say no to opportunities that could advance your goals. When presented with an option, ask yourself if it is good enough for today. If it is, move forward.

4 "Fail quickly." This ethos, embodied by the tech world, means that you make small moves based on the information you have. If one or more of those moves don't succeed, you can "pivot" and go in a different direction, because you haven't put all your proverbial eggs in one basket.

(5) Set limits—and enjoy them. Boundaries, such as a time limit for decision-making, help you focus on the end goal. Remember the S.M.A.R.T. goals when making decisions.

(6) After you've made a decision, own it. If things don't turn out the way you'd hoped, practice an "attitude of gratitude" rather than feeling regret. Learn from past decisions as you move forward.

The reverse-flowchart technique you read about earlier can really expedite your decision-making too, as well as choose the paths that minimize dependencies where roadblocks might appear.

Understand the 80-20 Rule
(The Quick Way to Make the Right Decisions)

The Pareto principle, also called the 80-20 rule, holds that life splits everything into an 80-20 ratio. Think about it: Do you interact with 20 percent of the people you know 80 percent of the time? Find that the 20 percent of the most unimportant tasks in your life take up 80 percent of your time (or vice versa)?

For your own business, it is likely that 20 percent of customers and 20 percent of your products will make up 80 percent of your sales. (And you may find yourself wearing 20 percent of your wardrobe 80 percent of the time.) Remember this "80-20 rule" (which some say is often 90-10), and you'll find yourself analyzing your opportunities, sales patterns, and making decisions in a way to strategically allocate your time, energy, and resources. At the same time, keep an eye on future growth potential from the 80 percent of lower-selling products as you expand your target audience or trends evolve.

TAKE ACTION TO CONNECT THE DOTS

As the Zen Buddhist philosophers know, living in the present with awareness and attention can bring magical results—especially when you know your S.M.A.R.T. goals. As you journey through your days, watch and listen for signs. Then leap.

If someone has offered to introduce you to a possible partner, a production space, or a farmer, don't wait days or weeks, or try to craft the perfect e-mail reminder. A two-line e-mail is perfectly OK. Better yet, pick up the phone and converse, no matter how much your finger's twitching to text. Follow up even if a connection does not seem quite related to your interests. As soon as possible.

For example: One morning, I went to a café, as I am wont to do, and decided to sit next to the café's coffee roaster. She mentioned she was going to Louisville, Kentucky. I brought up Bourbon Barrel Foods, which is based there. Realizing I was a foodie, she said, "You really need to meet Bob," a fellow sitting next to me. We started chatting, and Bob told me about Red Boat Fish Sauce, which we pulled up on my laptop. The company had a wonderful story, product, and branding. I immediately e-mailed the website link to food writer Ruth Reichl, who at the time was working with Gilt Taste, an online purveyor of artisanal foods. She leaped all over it, and Red Boat took sail. (See "Inside Scoop: Red Boat Fish Sauce Targets Several Channels for Sales Success," page 150.)

Sure, I was powered by caffeine. Even more, I was powered by the desire to introduce Gilt Taste to a cool new product and help this food entrepreneur be successful. If I had jotted a note to myself to write to Ruth later, I probably would have let the opportunity fade away.

INSIDE SCOOP:
MAMA BARETTA REACHES OUT FOR SUCCESS

Debra Baretta attended a food business workshop I gave, then followed up with several updates and requests for help. Our conversations make a great lesson in connecting the dots.

She started by sending me a nice e-mail: "I enjoyed your workshop yesterday and 'Liked' your Facebook page. I am thinking about entering The Next Big Small Brand contest" (a New York–San Francisco food company shoot-out I'd mentioned in the workshop).

Less than two weeks later, she reported: "I made the semifinals in The Next Big Small Brand contest. Thank you so, so much for telling me about the contest. If it weren't for you I would not have had this opportunity at all. " If it weren't for her follow-up, she wouldn't have had the opportunity either! Debra let me know that she didn't win but that entering that contest had led her to persevere and enter another contest. She shared some other exciting progress reports: "I will be headed to a radio station for an interview and am going to be proving how absolutely fantastic gluten-free vegan baked goods can be. I just created several new products to add to my existing line of breads, cookies, and pastries. I have a meeting at a 10,000-square-foot Meals on Wheels Kitchen. We may strike a deal, and then I will be able to increase production. At that point I will do sales calls and hopefully not kill myself again! But thank you so much for the tip to get referrals to accounts. I hate sales calls, but if someone refers me it's a little easier!"

Nine months later, in December 2012, an e-mail showed up in my inbox: "Mama Baretta wins Intuit prize!" The prize was a post about her company on Intuit's blog—priceless.

Debra's e-mails illustrate dot connecting in the making. By sharing her progress and goals with me, she was opening herself up to suggestions on her next steps. That, an open mind, lots of hard work, and following up led her to epic progress in just one year.

MIND YOUR MIND, SQUASH YOUR FEARS

Afraid of getting started? Or of taking a big risk and failing? Think positive. And if fear and insecurity do overtake you, ask yourself, "What am I worried about?" Here are some common fears, and answers that can help you overcome them.

The Fear	Tell Yourself . . .
Setting goals, then not achieving them	It wasn't a priority after all. *Or* I'm changing direction.
Losing money	I'll take my time and make a strategy with a set budget.
Success and greatness	I only have one life to live, so I should make it great. (Tap in to the self-help world to overcome your blocks.)
Shyness and starting conversations	If I don't speak up, I'll miss out on great information, and others will miss an opportunity to learn from and connect with me. (Read books to practice overcoming shyness, and join Toastmasters.)
Being perceived as rude by talking to strangers or eavesdropping	If I am friendly and curious, while still being respectful of others, striking up random conversations can only bring me synchronicity and advance my goals.

CONTINUE ▶

The Fear	Tell Yourself . . .
Rejection, or that people won't like your product	This helps me "fail quickly" so I can improve my product. *Or* They aren't my target audience.
Imposter's Syndrome—you aren't an entrepreneur, and people will see right through you	I'm absolutely qualified to create and market my product, and I'll gain even more confidence and knowledge as I go for it. (Reading the stories of career changers in this book will help.)
Lack of motivation	I will break overwhelming to-do's into smaller, more manageable tasks. *Or* I will take a hard look at my business and make sure it is still my dream.
Negativity and bad luck	I will focus only on the things I can control, and the rest will all work itself out. (Check the 10 Easy First Steps and Further Reading, page 245, for books I recommend or seek out a personal-development workshop.)

I've faced many of these same fears, and they still creep up at times. But I've learned to embrace them and then work through them. Part of my coaching helps entrepreneurs understand patterns they may have learned as a child that, in fact, are as outdated as frozen lima beans. Try some of these ideas and see if you don't feel your fears melt away. If they don't, let's chat.

INSIDE SCOOP:
PUNK RAWK LABS CONNECTS THE DOTS FOR SUCCESS

Alissa Barthel's journey into food entrepreneurship is a prime example of how dot connecting led her to create Punk Rawk Labs, her Minneapolis company that specializes in "living cuisine" (meat-free, dairy-free, gluten-free, sugar-free, unprocessed raw food).

After a toxic exposure and a car crash, Alissa attended a gourmet raw-food academy with hopes of improving her health. She began developing nut-milk cheeses as a dairy alternative. This led to an opportunity to teach an "uncooking" class at a co-op market (while still hobbling around on crutches). A market attendee named Julie noticed Alissa's state and offered to help out with the class. They got to talking and discovered they had similar dietary issues. They teamed up informally, and Julie began helping Alissa sell her living foods locally. Alissa raised money through a Kickstarter campaign to expand her business. Soon orders poured in from all over the world, and before long, Alissa realized she was in way over her head. Where to turn to for help? She remembered that Julie was a former record-store owner and had gone through small-business growing pains—and she also had a passion for living food. Alissa asked Julie to be her business partner, and Punk Rawk Labs has rocked ever since.

TAKEAWAYS

- The art of dot connecting (being aware of and open to opportunities and connections, and then taking action to make things happen) will serve you well as an entrepreneur.

- Setting S.M.A.R.T. goals is an effective way to define what you want and to make it happen.

- Research, both primary and secondary, is integral to building a good business, as are solid decision-making skills.

- Every entrepreneur will face fears; it's how you conquer them that counts.

GREAT BUSINESS ACTION PLAN

☐ Come up with a S.M.A.R.T. goal for the next step in your business, whether you're still searching for an idea or you're ready to find a production kitchen. Write it out using positive phrases, or use the reverse-flowchart method.

☐ Think about your connections: old, recent, and potential. How can you help them? How can they help you? Whom do they know?

☐ Dot connecting is not a solitary activity. Know your friends' and colleagues' goals and make sure they know yours, as part of staying alert for opportunities that pop up. Share resources with them, and make sure you each follow up on what you say you will do. Hold each other accountable.

☐ Start practicing the dot-connecting habits in your everyday life.

ON *GOODFOODGREATBUSINESS.COM*
Learn more about connecting the dots and valuable basic business and life skills.

STEP
2

COOK UP YOUR BUSINESS IDEA

CREATE YOUR MISSION, REALIZE YOUR VISION

BURNING QUESTION:
MUST MY FOOD REALLY SERVE A LOFTY GOAL?
(IT'S JUST FOOD!)

Certainly not, but it's easier than you think to make a difference with every choice you make in your business. When you use the best ingredients and more healthful recipes, you're helping people to be healthier. When you choose to buy local or, better yet, directly from farmers, you're helping growers and your community by contributing to the regional economy. Your product can also solve problems for your consumer—think of a portable but healthful breakfast item perfect for busy people who need to eat on the go, or a healthier version of a 100-calorie snack pack that helps folks trying to control their weight feel good about themselves.

STATE YOUR MISSION: WHY ARE YOU DOING THIS?

Your mission statement defines your company's reason for being—why the company you want to build exists and the needs it aims to meet. Good Food mission statements usually revolve around serving or helping people in some way. Fill in the blanks in this simple exercise to start outlining your mission:

For _____ (your target audience—all people, kids, parents, people on the go, etc.), we provide _____ (what your product is, in general) so that _____ (results). We commit to _____ (the actions your company will take to care for the people involved with your business and for the planet). To sustain the business, we will _____ (something related to your responsibility to earn enough money to keep the business going). We will work within and as part of our community by _____.

> Example: For *kids of all ages and all income levels*, we provide *affordable, simply nutritious, grab-and-go organic food* so that *people on the go can always eat well*. We commit

to *manufacturing locally while employing the older generation and training the new. To help our earth, we will manufacture and package using renewable resources as much as possible, and source from local farmers whenever possible to connect with and give back to our neighbors.* To sustain the business, we will *watch our spending and tend to our profits.* We will work within and as part of our community by *giving 1 percent of our profits to public education on nutrition within our home state.*

A mission statement should spark your energy to keep going, even when times get tough and nights get sleepless. Here are some real-life examples of mission statements.

- Two Degrees Food, which gives a meal pack to a child for every one of its energy bars sold: "Here at Two Degrees, we believe that everyday choices can make a big difference. Instead of grabbing just any snack, you can go for one that feeds your hunger and helps do the same for another. That's the power of our one-for-one model. For every Two Degrees bar you buy, we donate a meal to a hungry child." (Two Degrees Food's "Our Mission" page goes on to inspire and explain to consumers how they can make this mission happen.)

- Nuts About Granola, a granola company: "Nuts About Granola is made locally, sourced locally, and traded locally. We believe strongly in the power of a thriving local community, one which values where their food comes from and who makes it."

By the way, your statement need not be seriously sincere. If that's not your style, fun and irreverent works just as well, such as: "We make the best organic applesauce for people from 1-101, teeth or no teeth." Long mission statements may also be hard to remember, let alone repeat.

In his book *Art of the Start*, tech maven and author Guy Kawasaki suggests skipping the long statement altogether for a shorter mantra. Some food examples: granola and bar company 18 Rabbits' "See, Taste, Love"; Numi Organic Tea's "Celebrating People, Planet, and Pure Tea"; Brooklyn Brine's "Damn Fine Pickles"; and Equal Exchange's "Small Farmers. Big Change." Mary's Gone Crackers "Conscious Eating" is a shortened version of its mission statement: "To heal humanity and the planet by inspiring Conscious Eating." Notice how most of these easily double as a slogan or tagline for the brand.

COMPARE AND CONTRAST: TRANSFORMING BUSINESS IDEAS INTO DREAM LIFESTYLES

Once you know your mission—whom you're serving and why—your detailed vision of where you want to go with the company will begin to jell. Take these diverse preserves businesses, for instance:

- Using the marketing prowess he honed over years as an ad man in New York, Paul Cappelli created his Villa Cappelli brand of specialty foods in southern Italy near his family's hometown. Locals, including grandmothers, make the company's traditional Italian food preserves, olive oils, and sweets for export to other countries using local ingredients. Plus, a villa he restored doubles as an amazing home and luxury vacation rental. *La dolce vita!*

- Todd and Jordan Champagne parlayed a love for working with local growers into a multifaceted family business, Happy Girl Kitchen. Purchasing produce directly from San Francisco Bay Area farmers, they make their own brand of pickles and preserves. In addition to selling at farmers' markets and limited retail outlets, they offer jam and pickling workshops; run a café in the affluent community of Pacific Grove, California; offer contract manufacturing services for farms that want to preserve their harvests; and sell farm-fresh produce to DIY canners.

- You've likely seen Stonewall Kitchen's products labeled with a signature handwritten look. Company founders Jonathan King and Jim Stott got started selling jam at a Maine farmers' market in the early 1990s. Now a company with $50 million-plus in annual sales, its jams have been joined by sauces, books, and even kitchenware. Over time, the founders created a tourist destination in their York, Maine, location with a café and cooking school. The founders enjoy a wonderful semirural coastal lifestyle while tending to their healthy business and beautiful gardens.

So you see, jam is often merely the means to an end—the end being fulfilling your personal missions and achieving your vision.

LEARN THE ABCS OF HOW YOU CAN MAKE FOOD

Before the paddle hits the kettle, it's important for you to know some of the most common ways food products get made, and the role or roles you might take on in the process. Will you be an Artisaneur, a Business Builder, or a Community Builder? Read on to find out.

A Is for Artisaneurs

Artisan-entrepreneurs (Artisaneurs for short) are the makers, bakers, and crafters, people happiest when they are dusted with flour, their hands cramped from stirring bubbling sauces, or their fridges and pantries bulging with the season's bounty awaiting pickling. The downside of making your product yourself? The workload. Capacity constraints. Higher prices due to lower volume. In short, you'll be living those 5 Perils and Paradoxes you read about on page 19. As demand grows, Artisaneurs need to either grow the business (i.e., hire more people and invest in more equipment) to keep on crafting (as a "Community Builder"), or transition to a co-packer and outsource production (as a "Business Builder").

GOOD IDEA:
START AS A HOME-BASED BUSINESS

More than 40 states have laws that allow home-based food businesses. Called "cottage food," "homesteading," or "homemade food" laws, rules related to inspections, what you can make, where you can sell, and how much you can earn per year vary wildly from state to state, and often from county to county. Still, these laws are a boon for testing your concept, both for market acceptance and to see if a food business is really for you. For example, Julie Rabinovitz started her gluten-free business, Tasty Bakery, out of her Ann

CONTINUE ▶

Arbor, Michigan, home. Cramped quarters notwithstanding, the setup let her (1) promise no gluten was present (a tall order when sharing a commercial kitchen with other food entrepreneurs), and (2) start slowly without much upfront expense by selling at a farmers' market. Eventually, she found a part-time bakery to help her company grow with demand.

B Is for Business Builders

Many food brands of all sizes contract out their manufacturing to companies called co-packers. This model has helped many a food entrepreneur grow a thriving business. For example, Clif Bar has always preferred to contract out its production so the company can focus on other aspects of building a sustainable business. (Only in 2013, after more than 20 years in business, did the company announce plans to build a plant, in Idaho, to manufacture part of its product line.) Sonoma Syrup's Karin Campion teamed with a co-packer to make her natural-flavored syrups, allowing the architect-turned-food entrepreneur to run her company from home while her kids were growing up. The "Business Builder" model of production appeals to entrepreneurs who prefer to focus on sales, marketing, and building customer and community relationships rather than running a food-production facility. Even if you decide to work with a co-packer, you'll want to oversee production runs to ensure the product meets your expectations for quality, flavor, and presentation. (If you don't believe me, see "The Joys of Good Co-Packers Making Your Food (for Business Builders)," page 121.)

C Is for Community Builders

All Good Food entrepreneurs tend to love community. Here, *community builder* refers to entrepreneurs growing a local food-manufacturing business, perhaps with a retail storefront or café. This model connects you with your community, creates local jobs, and gives you the flexibility to rent out kitchen space, experiment with and extend your product lines, and shift your business however you see fit. For example, the founders of Savory Creations started out making their concentrated broths with a co-packer, but they found themselves wanting to be more involved in the making of their product. They realized that in addition to letting them be more hands-on with their production, running their own facility would allow them to make custom products and to innovate at will.

This is a great example of how your production methods might change along with your company strategy. Learn more about Savory Creations on pages 62 and 225.

Setting up and running your own production facility is costly, but it can offer unlimited rewards. To offset costs, you could band together with a few like-minded souls to start a for-profit cooperative, or a socially minded venture. New York's Hot Bread Kitchen is a nonprofit that helps foreign-born, low-income people break into the food industry. To offset operation costs, the organization sells multiethnic breads made by its trainees (and the baking helps the trainees build experience they can use later).

Community Builders can also act as co-packers for other companies, to provide another revenue stream in addition to selling their own products. This model works best with foods that use the same equipment to make and package, such as a bakery like Tate's Bake Shop, which produces nearly two million cookies a week. As another example, Anthony Flynn and his mom founded YouBar in Los Angeles to help both everyday consumers and food entrepreneurs customize, manufacture, brand, and launch natural energy, protein, and meal-replacement bars as well as trail mixes and cereals. Tim Ferriss, author of the *4-Hour Work Week*, tapped into YouBar's co-packing services, perfectly illustrating his "4-hour" concept—an entrepreneurial business that can run with very little oversight. Customers order the company's "Training 33" bars online. YouBar makes and ships them out. Tim can go about his writing and other endeavors. Within five years, the demand for YouBar's customized products led the company to expand from a tiny apartment-size space to an impressive 8,000-square-foot production facility in downtown Los Angeles with annual sales in the seven figures.

With your own facility, you might choose to produce food similar to your own for stores as a "private label" brand. You've seen the results of this common practice on the shelves at chain stores: Whole Foods has its 365 Everyday Value, Costco's has Kirkland, and Trader Joe's has its well-known name in all sorts of fun permutations. The private-label approach can be a win-win—an efficient way to make money from unused factory capacity. Still, small food manufacturers need to weigh the cost, benefits, and revenue gained by a private-label business deal. For example, your private-label brand may compete with your own branded line, which could eat into profits. The Private Label Manufacturers Association (PLMA.com) is your go-to place to learn more.

So What's Your Food Business Personality?

After reading about the various models for producing food products, which do you think fits you best? Your answer may direct what you choose to make and how you choose to make it. Why? First, products vary in complexity, from easy-to-make and hard-to-ruin foods to temperature-sensitive, easily spoiled, difficult-to-ship, potential-to-kill-people foods. For a long time, I dreamed about being a cheesemaker. A week at a goat-cheese farm cured me. Monitoring vats of milk, turning cheeses, wearing galoshes in sanitized rooms, and taking care to monitor storage temperatures was simply not for me. Eating goat cheese is a totally different story! I'd be much happier hiring an expert to transform my vision into delicious cheese wheels, while handling all the production details.

Are you up for handling food that can melt in summer, wilt in a day, or be subject to a recall if salmonella sneaks into production? That question leads well into choosing how you'll produce your food. If you find yourself less than retentive in the cleanliness and uniformity department, consider the co-packer route. Remember, connect the dots and you'll find a way! So what are you thinking?

- **I'm an Artisaneur. I want to craft the product myself, and I love the freedom of keeping it small and getting my hands dirty.**

- **I'm a Business Builder. I want someone else to make the food that I will brand and market.**

- **I'm a Community Builder. I want to manufacture Good Food, with employees and maybe a retail storefront or restaurant.**

- **I want to be a contract manufacturer (a co-packer) to help other companies bring their Good Food dreams to life. I could also manufacture for private-label store brands.**

- **No idea, that's why I'm reading!**

You'll read more about getting your food into production in chapter 8.

TESSEMAE'S ALL NATURAL BECOMES
AN ACCIDENTAL MANUFACTURER

The tale of Tessemae's All Natural is like so many you've heard before. Greg Vetter's friend obsessed over the fresh lemon-garlic dressing Greg's mom made—so much so that he sneaked into Greg's house to snag a jar of it from the fridge. That simple act of thievery was enough for Greg to ditch his sales career, pursue his entrepreneurial urge, and transform his mom's recipe into a business.

Whole Foods took the lemon-garlic dressing on, placing it on an obscure shelf in the refrigerated section and pricing it at $6.99 for 8 fluid ounces. The store asked if Greg could lower the price to $4.99. Greg demurred, both because he wouldn't be able to recoup the cost and because he felt that Tessemae's products, made with all fresh ingredients, were worth more. Whole Foods lowered the price anyway, offering Greg the same payment he had been getting at the higher retail price. As word got around, sales grew and grew.

Armed with a line of credit from the bank and a plan for growth, Greg approached co-packers who could handle large production runs. The first co-packer promised the dressing would taste exactly like the original, and charged a hefty fee for testing. The recipe was a failure. Greg found a couple more co-packers who wouldn't charge him for test batches. They did, however, want to modify his recipe to use dried garlic, xanthan gum, and other additives, which made the end product taste nothing like the original. Greg realized the key to the business was sticking with fresh, homemade ingredients. He reflected on his business and made a decision: Tessemae's would become a food manufacturer.

The company quickly grew, and its product line now includes dressings, marinades, and spreads that are sold in stores and restaurants in numerous states. Because it owns its own facility, Tessemae's can buy extra ingredients to be sure to always have enough on hand, and then it donates any leftovers to charitable causes. The big-picture goal is to launch a significant and lasting Good Food revolution in America's schools.

WRITE YOUR VISION STATEMENT:
WHERE DO YOU WANT TO GO WITH THIS?

A vision statement paints your long-term view of where you see your business in ten years (or twenty or thirty). Knowing your desired outcome lets you backtrack into a roadmap to getting there. Your vision helps you define success simply: your vision achieved. To illustrate how a vision statement can guide you, look to Zingerman's, a fabulous Ann Arbor, Michigan–based deli and mail-order company that set the standard for sourcing artisanal products directly from producers around the world.

The Zingerman's team routinely drafts vision statements when defining goals, whether monumental projects or day-to-day tasks such as planning a team outing. Cofounder Ari Weinzweig literally wrote the book on writing vision statements, *A Lapsed Anarchist's Approach to Building a Great Business.* (If an anarchist can plan the future, so can you.) Since its 1982 founding, Zingerman's vision was to grow while still staying intensely focused on its local community. This vision has come to fruition. Today, Zingerman's is a local "community of businesses," with only-in–Ann Arbor retail locations ranging from a coffee roaster to a deli to a creamery. In addition, it runs a mail-order food business, offers "great business" training programs, and organizes cool food tours around the world. This combination generates more than $30 million in annual sales for the company. If you've ever felt torn between supporting your local economy and becoming a big business, let this success story be your model.

You may have no experience in the food business—or money to invest. Still, do yourself a favor and conceive a truly audacious vision, as Jim Collins advises in his book *Built to Last: Successful Habits of Visionary Companies.* For you, audacious may mean selling a thousand jars of salsa in a year. Or bringing in $100,000 a year in sales. Or maybe you envision having a $100 million food business in ten years. Why stop there? The Equal Exchange co-op, which sells fair-trade chocolate, tea, coffee, and other goods, set a twenty-year goal to create a "vibrant mutually cooperative community of two million committed participants trading fairly $1 billion a year" in a "way that transforms the world." For you, audacious can be less about money and more about changing the status quo. Claire Herminjard switched careers in her twenties, setting out to create an organic, non-GMO meat brand using pasture-raised dairy cows for which she would pay family farmers a premium.

(Previously, older dairy cows would often end their lives as convention-ally raised cattle.) She worked out a plan, reached out to make connec-tions in the dairy-farming world, found a home for rent across the street from Straus Family Creamery, an organic dairy in rural Marshall, California, and embarked on creating Mindful Meats. With the complicated U.S. Department of Agriculture (USDA) regulations around meat process-ing, that is no small feat. Her vision of a future "in which everyone has access to sustainable food choices, and the agricultural industry finds balance with our environment" is hairier than a cow. It's audacious. And it guides every decision she makes.

Give your own vision statement a try. Settle down in your favorite cozy spot. Turn your phone off. Write as if you are in the future—five, ten, or twenty years from now—looking back at how far you've come.

Be sure to include a lot of details. Some people find writing as if they are in the present incredibly powerful. Your vision would read: "I am sitting at my Mission-style antique wooden desk, on a video-conference with our Parisian chocolate partner, while enjoying watching the sun rise as I enjoy a cup of house-roasted coffee." Oh wait, that's my vision. Use these questions to guide you:

- How does your food business fit into your life? Is it your calling or a side project? If it's a side project, does the business earn enough to be your main source of income?

- What do people—including customers, the press, your family, and your funders—say about your company?

- Who and where are your customers? How are you serving and help-ing them?

- What impact is your business having—on your local community, the country, and the world?

- Does your company make the product, or do you contract produc-tion out to focus on marketing, sales, and other activities? If you make the product, how vast is your operation?

- Is your offering seasonal or year-round?

- Where is your home and office, and what are they like? Or did you choose a nomadic lifestyle?

- What are you doing all day, when you're working and not working?

- What fulfills you about the business? What great accomplishment do you look back on?

- How are you doing financially?

- What are your partners and colleagues like? Are you collaborating or going solo?

- Do you still own the business or was it acquired? If the latter, what is your involvement after you sold it, if any?

A day or so after answering the questions, review what you wrote. Do your answers reflect your (and perhaps your partner's) vision? Or do you detect a hint of someone else's vision in there, an idea of where you "should" be instead of where you want to be? When drafting a vision for my short-lived food business, I realized it looked good "on paper," defining success in a way other companies had. But it had no bearing on what would really make me happy. Back to square one! Review and update your vision as often as you like.

Vision Shortcuts

If you're stumped, one of these exercises might help free your mind:

- Borrow from role models, in the food business or otherwise. If you're a career changer, think about Julia Child, who hit her stride in her forties. (For a boost of Julia's devil-may-care audaciousness, take a look at Karen Karbo's *Julia Child Rules*.)

- Cut, paste, and collage your vision to illustrate your desires. Go digital or old-school. Grab some magazines, scissors, glue, and a piece of pasteboard. Piece together words and images that speak to what you want to create. Then post it somewhere you'll see it often—maybe even as your phone's "locked screen" image!

- Chat with producers at the farmers' market or the owners of your favorite businesses, whether local or online. Listen closely. Are they complaining? Do they have any regrets? Is your vision realistic?

ASKINOSIE CHOCOLATE, STONE-BUHR FLOUR, AND LOTUS FOODS DRAW INSPIRATION FROM WHAT'S RIGHT IN FRONT OF THEM

Many entrepreneurs got their start by seeing signs on the open road, then connecting the dots to bring their businesses to fruition—often with no foresight to start a food business! (Did you ever notice how many food-company histories kick off with trip-inspired epiphanies?) While mulling over a career change from lawyer to cupcake maker, Shawn Askinosie followed a sign—actually, bumper stickers—on a road trip. The cupcake idea became history, replaced by inspiration to start a chocolate company. Never mind that he knew nothing about chocolate manufacturing. He learned the trade and started Askinosie Chocolate, a Good Food poster child. He works directly with growers, shares a percentage of the profits with them, and gives them unparalleled insight into his business. In addition to supporting the local community, Askinosie's Chocolate University bridges cultures by flying local high school kids from Missouri to Africa to learn about cacao farms.

Josh Dorf had just read Michael Pollan's *Omnivore's Dilemma*, and as he road-tripped through eastern Washington, thoughts of food systems and the way Americans eat filled his mind. He passed miles of wheat fields wondering, "How come our wheat comes from Montana and not from here?" Around the same time, a group of farmers in the region had started a pilot program to mill their local hard wheat into 50-pound bags for a Spokane, Washington, baker. Dorf reached out, met the farmers, and was enchanted by them and their business model. He connected the dots and after a year or so, he created FindTheFarmer.com, a website that profiles the family farms that grow the grain for his Stone-Buhr Flour Company.

Caryl Levine and Ken Lee were on vacation, roving through China in pursuit of inspiration to start some kind of business together. They sat down to two bowls of very rare black rice that had a nutty flavor and hints of floral at the finish. The duo returned to the States "with ninety ideas," but that black rice stuck in their minds as something they would want to continue eating at home. Neither had a background in food, yet what they saw in China spoke

CONTINUE ▶

to their desires for social entrepreneurship: "Farmers were only growing what was being bought. Our vision was to keep the bio-diversity of rice alive while helping the small family farmer earn an honorable living." They formed Lotus Foods to do just that, partner-ing with Cornell on an initiative to help farmers grow more rice with less water and building demand for that rice. This exciting initiative so inspired me that I dabbled with my own line of black rice snacks, under the name The Nutless Professor.

OUTLINE YOUR GUIDING PRINCIPLES: YOUR RULES OF THE ROAD

Guiding principles intertwine with and support your mission in day-to-day business operations, adding clarity to what your company will and won't do. That clarity can really simplify decision-making. Some com-panies combine their mission statements and guiding principles. The principles may relate to leadership, teamwork, excellence, integrity, accountability, compassion, and caring for the community. They can also include your product's promise, such as never using genetically modified ingredients. When prices for organic fruit go up after a crop failure, you may feel pressured to substitute conventional fruit from abroad. A guiding principle to be 100 percent organic will remind you to "just say no." At their Brooklyn headquarters, Mast Brothers Chocolate displays a series of guiding principles on artsy square tiles on a wall. This approach reinforces the bean-to-bar chocolate makers' informal culture while reminding employees to "be honest and transparent, inno-vate through simplicity, and waste nothing."

In the spirit of Good Food, your principles will likely revolve around your Promise. Often called "the triple bottom line," the Promise includes three considerations that add up to sustainability:

- **PLANET.** How will you help the planet or avoid harming the environment?

- **PEOPLE.** How do you enhance the lives of employees and cus-tomers? Your mission might include sharing profits; operating as an open book, giving employees visibility into company finances, and assuring customers they can trust your business choices.

- **PROFITS.** How can you fulfill your mission while sustaining the business to meet the needs and expectations of any investors?

The successful small companies that Bo Burlingham profiled in his book *Small Giants: Companies That Choose to Be Great Instead of Big*— including Zingerman's—share some commonsense qualities that lead to a great company culture: a desire to buck trends, a good sense of perspective, a belief in a better tomorrow, a willingness to go the extra mile and stick with things for a long time, the ability to maintain quality relationships, and, last but not least, having fun and appreciating everything.

Draft your guiding principles early on to help guide your business planning. When writing them, answer questions such as: What does your company stand for? What will your company never do? What will your company always do? You can modify your principles as your plans or the environment around you changes. Start with this fill-in-the-blank exercise:

- We enjoy our work by . . .

- We help our community by . . .

- We care for the planet by . . .

- We make high-quality foods and services for our customers by . . .

- We balance profits with human needs and daily realities by . . .

TAKEAWAYS

- You can approach entrepreneurship in several different ways, depending on your personality and goals: as an Artisaneur, a Business Builder, or a Community Builder.

- Having a mission statement for your business is important: It clarifies what you're doing, why you're doing it, and for whom. And guiding principles will help keep your business on track.

- Having a vision for where you want your business to go helps project a positive outcome for everyday activities as well as for big decisions.

GREAT BUSINESS ACTION PLAN

☐ Write your mission statement.

☐ Write your vision.

☐ Outline your guiding principles.

☐ List five people who can help you today to make your vision real, as well as five more people who should be involved in your business planning process (including your family). Test drive your mission and vision on those people and get their feedback.

☐ Try volunteering or getting a job at a food business by using your current skills. Or perhaps try a role unlike any you've had before, to stretch your skills.

☐ Start connecting the dots: Watch for signs and follow up immediately as opportunities present themselves.

> ### ON *GOODFOODGREATBUSINESS.COM*
> Get a quick start with the links to resources
> mentioned in this chapter.

CHAPTER

FIND YOUR NICHE

BURNING QUESTION:
DO I REALLY NEED A BUSINESS PLAN BEFORE I START?

Yes and no. You need some sort of plan to avoid being another under-researched business on the fast track to folding before you've barely even started—a phenomenon facing many entrepreneurs (food or not). But you don't have to start out with a polished 20-page business plan—that will come later. While reading this book, you'll think about what you want, and by the time you reach the last chapter, you can get down to actually writing your plan.

3 LITTLE BIG QUESTIONS: WHO, WHAT, HOW?

Three key pieces of information will get you started toward fulfilling your mission and carving out your niche: knowing whom you're serving (your customers), knowing who else is serving their needs (your competition), and deciding how you'll create an irresistible 5 Staples food mix (your product strategy). By the end of this chapter, you'll look at food products and shopping in a completely new way.

PICTURE YOUR CUSTOMERS

To perfect your product, you must have a crystal-clear understanding of your customers and their needs. Are they granola-loving, natural-food eaters or pleasure-at-all-costs gourmet-food lovers? Or are they both? Natural consumers value nutrition and sourcing information before flavor, according to Kathryn Peters of SPINS, a natural-products-industry market research and consulting firm. Gourmet consumers do just the opposite; they are lured by taste and presentation. These days, more consumers cross those lines than ever before, thanks to stores such as Whole Foods and Trader Joe's, which sell healthful food that tastes good. I try to eat simple natural foods on a daily basis, saving the bacon-caramel-chocolate bars for weekends . . . usually.

The type of customer you want to serve will direct all the decisions you make about your 5 Staples mix of product, price, promotion, placement, and promise. As a businessperson, you should look at your customers from two different angles:

- **DEMOGRAPHIC.** Specify factual characteristics, such as age, gender, ethnicity, and income level—data that are manna to marketers. If your foods might appeal to affluent 50-year-olds of any ethnicity, you might advertise in or pitch a feature about your company to *Saveur* magazine, whose readers (in 2012) had an average age of fifty-two and an average household income of $136,145. Identifying the demographics of your target customer helps you target your 5 Staples mix at a very specific level—which is awesome when you're on a tight budget.

- **PSYCHOGRAPHICS.** Identify desires, needs, behaviors, aspirations, lifestyles, and attitudes. For example, affluent foodies may aspire to buy all their food locally, but, in reality, do so only 20 percent of the time. Why they are not buying more local products? The answers could help direct your product offerings. If they can't make it to the farmers' market to get local food because of its limited hours, you could launch a service such as home delivery. Or if you're marketing to busy restaurant chefs, you might similarly offer a daily delivery service.

Knowing your ideal customer will also help you understand your competition better. One of my favorite foods is wild Alaskan smoked sockeye salmon, which is naturally wood-smoked with brown sugar and salt—and most important, no preservatives. What artisan makes this delicacy? Kirkland, more commonly known as Costco. Well, technically, Trident Seafoods is the maker, and their salmon is packaged under Costco's private-label brand. Say you're selling wild-caught salmon that you smoked (and perhaps that you source directly from indigenous fisherfolk). Does your customer compare your foods to Costco's? Or is she so drawn to your story, the terroir, and your direct relationship with the source—and affluent enough to afford your higher price—that, in fact, the two products are not actually competition? In this case, online sellers, perhaps the fisherfolk themselves, might be your competition, rather than the nearby Costco.

As you can see, defining customers in general terms such as "people who shop at farmers' markets" or "people who eat at restaurants" is a good start. But which people? Old, young? Affluent, lower income? Locals, tourists, or both? Why will they buy something, and how will they choose your food over its alternatives? Remember also that there is a market for products that appeal to consumers within certain places: large venues such as convention centers, sports stadiums, concert halls, military commissaries, and schools. The closer you get to "knowing" your customers, the better you'll know how and where to serve them.

You might also find a lucrative niche selling to food-service establishments, such as restaurants, hospitals, hotels, and corporate kitchens—particularly for premixed ingredients used for cooking, such as sauces and rare spice blends. You benefit by eliminating costly fancy packaging and many promotion-related expenses. And although the profit margins in the food-service market are smaller, the volume you can generate selling to restaurants, hotels, or stadiums can be significant. Selling to food-service establishments might also include retailing bulk-packaged products at warehouse clubs, such as gallons of flavored olive oils and gourmet pasta sauces.

Breaking in to the food-service market has its challenges: At the high end, the chefs often make all their food from scratch, and thus they won't be interested in what you're offering. In this case, your would-be customers—the chefs—are your competition. At the low end, the chefs may be price sensitive enough that specialty products aren't an option, because they can't sell their own foods at a price that would allow for profit.

Design Your Dream Customers

To help you define your customers, try this exercise: Paint a detailed picture of your end customers, called a "persona," to make them seem real. The most popular products and services (as well as brands) emerge from such persona exercises. The goal is to bring your ideal customers alive in your mind. Personas help you focus all of your efforts, time, and money rather than a "throw it out and see what sticks" recipe for failure.

Create fun nicknames for your personas—this will help you remember them and refer to them when making decisions. Some examples of fleshed-out personas, and the products that they might each need, are:

- MOMS WHO MARATHON—affluent, active, health-conscious mothers, ages 24 to 37, with young kids. Product: On-the-go snack packs that provide nutrition for both moms and kids.

- **BODACIOUS BOOMERS**—aging (in their 60s) baby boomers who need healthful, affordable snack foods that provide nutrition but that don't overtly allude to aging. Product: Calcium-loaded caramels.

- **GOOD FOODIES**—hip urban professionals ages 24 to 48 for whom price is no object, and sustainable, delicious food is everything. Product: Weekly meal-delivery service with ingredients sourced exclusively from local farmers' markets.

- **MASS-MARKET MASTER CHEFS**—chefs of large food-service venues seeking high-quality, low-cost foods that are shortcuts to gourmet dishes. Product: Unique spice blends that can serve as the base for soups, sauces, or stews.

- **RAGING ROAD TRIPPERS**—adventurous men ages 29 to 69 who relax by taking long drives and power up by eating convenient all-natural snacks. Product: Jerky made from exotic meats such as wild boar, alligator, and venison.

- **DISCRIMINATING RETAILERS**—high-end deli owners seeking ready-to-eat ethnic sandwich meats or condiments. Product: A range of spicy and savory spreads for sandwiches—chipotle mayos, habanero mustards, arugula pestos.

- **WEEKEND CHEFS**—people who pull out all the stops once a week to cook or barbecue a grand feast at home. Product: A line of gourmet marinades, dry rubs, and finishing salts.

How are you to know who wants what? You don't, though research and observations should guide you. The more narrow your persona, the smaller your market. But when starting small, limited can be good. And research can help you define your target customers even more clearly. For example, the 2012 Mintel/Specialty Food Association Specialty Foods Consumer Annual Report survey revealed that an equal number of people who were surveyed buy specialty food to use as part of meals at home as to snack on outside of meals: 68 percent in both cases. The same report found that younger consumers lean toward snack and convenience specialty foods.

Your customer personas will also help you make quick packaging decisions for quandaries such as: "Would 'Young Dad Dave' be OK with having to find a clip for his bag of garlic pretzels? On the chart that follows, use your best guesses to create some personas who would buy your product (photocopy it if you have more than one product in mind):

Customer Nickname			
Gender and Age Ranges			
Education Level			
Lifestyle/ Psychographics			
Income			
Where They Shop 80 Percent of the Time			

HOW TO FULFILL YOUR CUSTOMERS' DEEPEST NEEDS

How quickly we can go from a Zen-like state to miserable, for lack of food, sleep, or a bathroom. Psychologist Abraham Maslow unraveled the mystery of what makes humans tick in 1943, proposing a "hierarchy of needs." In a nutshell, the most basic human needs and motivations have to be satisfied before we can pursue the loftier desires of self-actualization. First, we need to satisfy our physiological basics, such as food, water, and shelter (yes, and sex); after that we need safety, work, and well-being; love, friendship, and belonging come next, followed by esteem and confidence; and the final step is self-actualization (realizing your full potential). Self-actualization frees you to be creative, spontaneous, and open-minded.

Why must we have pricey smartphones? What human needs do they serve? Freedom. Connections. What need does a breath mint fulfill? The little candies help you socialize after you've eaten a garlic-laden meal, or energize you when you need a quick sugar fix. By helping people effortlessly fulfill their most basic needs, a food company can free customers to live their lives and pursue happiness. Little unexpected surprises such as poems on a chocolate wrapper or Zen sayings on a tea bag's tag can produce a self-actualized experience. So can handing the creativity reins to customers, letting them design their own chocolates (as Austin's Piq Chocolates does with a trendy 3D printer, no less) or energy bars (as does YouBar). Finally, connecting directly with your customers through social media, whether you are chatting about recipes that use your products, informing them about how the fair-trade arm of your business works, or showing them how your products can help their kids eat better, can help customers feel like they are part of a bigger cause and understand that your food is not only delicious but also meaningful.

Chip Conley applied Maslow's hierarchy to inspire excellent customer and employee experiences at his ultra-hip Joie de Vivre boutique hotel chain. The idea, which Chip wrote about in his best-selling book *Peak*, proposes that by fulfilling your customers' unrecognized needs, you might actually help them reach their full potential. Remember, too, that moment by moment, we can go up and down the hierarchy of needs. Consider this example: Jane arrives at the store hungry and grumpy, buys and inhales a pack of Nuts Plus Nuts Thai spice cashews, and then is inspired by the package's label to research the company, learning about the cashew growers' story—and in the process, she moves from physically satiated to intellectually stimulated.

THERE'S A BUSINESS FOR EVERY CUSTOMER NEED

As someone who thinks about coffee way too much, I've observed that different coffee brands and experiences serve different needs. The craft coffee roasters who produce very limited batches and have few café locations charge more—and their customers are willing to pay in both money and the time to wait for a hand-dripped brew. While few will become multibillion-dollar companies, many do sell in the millions of dollars a year, great business lessons on the 5 Staples Mix:

- excellent product

- a premium yet doable price

- natural promotion, via the media and word of mouth

- limited placement, creating desire (the scarcity principle)

- the promise to roast and brew only the best coffee, usually sourced directly from the farms.

Once you start viewing your business, customers, employees, and your own life in terms of Maslow's hierarchy, moods and motivations become crystal clear.

DISCOVER YOUR COMPETITION

The Good Food industry breeds friendly competition—an abundance and "we're all in this together" kind of camaraderie. Most entrepreneurs are just thrilled to be pursuing their passions. They feel a greater purpose in making delicious, wholesome foods. Many Good Food makers often engage in "co-option," or co-operative competition for a greater good, whether to pass legislation or to achieve group-buying discounts. Numi Organic Tea's cofounder Ahmed Rahim sums up this good-energy sentiment well: "Wouldn't we rather be friendly with others in our industry than be enemies?"

You do need to know your competition. Your competition is *all* of the alternatives to your products. Look back to your customers' desires and needs to understand the competition you face. Why? Psychology drives buying behavior. When deciding which food to buy, we might consider our health and body perceptions, if the food will make us feel good mentally (like potato chips) or physically (like kale chips), and the cultural eating habits or messages drummed into us through advertising. Landing on the right 5 Staples mix for food products is a lot more complicated than selling jewelry or sneakers. That's also why your competition is not just the foods that are similar to yours. Consider these other types of competition:

- Hidden competition. These are the not-so-obvious alternatives, such as hummus instead of vegan cheese. Gourmet frozen meals compete with local restaurants. The DIY movement and homemade-food exchanges may adversely affect sales for companies that make fermented vegetable products. Refrigerated food cases at supermarkets selling salsas and salads also compete for customers who might otherwise buy bottled salsa.

- Inertia, or "doing nothing," is a huge competitor, in every product category. We enjoy eating familiar comfort foods. As a Good

Food businessperson, your biggest weapon against inertia is very low-tech: sampling! You can win over those customers hesitant to change their habits by addicting them to your better-tasting, better-for-you Good Food. (More on this in "Your Number-One Selling Tool: Samples," page 194.)

- Customers' belt tightening, or choosing to spend their money on things other than food, competes with your business too.

PLOT YOUR COMPANY AND PRODUCT STRATEGIES

Your vision, mission, and guiding principles all inform your company strategy, or overall plan. That plan, in turn, directs what you're creating for your target customer and how you go about doing it. For example, Mary's Gone Crackers created its natural, sweet-and-savory snacks to serve gluten-free eaters. The founders left their comfortable yet traffic-plagued San Francisco Bay Area suburb for rural Gridley, California, where they opened a production facility in a more affordable area near the company's rice growers. This strategy helped the team build close relationships with the growers and avoid high shipping costs for rice, resulting in a more accessible price for the product line. Its "Conscious Eating" mantra, its mission, and the strategies undertaken as a result guided and enabled Mary's Gone Crackers to grow rapidly over ten years and to keep pace with the growth of the gluten-free market.

Step 1: Set Your Big Picture Strategy—Go Broad or Go Deep

A fundamental strategy question all companies face is: Go broad or go deep? A broad strategy calls for a series of product lines. A deep strategy is all about focusing on one type of food. Take pickles, for instance. McClure's Pickles went broad, going beyond pickles to add potato chips, relish, and Bloody Mary mix to their product line. Rick's Picks went deep, making only pickled vegetables (albeit a variety of vegetables). Your product strategy will impact lots of decisions around your 5 Staples Mix, including your brand and name, your production facility, funding needs, and a whole lot more.

Let's take a look at the pros and cons of each approach.

Considerations for a Broad Product Line

The pros of a broad, diverse product line can far outweigh any cons. Some benefits include:

- GREATER EXPOSURE. Your line has more visibility because it takes up more space on store shelves, called a "brand block."

- LOWER RISK. If sales of a trendy product fall, your other products can make up for the shortfall while you eliminate the less popular item, as so many beverage makers have mastered.

- ONGOING REVENUE. You can balance products with seasonal appeal or limitations, such as holiday candies, with foods consumers will buy year-round or that are easier to deliver in hot weather. For example, Chicago company Cake developed a line of giftable, easily shippable cookies to offset its slower chocolate sales in summer.

- MORE POTENTIAL. You can appeal to more customers with different products, sizes, assortments, and flavors as well as diverse markets, such as consumer, business-to-business, and food service.

The downside? When products use different ingredients, packaging, or production methods, reaching economies of scale—meaning more efficient production with larger volume—may be difficult. You may work more and produce more, but you don't profit as much as if you had a smaller product line.

If the idea of a huge product line gets your heart (and wallet) going, find a way. Don't panic; Stonewall Kitchen wasn't built in a day. That company found success with a broad line by making some of its own products and contracting others out. Take your time and grow your business at a sustainable pace.

Considerations for a Deep Product Line

A dedicated and deep focus on one or two amazing products offers a number of advantages best summed up as: "It's easy!" The benefits of depth over breadth include:

- EASIER PROMOTION. Making a name for one amazing product is a lot easier than promoting a whole line. Companies such as Heritage Shortbread, Sir Kensington's Gourmet Scooping Ketchup, and all those cupcake shops have found great success with a single focus.

- EASIER PRODUCTION. Master one recipe, then slice it and dice it into different sizes and packages to expand the sales opportunities. Consider packaged cereal, which first came in large boxes, then single-serving boxes for lunch boxes and travelers. (Cereal companies have gone broad as well—think cereal bars).

- **LOWER COST.** Your ingredients and packaging costs get lower as you buy larger volumes of the same items. Production costs are lower, too, with fewer production processes. For example, Rick's Picks brines lots of vegetables in lots of jars—their operations are quite streamlined.

The downside? When you bank your business on one product, that product needs to be really excellent, addictive, and lasting, lest you be remembered as a one-hit wonder.

Decades-old Nory Candy, based in California's San Fernando Valley, exemplifies success going deep with a niche product (Turkish delight, a chewy Middle Eastern sweet) and niche distribution (largely in international markets). Nory Candy's kitchen has just a few copper kettles and a couple of candy makers crafting and packing its high-quality sweets, which are made with California nuts. Because owner Armand Sahakian's product focus limits ingredients and production processes, this small operation can serve a niche nationwide for international markets as well as online customers. A focus on one candy category gives Armand freedom to cost-efficiently innovate flavors and packaging.

Combining a Broad and Deep Strategy

Once your company is established, your product strategy—and your customer profiles—might be both broad and deep. Think of companies with a range of product types in many flavors and/or packages, such as scoopable ice cream, ice cream sandwiches, and frozen treats on a stick, each in five flavors.

Your plans may unfold naturally over time, as they did for former schoolteacher Beverly Takizawa and her husband, Douglas. They started Savory Creations, a natural, concentrated broth company, by hiring a food scientist to develop recipes and surveying restaurant chefs to confirm their interest. Two years later, they came out with a line of broth products (a deep strategy) targeted to professional food-service chefs. After enjoying the product for professional use, chefs suggested to Beverly and Douglas that they create a consumer-friendly concentrated-broth product line packaged to sell in retail stores (effectively broadening their product line). As a side benefit, the company can say on its retail packaging that the broth is "chef tested, chef approved."

Savory Creations' tactic of repackaging similar products for different target markets served it well when the 2008 financial disaster hit. The subsequent recession meant that people ate out less and food-service sales dropped. Retail sales climbed, however, because people were eating at home more frequently.

JUSTIN'S NUT BUTTER CONNECTS THE DOTS BETWEEN CRAVING AND BUSINESS

Justin Gold was on track to be a lawyer in Colorado when he realized that office life did not sync with his personality and interests. He decided to take a year to find himself. As a vegetarian and an outdoor athlete, he found himself eating a lot of peanut butter, and he started making his own, adding honey, agave, or coconut. Justin loved the process, and the results, as did his taste-testers (his roommates and the chefs cooking in the restaurant where he worked). He carefully recorded his recipes and all the feedback, both good and bad.

With a vague notion of developing a national brand, Justin started making flavored peanut butters with natural ingredients, trusting his intuition along the way. "I knew this was what I wanted to do," Justin says. "I had a gut feeling it was really a good idea." He researched how to trademark his products and get UPC codes. He sought out guidance through one-on-one consultations and business-plan-writing workshops at his local Small Business Development Center. He found a mentor to help with his business plan. Simultaneously, Justin gave samples of his nut butters to anyone who would taste them, and he recorded the feedback.

Before long, Justin realized his strengths were selling and marketing. His weaknesses: food safety and consistency. So he partnered with a local manufacturing company, put his equipment in their facility, and taught the company how to make his product. The co-packer also had a full-time food scientist, mechanic, and other staff Justin couldn't afford on his own.

Justin soon encountered a classic growth challenge: Sourcing the right raw materials at the right price, resulting in a consistently great (and available) product. The business began faltering. Then

CONTINUE ▶

one day while mountain biking, Justin had a protein craving, and this sparked an idea: Why not package his nut butters into convenient squeeze packs in addition to the jars he already carried?

This small innovation proved brilliant on many levels. Justin differentiated himself on the market by creating the single-serve peanut butter pack. Customers would think of his brand more often. And they would replenish their supply more often than they do with jars of nut butter. Plus, the squeeze pack created a category of innovation, compelling for active lifestyle stores such as REI and for bakeries to offer as an alternative to butter. Consumers could also try something new, such as almond butter, at a low-risk price, since the squeeze packs retail for about $1 each. And once consumers got hooked, they would buy the full-sized jars of almond butter at $10 a pop, benefitting retailers used to getting $3 for peanut butter.

There was just one glitch: Squeeze packs weren't sustainable, and they didn't align with Justin's promise to care for the planet. Justin also learned that millions of squeeze packs end up in landfills every year—and no one was focusing on this issue. He invited a group of major food companies that used squeeze packaging, as well as retailers and packaging manufacturers, to meet with him, and at what they dubbed the Sustainable Squeeze Pack Summit the group agreed to start experimenting. Within one year, several companies presented sustainable solutions. In 2012, Justin's Nut Butter, working with Cadillac Products Packaging Company, began testing a fully compostable pack made from 60 percent renewable materials.

As the squeeze-pack business grew, Justin expanded his company vision into candy, against the advice of his advisors. He formulated a recipe for peanut butter cups, the USDA certified it as organic, and he started making the products. Justin's gut proved right again: The peanut butter cups quickly topped the company's sales charts, with the Specialty Food Association awarding the Dark Chocolate Peanut Butter Cups a Sofi (Specialty Outstanding Food Innovation) Silver award, the industry's equivalent of an Oscar.

Justin largely attributes his great business to being in the "right place at the right time." For Justin, that right place is Boulder, Colorado, and this is why:

- The community cares about local and organic foods—so he did well at the farmers' market.

- He had access to mentorship. People from many successful natural foods companies based in Boulder helped Justin refine his ideas while he learned sales and product development.
- Boulder is home to many high-net-worth individuals who like investing in local entrepreneurs. (A Whole Foods Producer Loan helped too.)

In 2012, the company had 12 employees and almost $20 million in sales. That year, Entrepreneur.com named Justin a finalist in its 2012 Entrepreneur of the Year contest.

Justin Gold's success exemplifies connecting the dots: Through following his passion, exploring his options, listening to his intuition, talking to lots of people, and synchronicity, he was able to succeed. His focus, drive, and follow-through led him to make Good Food that quickly transformed into a great business that delivers on its promise to help people and the planet, while also producing a sustainable profit. Who knew nut butter could be so inspiring?

Decision Guide: Possible Product Strategies
The depth and breadth of your product line is just one aspect of a strategy. Whether you've already landed on your big idea, this chart might spark ideas.

Strategy Focus	Examples	Benefits to You	What You Need for It to Work	Possible Pitfalls
Single-serving size; on-the-go pack	Cooking-sauce packets; 100-calorie cookie pack; meal bars; nut butter squeeze packets	Niche, highly targeted marketing; can serve as "samples" for your products; high profit margin	Distribution in warehouse stores, vending machines, counters, and other grab-and-go locations	Hard to compete with high-volume brands that have lower production costs
Easier-to-use packaging	Squeezable fruits; squeeze bottles that sit upside down for faster squeezing; shelf-stable puddings	Tap in to a big market with useful, differentiated packaging that sets you apart	Funding for packaging development, plenty of "usability" testing on packaging, great marketing	Expensive-to-produce custom packaging, funds for consumer education

CONTINUE ▶

Strategy Focus	Examples	Benefits to You	What You Need for It to Work	Possible Pitfalls
Exciting and trendy	Kombucha, bacon jam, cheesecakes in a jar	Exciting for press and retailers seeking "new" and adventurous eaters	Samples, press raves, good placement in stores, serve a huge customer need (health, convenience, pleasure)	May be fleeting trends; infrequent use; can confuse retail buyers (no obvious department to place them in)
New twists on old favorites, often better-for-you versions of "junk" foods	Cheesecakes in a jar, non-GMO popcorn, natural candy bars, locally sourced ice cream	Easy for customers to "grasp" the food concept and "risk" trying, serve customers seeking healthier alternatives to favorite foods	Compelling descriptions, good ingredients, better tasting than the original versions, affordable yet profitable prices	Comparisons to conventional, cheaper-to-produce products
Dietary choices	Gluten-free, vegan, low glycemic index, sugar-free	Easy to communicate to a highly targeted customer group	Niche marketing, recipes that are delicious despite the health benefits	Can be expensive to produce for a limited market
Lifestyle	Calorie-free noodles, carb-free bread, immune-boosting gummy candies, fair-trade and organic foods	Aligning with trends leads to higher sales, the satisfaction you're helping consumers and suppliers	Great marketing and sampling campaigns (or mainstream press and blogger raves) to build consumer confidence	Expensive to produce and develop the products, with much nutrition testing required
Experiential and novelty	Cookie mixes, flavored salt-tasting kits, chocolate sampler with wine-pairing instructions, customizable foods	Often easier to make, more shelf-stable (e.g., cookie mix vs. baked cookies), giftable at higher price points	A unique twist, bundled gift packs for highest price points	Competition from high-quality store brands, consumers who want to assemble their own kits or samplers

Step 2: State Your Value Proposition—What's In It for the Customer?

Think of your favorite brand of your favorite food product. Why do you love it so much? You have just verbalized that food's value proposition, often called the unique selling proposition (USP). The USP of your product combines traits that make your offering different from any others. The USP does not overcome all the other ways potential customers might spend their money, but it helps your brand stand out among similar products.

Examples:

- Organic hazelnut cocoa spread, a healthful indulgence for breakfast through dessert with just Oregon hazelnuts, cocoa, and sugar. (The competition here is Nutella, which contains palm oil and vanillin, yet to many consumers offers an irresistible value proposition: memories of a trip to Europe.)
- Snackable 100-calorie fruit rolls kids will love, made with 100 percent local, organic fruits dried at low temperatures to preserve the natural nutrients and bright colors.
- Gluten-free, organic cornmeal pizza crusts priced well, ready to use, and flexible enough for any toppings. Have delicious pizzas or appetizers ready in minutes.

When considering your value, try skipping phrases such as "artisan" and "handcrafted" to focus on the tangible value to the buyer. What is a "small batch" anyway? Value phrases include "fresh" ("made fresh to order"), "rare" ("grown organically in the Jones family's 100-year-old orchards"), and "99 percent fruit" ("slow-cooked over three days for intense flavor and natural spreadability. Twenty-five peaches in every jar!").

Simultaneously consider your value proposition to retailers, which may turn out to be the same as your message to consumers. Project ahead to the time a retail buyer hears about your product. One company promises its ready-to-eat, bagged lettuce will "protect category profitability." Retailers operate on very slim margins. Every penny counts. A message that stores can reduce spoilage, and therefore losses, gets attention. Combined with the value to consumers of easy healthful eating, the products cover the bases. That's also how flavored almonds packed for snacking and tossing into meals have made inroads into the produce section. Produce shoppers tend to have healthful eating in mind. Almonds are healthful. Selling in this part of the store, beyond the bulk bin or baking aisle, reaches new customers and gives stores new profit potential.

OCHO CANDY GROWS ON FOUR KEY PILLARS

Denis Ring and Scott Kucirek combined their passion for Good Food with their business backgrounds (Denis having developed private-label brands for Whole Foods and Safeway) to start Five Star Organics. Their Ocho Candy line was the first line of all-organic, mainstream-style candy bars on the market.

See how the four value propositions they wanted to offer consumers guided Ocho Candy's development:

(1) **Tastes good.** These candy bars blew my mind. The company is committed to making the bars in a way that maintains the center's softness—even though this meant a more laborious production method that's unlike other candy bar manufacturing. For Denis and Scott, flavor, texture, and the overall eating experience trumped ease of manufacturing. Real ingredients such as ground coffee, rather than flavorings or extracts, fill the bars. It's more expensive to produce this way, but they can still make the numbers work as their popularity, and production volume, increases.

(2) **Organic.** The 100 percent-organic value proposition for candy bars is unparalleled, at least today.

(3) **Affordable.** Organic eaters and parents seeking healthier-for-you treats know that Good Food costs more. The bars sell for around $2, which is about average for a natural candy bar and equal to the price of a candy-store bonbon.

(4) **Fun.** The company wanted a bright, cheerful, colorful approach. Early on, the product had to stand out on shelves while the company simultaneously built awareness, mostly through sampling. The name "Ocho" is fun and easy to remember. Denis noodled over names for many months. He knew that people remember numbers; for example, most refer to Whole

Foods 365 Everyday Value brand as "365." Ocho was perfect because the "O" can stand for organic, while the "cho" brings to mind chocolate. The potential appeal to Spanish speakers was a bonus. "It allows the brand a bigger identity than what we have in North America," Denis says.

Step 3: Define Your Product Line

Ready to get audacious? Take a stand and outline your short- and long-term product offerings, even if it's just preliminary.

Here's an outline for what you should cover:

- PRODUCT. List your products, with one line per product size.

- VALUE PROPOSITION TO CUSTOMERS. State what's in it for them. Your value proposition should vary by product size, because you're offering different features and benefits.

- POSITIONING. State what differentiates your products from the competition—something you'll need to do when talking to a potential buyer who says: "We already stock an XYZ. Why should we carry yours?"

- FEATURES AND BENEFITS. Every customer buying decision revolves around evaluating product attributes, called "features," and what the customer gets out of the product, called "benefits." Your promised features and benefits will direct your ingredients and packaging decisions and are integral to your marketing. Based on the value proposition you have in mind, you can outline exactly how you'll deliver on your promise. Take the following olive snack-pack example:
    - Convenient 30-g/1-oz resealable foil pouches of delicious marinated olives
    - Naturally healthful with no preservatives and only 50 calories per pack
    - Vegetarian, vegan, kosher, and lower in salt than other olives
    - Perfect for lunches and picnics
    - Easy to eat as they're pit-free; great for kids

- **EXPECTED PERCENTAGE OF REVENUE.** Take a wild guess as to the proportion each product or size will likely comprise in your overall sales mix. This column should total 100 percent. (Don't be surprised if your projection follows the 80-20 rule, with 20 percent of your products generating 80 percent of your revenue. Refresh yourself on this concept in "Understand the 80-20 Rule (The Quick Way to Make the Right Decisions)," page 31.)

Get a quick start with the Product Planning template on GoodFoodGreatBusiness.com.

PROVE YOUR IDEA: YOUR TASTING-PARTY SHOOT-OUT

Everyone's saying, "You should sell that!" But should you? A tasting party gives you a better idea of how marketable your food might be. Food business consultant Anni Minuzzo outlines how to arrange a competitive-analysis tasting party, where you'll compare your goods to other similar foods. Think how much money you can save by getting any feedback and suggestions *before* going to market! Here's how to go about the party:

- Identify your three most significant competitors.

- Purchase enough of their products for a blind taste test. Remove the products from their packaging and place them in containers with labels such as A, B, C, etc. Include your own product.

- Invite six to ten tasters, ideally those who reflect the primary consumers for the products. For complete honesty and objectivity, it's best to choose strangers. Try to schedule breakfast-centric foods for the morning and tastings of desserts and savory and spicy foods later in the day. You don't want palate confusion coloring tasters' feedback.

- Create a feedback sheet to give the tasters. The sheet should list various categories to assess: appearance, texture, color, flavor, aftertaste. Include space for general comments. You might even want to ask for ideas for the product name.

- Guests can taste at their own pace, or you or a friend can moderate the tasting, directing when to taste what.

After the test, show the tasters the packaging, including your own if you have a rough prototype (see "Test Your Packaging," page 97) or even just a sketch. Ask tasters to discuss what they like and don't like about the packaging and brands. Listen closely to their first impressions. Ask about type legibility, logo, colors, pricing, nutritional appeal, and visibility on a store shelf. Accept feedback on your own products openly and without defensiveness, and consider how you might use feedback about other products to your advantage.

You can decide whether to tally the tasting results while your guests are present. They may want to know. I've enjoyed sharing such test results to get real-time reactions, see facial expressions, and ask for suggestions. Using the feedback, consider how you can improve your product and competitive position. Be sure to consider any biases and whether the tasters truly represent your target customer.

TAKEAWAYS

- Understanding the customers whose needs you wish to serve is extremely important; demographics and psychographics can help you do this.

- Knowing who and what your competition is will also help you direct your product to better fit your customers' needs and wants.

- You can choose to go broad or to go deep with your product strategy. Or both. The simpler the strategy, the easier, cheaper, and faster it is to achieve and the lower your risk.

- A strong value proposition and strong positioning that differentiates you from the competition makes you most attractive to buyers.

GREAT BUSINESS ACTION PLAN

☐ Define the customers your company will serve.

☐ Draft your general strategies for how you'll develop your business the first three years.

☐ Make a list of current competitors (including hidden competitors). Embark on competitive product research to find competitors you didn't know about. Try tapping into local business students for research help. Your food business could be their dream project.

☐ Identify your product line with value proposition, features and benefits, and positioning for each target audience.

☐ Test your product ideas; if you have prototypes, have a Tasting-Party Shoot-Out against competing products.

☐ Contact the Small Business Administration (SBA) for help at SBA.gov, through Service Corps of Retired Executives (SCORE) and/or Small Business Development Centers (SBDCs).

☐ Refer to SpecialtyFood.com for research studies and articles on trends by food category as well as to see Sofi award winners. See who's winning Good Food Awards at goodfoodawards.org.

☐ Talk to store buyers; listen for signs pointing to unmet opportunities.

ON *GOODFOODGREATBUSINESS.COM*

Get a quick start with the Product Planning and Research Template and Checklists spreadsheet along with links to the resources mentioned in this chapter.

CHAPTER

BRAND YOUR BUSINESS

BURNING QUESTION:
I'VE GOT A COMPUTER. CAN I DIY MY BRAND?

Maybe, with a big "but" and "if." If you're artsy and your brand revolves around rubber stamps and craftiness, you might be able to do it yourself. But, for most businesses, you'll have just one chance to make a great impression—and you don't want to blow it with a design that doesn't do your product justice. A onetime investment in a high-impact brand can take you a long way. Plus, you'll focus your time on more important things, such as building your business.

WHAT BRANDING IS AND WHY IT'S IMPORTANT

What do "potato chips" bring to mind? Close your eyes for a second and certain colors, package textures, chip shapes, flavorings, or logos may drift by along with the visceral memory of a gas station on a long road trip. Now think of a couple of different potato chip makers and the differences in their products, packaging, pricing, and where they sell. Maybe you even have different impressions of the companies and their chips—some chips may be more "natural," while others are highly processed. All of the attributes you associate with a brand, including its ingredients, make up a brand's identity or image. A strong brand separates your product from the competition, makes it stand out, and evokes fond feelings in your target customers.

A brand comprises your name, logo, packaging design (including its colors, typography, and look), and the tone and voice of your written communication. Aspects of your product can represent your brand as well. That's why you need to align your brand with your 5 Staples mix. In fact, a November 2012 Kettle Brand ad campaign reminded us that other food makers "can copy our style but they'll never have our substance." Where you sell, at what price, and your product quality are inextricably tied to how people perceive your brand. (Have you ever unexpectedly seen rare foods or luxury goods at a drugstore and changed how you perceive those brands?)

Your efforts will build your "brand equity," which is the value underlying your company name and image. Brand equity creates loyal customers who will buy your product again and again, and, if you are lucky, some of those customers will sing your praises to others, effectively doing marketing for you. When you hear of one company suing another over a name or logo that's too similar to theirs, it's because the business is protecting its brand equity. On the flip side, "generic" products don't have brand equity to rely on; their makers put no money into building their brand name, and therefore these products can be sold for lower prices. The parent company selling the generics under their name needs strong brand equity, however. Otherwise, consumers might not trust the generic.

Emir Kiamilev, who rebranded his Amella Caramels to expand the company's opportunities, says: "Great branding means you're able to command a high price in the marketplace. It gives funders assurance that tomorrow someone won't be coming out with a lower-cost 'me too' product that people will switch to." If your product has strong brand equity, consumers will more likely think "I want the real thing" and buy it over its competitors. Finally, if, down the line, you want to sell your company, brand equity will be important. Read more about the Amella strategy in "Inside Scoop: Amella Caramels Remixes for Marketing Success," page 187.

INSIDE SCOOP:
DROGA CONFECTIONS BRANDS STRATEGICALLY FOR GREAT FOOD GIFTS

When Michelle Crochet set out to turn her mom's salted peanut-rocky road recipe into a business, she set her sights on retail sales as her target market. Drawing upon her experience as a food buyer for Williams-Sonoma, Michelle crafted a 5 Staples mix focused on selling in stores where old-fashioned candy lovers would value natural, simple ingredients as much as delicious candy—and would pay the premium for such quality.

First, she perfected the Good Food aspect of her recipe, using organic brown-rice syrup instead of corn syrup, and local California wildflower honey, which she buys direct. Michelle strategically names her organic dairy source on her website and packaging.

"Customers know those ingredients because they buy them in the local market. They can see that we're using simple, natural ingredients."

Next, Michelle approached packaging with an eye toward maximum appeal to retailers. Her brightly colored, eye-catching packaging pops off the shelves. The boxes are shrink-wrapped, increasing their shelf life, which extends Droga's appeal to wholesale customers too. "A few months versus a few weeks definitely makes our product more viable for the marketplace and allows me to grow my business," says Michelle, noting that candy made using classic methods results in a delicious product that will stay delicious for a few months. This is a nice example of turning a product-quality story into a real value proposition different from brands that rely on preservatives for shelf life. To increase sales in the gift market, she created a package beautiful for giving as is—no need to wrap it or add a bow.

DRAFT A BRANDING STRATEGY

As Justin's Nut Butter (see page 63) expanded its product line and distribution, the time came to leave its original homegrown look behind. A clear strategy directed Justin Gold's creative team. He explains, "I wanted to turn my farmers' market brand appeal into a national brand appeal. I wanted it to be fun and goofy, yet reliable and safe. The brand had to communicate: 'This is the best nut butter ever, and it comes from people who are laid-back and silly, yet who mean business.'" Mission achieved. The designers chose to use a playful script type, without an icon or mark, as the logo. Each package identifies the flavor with a charming nut illustration against a clean, white backdrop.

You'll embark on similar strategic thinking as you write your branding strategy, which outlines goals for your logo, overall look, naming, and even packaging direction. Consider your designers to be part of your team. The more they understand your goals, the better they'll rock your designs and feel part of your success. Your strategy document should include:

- Background information on you, your products, and your company

- The target customers who will be buying your products

- Unique selling proposition or value proposition that sets your brand apart in the marketplace

- Key words describing your brand's spirit and style, such as "healthful, indulgent, friendly, earthy, simple" or "breezy, personable, friendly, energetic"

- Logo direction, such as if you want an icon or just text, and any preferred color palettes. You should also include constraints, such as if you want the logo to look good when it's in black-and-white. Be sure to specify that you want Web-ready as well as high-resolution logos and graphics for printing on banners, clothing, and brochures.

- Your closest competitors, which helps the designers see what products may be on display alongside yours

- Designs you really don't want to see, such as "a chalkboard look," "1950s-style kitsch," or "a supermarket look with bright, garish colors"

- Brands you admire that exemplify what you're going for, whether food brands or nonfood brands

- Packaging and labeling requirements, including eventual internationalization plans that could multiply the space you need to jam in multilingual information

You'll find a Branding Strategy template on GoodFoodGreatBusiness .com. As you might have guessed, much of this planning can plug neatly into your overall business plan.

GOOD IDEA:
BE A STORE DETECTIVE

At the same time as you conduct your competitive-product research in stores, you can audit packaging for products within your category and perhaps beyond. What you see may very well answer "What should my look be?" The idea here is to evaluate which products quickly catch your eye, see how well they fit and stand out on the shelf, think about how your prospective customers might react to your competitors' company and product

---

NAME AND TAGLINE YOUR COMPANY AND PRODUCTS

In addition to identifying your branding goals, you need to name your brand. In a perfect world, you'll approach the verbal and visual aspects of your brand at the same time, for efficiency and unity. But in some cases, you may have a name before a brand strategy, or vice versa. Whatever order you tackle things, always think strategically about your goals and focus on the brand experience you're trying to create.

The best brand names are simple and conceptual, according to Alexandra Watkins of the San Francisco naming company Eat My Words. Alexandra shares some of her tips for names that work:

- Articulate the personality of your brand in three words, such as you did for your mantra (see page 40), and then use that as a litmus test for names.

- Make your business name easy to say (for word of mouth) and spell (for searching), especially if your target customers include non-native English speakers.

- Avoid the temptation to base your company name on available domain names.

- Paint a memorable mental picture with your brand, such as Krave Jerky or Le Caramel. People remember pictures more than words.

- Project ahead when including the product in the company name. You might assume the company Just Tomatoes makes just that—rather than the vast line of freeze-dried fruit and vegetables that, in reality, comprises the product line.

- Keep names short if possible, such as Nutorious or Lotus Foods. While longer names—such as the very visual Brown Butter Cookie Company and Jeni's Splendid Ice Creams—can work, be aware that consumers might shorten them and just say, for example, "I just inhaled a pint of Jeni's."

- Create a positive brand experience and an emotional connection. What do you want your customer to feel when they purchase and then give or consume your foods? Or receive your food as a gift?

- Avoid acronyms unless you've got an ad budget, like TCBY. Generally, though, acronyms just aren't tasty.

- Consider how your brand name and/or logo might look on merchandise such as T-shirts or tote bags. Eventually, if you have a cool enough name and brand, people will pay *you* to wear your brand.

Take a look at how the following brand names embody different goals/themes. Do any of these themes appeal to you?

Theme	Examples
Evoking a lifestyle	KIND Healthy Snacks, Caveman Cookies, Blue Lotus Chai
Product benefit	Tasty Brand, Invisible Chef, Vibrant Flavors
Founder's name plus food	Dave's Killer Bread, Zhena's Gypsy Tea, Rick's Picks
A family name	Effie's Homemade, Tate's Bake Shop, Pennington Farms
Puns or attitude	Three Tarts Bakery, My Husband's Nuts, White Girl Salsa
Real place names	Sonoma Syrup, Rogue Creamery, Royal Hawaiian Honey
Conceptual place	Earth & Vine Provisions, Saffron Road, Pepper Creek Farms
Specific food	Artisan Biscuits, SugarVeil, Olli's Salumeria
How it's made	Bourbon Barrel Foods, Rustic Bakery, Brooklyn Brine

Or you could combine a variety of themes, as did Callie's Charleston Biscuits.

Brand and Naming Hierarchy

Start with a brand hierarchy, which is like a family tree starting with the company name down to product lines and flavor names. Peeled Snacks, a dried-fruit-snacks company, has aligned its desire to make healthful snacks fun with its product names: Cherry-go-round, Apple-2-the-core, and Banan-a-peel.

A company name and logo can only get across so much information—that's where taglines can come in handy. A tagline is that descriptive phrase you often see tacked on to a logo; it further identifies your brand. The tagline might reflect what you do (the offbeat "Shameless Exploitation in Pursuit of the Common Good" from Newman's Own), what you stand for (Vosges Haut-Chocolat's "travel the world through chocolate"), or what's in it for the customer (the oft-photographed "You Can't Beat Our Meat" from a Los Angeles meat company).

Your tagline's tone and message all come back to the direction in your branding strategy and your competitive positioning. You can go without a tagline, but it helps people describe your company and products in terms that you control. Without a tagline, consumers and promoters may go mute, particularly when it comes to foods carving a new niche. Is it a natural meal bar, an energy bar, a nutrition bar, or a fruit-and-nut candy bar? Make word-of-mouth marketing effortless for your followers. If you were feeling supercreative when abbreviating your mission as a mantra (see "State Your Mission: Why Are You Doing This?" on page 38), you might very well turn that mantra into your tagline, provided the phrase resonates with your customers. Chipotle Mexican Grill's "Food With Integrity" tagline is both central to the restaurant chain's marketing and clearly doubles as a mantra, not to mention a guiding principle for their ingredients sourcing.

TAGLINES VS. SLOGANS

How are taglines different from slogans? Taglines usually stay the same for years, if not forever. Slogans tend to be shorter term and more marketing campaign–based, changing over time, as we've seen in mainstream advertising.

Cheap and Fun Exercises for Names and Taglines

When embarking on naming your company, never discount a crazy idea—it may be a stroke of genius in disguise. Go ahead, take a road trip to nowhere and see if inspiration strikes you along the way. Soak in a hot tub. Daydream while cooking. Or take the popular shortcut of picking your friends' brains. Schedule a dinner-party brainstorming session. Fill your guests in on your target market and goals. (I'd skip the nondisclosure agreement; if they'd wanted to start a black-bean brownie company, they probably would have.) Make a poster with your company name and product-name headings. Suggest they write ideas on sticky notes, or shout them out loud. The number-one rule is no criticism and no "nos" or "buts," especially from you.

Time pressure can produce wonders. Rachel Flores and Bill Waiste of P.O.P. Candy in Santa Monica, California, were in a crunch to come up with a name for their candy company when they had a last-minute chance to sell at a farmers' market. They brainstormed, striving for a name that said "community" and was short and hip. Billy suggested Pacific Ocean Park, after a local Santa Monica landmark. Rachel exclaimed "P.O.P.," and a name was born.

The name "Nutless Professor" came to me like a beacon in the night as I cooked up a batch of my nut-free black-rice snacks. My major brand goal was for kids to learn more about where their food comes from. After blurting out the name to an audience of marketers with whom I was holding a product-tasting and brainstorming session, their laughter convinced me I was on the right track. If laughter is the best medicine and you're making good-for-you food, perhaps a smile is the ultimate litmus test.

If a play on a popular food brand comes to mind, you might verify that your name is no threat rather than finding out the hard way (as did a restaurant briefly named McDharma's).

Test Your Name, Logo, and Tagline

Do some casual testing before investigating trademarking. Ideally, coordinate testing your overall brand along with testing your food products. After all, when you're out selling, customers will be judging your full offering, from the first glance on the shelf to reading your packaging and on through the eating experience. Venture beyond your friends and family, ideally with retailers and other customers. You're seeking unbiased feedback from people who are new to your concept—not warm fuzzies and self-esteem boosting.

When testing your foods, call them by the product names you're thinking about. Watch testers' reactions as they say the names out loud and comment on your tagline. Is the name too close to competitive products? Do the names easily roll off the tongue? Are some avoiding saying the names to avoid mispronunciation? Italian-named Ghirardelli Chocolate struggled with just that, over a century ago. They created posters to get people to "Say Gear-ar-delly!"

Get a quick start testing with the Branding Feedback template on GoodFoodGreatBusiness.com.

Design Your Logo and Look

After confirming that your name works and is legally available (read on for more on the last one), you will embark on logo design, brand colors, typography, and an overall look for your brand, based on your branding strategy.

You may work with a graphic designer who specializes in branding. Or you may find a packaging designer or firm that can handle all of your branding and marketing needs. (You'll read more about vendors in chapter 13.)

Be sure to test the logo in all sorts of scenarios: online, print, T-shirts. Share several versions with friends and colleagues for feedback.

Verify Availability and Own It

Your names, logo, and potentially other aspects of your brand, including packaging concepts, comprise your company's intellectual property—one of the key company assets that you will promote. You need to know that your desired names and taglines are legally available.

You can do a quick text and/or image trademark search on USPTO .gov or through a trademark specialist (a company that guides new businesses through the trademark process). If your name looks free and clear, go ahead and spend $10 or so to reserve your Web domain, along with any similar variations. The Systems Checklist on GoodFoodGreat Business.com lists a few domain services along with my two cents.

Trademark registration costs several hundred dollars per item and provides protection against infringement. Simply adding the ™ symbol to your company name may protect you in certain geographical areas, but if you're banking on company growth and expansion, register the name for the highest level of protection. Services such as cooking lessons or parties may be protected with a service mark (℠) before registration is complete. Try to handle all of the legal work related to protecting your brand at once—it will save you some time and bucks. Needless to say, for the final word, please check with your designer, a legal service, and/or USPTO.gov.

WRITE YOUR AUTHENTIC STORY

Much like your company name and visual brand identity, your story serves as the foundation for your in-person pitches, the "About Us" or "Our Story" page of your website, and the section at the bottom of your press releases called "boilerplate." You'll use snippets of your story for your social media profiles and for any marketing materials you print up for events.

Start working on your story as you develop your brand. Telling your story can also give you context to see if you really like your potential company and product names. Draw from the work you've done in outlining your vision, mission, product strategies, and value proposition, which defines what you're making and for whom. Most important, your story should highlight a "grabber" to draw the reader in:

"We take our fishing boat out over the continental shelf and harvest 1,000 pounds of salt water at a time." So began Bob La Mar's pitch at the Mendocino Sea Salt & Seasoning farmers' market booth. Clad in a cowboy hat, boots, jeans, and a denim shirt, Bob flawlessly and sincerely would tell the story of how he and his wife, Lora, transform the water to flaky sea salt, as well as how the business got started (see page 16).

You may have a fun story of how you took the plunge into entrepreneurship. You very well may not. If the reality is that you needed to make money and started making thin gluten-free cookies with local butter, organic sugar, and sea salt at fewer calories per bite, you can still write a delicious story that will entice consumers. Check out other companies' stories, then write your own—in a voice reflecting your brand—including the following elements:

- Your inspiration for starting the company.

- What you're making. Like bean-to-bar chocolate makers, the La Mars' challenge was communicating they were not simply repackaging purchased salt, another lucrative business model.

- The value you're offering and to whom. Here, you want to keep benefits related to your commitments to the planet and people (recyclable, renewable, Fair Trade) secondary to the food itself. The "good" is good, but the food must be delicious and fill a need too. Two Degrees Foods and Tom's Shoes need to deliver great quality as well as delivering on their promise to make donations with every purchase.

- Your guiding principles (see "Outline Your Guiding Principles: Your Rules of the Road," page 50)—explain what you promise to do and what you promise to never do in a storylike way.

- How you see the company evolving in pursuit of its goals.

- How you're involved with your community and causes, and other aspects of your social mission.

As you did in writing your value proposition, avoid buzzwords such as "artisan," "small batch," and "handcrafted." Instead, paint specific pictures, perhaps your tireless quest for the best ingredients, and the methods you use to make your Good Food—if, and only if, your process is central to your unique value. In the end, your food's deliciousness trumps a cute story. Think about using "we" rather than "I," even if the company is only you at this point—since down the line, you will likely have a team or a co-packer.

Here's a story I love: Anchored by the trademarked tagline "Love Just Tastes Good," San Francisco's Love & Hummus Co. carries its theme of love for people, pure food, and the planet throughout its website and other marketing copy. For example, "We love to take care of both your hunger and the planet by using only the finest organic ingredients to fill each and every recyclable glass jar." When founder Donna Sky gets in front of people at an event, her mission comes to life as she exuberantly explains her commitment to people and the planet through an organic product packed in jars.

TAKEAWAYS

- Having a branding strategy will help differentiate your company in the marketplace and appeal to your target audience.

- Your company and product names and tagline should be simple and conceptual to draw in the consumer; testing your names on your target audience is a smart move.

- Make sure any names you want to use are legally available so you can trademark them.

- Writing an authentic story early on will help you bring your branding strategy to life and clarify your vision and company strategies.

GREAT BUSINESS ACTION PLAN

☐ Get out and online to do competitive brand and packaging research.

☐ Think of three companies whose brands match with what you're looking for in your brand and customer experience. Research how they developed their brand identities and other creative elements (their websites, writing, etc.).

☐ Write your branding strategy. Determine how much you can budget toward branding, based on what your likely approach will be. Research and contact potential branding firms or freelancers (see "Build Your Support System: Commune, Contract, and Hire," page 209).

☐ Come up with your company and product names.

☐ Verify name availability and reserve the names and domain names.

☐ Write your story.

☐ Reality test your branding strategy with three people familiar with your company vision and who match your customer profile. Ask for honest feedback.

ON *GOODFOODGREATBUSINESS.COM*

Get a quick start with the Branding Strategy and Branding Feedback templates, Research Template and Checklist, and Systems Checklist, along with links to designers and other resources.

STEP
3

MAKE YOUR FOOD PRODUCTS REAL

PACKAGE YOUR PRODUCT

BURNING QUESTION:
WHEN DO I START WORKING ON PACKAGING?

A better question might be: When do I stop? Start thinking about packaging early on, as you craft your value proposition. Then revisit it when you prototype, learn more about production and your customers, and get a real grasp on the costs. You'll be able to finalize your packaging once you determine that your plan fits with your 5 Staples mix and that the packaging itself fits on the shelves of the retailers where you hope to sell.

THE POINT OF PACKAGING

What does the word "packaging" bring to mind? A floating island of trash? Alas, for most food products, you can't get around having some kind of container. Even at the bulk bins, the plastic bags you fill up with granola and rice are a form of packaging.

Farmers' market sellers can happily minimize packaging, because the producer is right there to make the sale. In most retail situations though, package design directly influences buying behavior. *Packaging World* magazine's *Labeling Playbook* puts hard numbers behind this fact: A whopping 70 percent of purchase decisions are made in the store, and 35 percent of purchases go to the products with the most eye-catching packaging. Package designer Rowland Heming notes that more carefully considered purchases tend to use shape and texture to awaken the senses and entice customers to spend extra in return for a more unique value proposition. Think about what goes into liquor- and perfume-bottle designs. Impulse purchases, the ones you try to resist but just can't, lean toward bold designs and information to quickly communicate the brand and product value as potential buyers cruise by. For example, the company Torie & Howard coupled organic hard candy with unusually beautiful tins. Their design makes the tins equally appealing to pull out at the opera (to stop that dry cough) or display atop an office desk. More important, a retailer's display by the cash register looks sharp, with colorful tins stacked high, ready for the shoppers to "grab and go." Torie & Howard's agency, Silver Creative Group, did an amazing job integrating the brand into an equally colorful, animated Web experience.

INSIDE SCOOP:
SWEET REVOLUTION MAKES A BIG IMPACT WITH A SMALL FOOTPRINT

For fans of Sweet Revolution's maple honey caramels, the brand's name evokes a white waxed wrapper protecting a rich, salty, USDA-certified organic caramel. A goal to "leave only footprints" on the earth drives artisaneur Anastasia Hägerström's packaging choices. I was stunned the first time I saw Anastasia hand-stamping the Sweet Revolution name on the compostable cardboard box, packing her hand-cut caramels inside, then wrapping the box with string before sealing it with red wax—artisanal to the core. That wax seal is unique and sets her apart. "When I was making Sweet Revolution, I was taking a class in Greek mythology," she explains. "That's where the idea of the seal came from. Every time I stamp it, I remember the depth of character in the Greeks." For her honey maple caramel sauce, she chose standard wide-mouthed jars because they're both cute and easy for the customer to reuse.

Anastasia focuses on direct-to-consumer sales and relationships with retail vendors who can turn the product over quickly, due to the candy's short shelf life. Handmade means high cost. So she partners with companies such as Dean & DeLuca whose clientele appreciates—and can afford—a premium, gourmet, and certified organic caramel in artistic packaging.

Anastasia relocated Sweet Revolution from San Francisco to the East Coast, a move that served both personal and business goals: She wanted a more rural life and to be closer to the source of her ingredients, her packaging suppliers, and her major customers. The result? Lower production and wholesale costs, thanks to lower shipping expenses. Just as important, she can feel she's taken steps to leave the smallest carbon footprint possible.

DEFINE YOUR PACKAGING ELEMENTS

Start by thinking about all the purposes your packaging will serve. Here are a few possibilities:

- **PROTECTION.** Packaging keeps food clean and compliant with Food and Drug Administration (FDA) and local sanitation rules.

- **BRANDING.** Package material, package design (its shape), and graphic design identify your brand.

- **PRESENTABILITY.** Will your product be given as a gift, displayed on the kitchen table, or stacked in a basket? The more unique, delicious, and known your food product, the less buyers will critique its packaging.

- **UTILITY.** Envision how your product will be carried and stored—not to mention how it will be consumed. Will it be poured, scooped, spread, or thrown in the mouth by the handful? Will the eater want to reseal the package, or would he prefer single-serving packs?

- **COMMUNICATING INFORMATION.** Aside from text that tells your company's story, packaging helps you comply with FDA rules for displaying details about ingredients, weight, origin, allergens, and other information that informs and protects consumers.

- **EXTENDING SHELF LIFE.** A longer shelf life makes life easier for you, resellers or distributors, and customers storing your products. Most packaging materials—plastic, metal, paper, glass, etc.—come in different thicknesses. Thicker packaging usually costs more but offers durability and a longer shelf life for your products. Little (and expensive) tricks, like lining paper bags or plastic cans with barrier film, add to shelf life.

Keep your first round of packaging simple, unless your business is well funded and you're planning to quickly expand into retail. Food entrepreneurs often start with ready-made packaging, which usually costs a fraction of what customized packaging does. You can easily customize ready-made boxes, pouches, bags, or jars with branded labels and tags. You'll find some suppliers listed in "Produce Your Packaging," page 98. Santa Monica, California–based P.O.P. Candy began printing "special occasion" stickers—such as "Love you," "Congrats!" and "Moms rule"—to dress up its tins for gift giving. Tin sales shot up, confirming what the candy makers believed: Easy gifts equal easy money.

Packaging and Filling Go Hand in Hand

Your packaging idea may seem really simple. But keep your finger off the "Buy Now" trigger before confirming how you or your co-packer will fill the packages. Take spices, for example. You'd think blending and packing spices in metal tins would be a no-brainer. On the contrary, one spice co-packer told me, "First, tins often don't seal 100 percent. Air and humidity get into the tin, reducing the spice's shelf life or requiring an extra seal. Plus, tins are very labor intensive and expensive to work with." The suggestion? Those typical plastic bottles, for which the co-packer already had automatic-filling equipment. Not quite the desired high-end brand experience. In cases like this, decision paths could include:

- Finding a co-packer who is able to package in well-sealed tins. This task becomes more difficult the more specific your requirements, such as wanting a co-packer near you who is certified organic, fits in your budget, and can handle large volume.

- Packaging your spices yourself. (To begin with, however, you'd need to plan for a licensed facility, an efficient way to pack the spices, a budget for labor, and the list goes on.)

- Finding a company that specializes in packing food. (In this case, you'd either mix your spices yourself and get them to this packing company, or your co-packer will do the sourcing and mixing and deliver the spices for packing.)

- Finding other packaging that would be acceptable and that your co-packer can manage.

The Packaging for Your Packaging

Allot plenty of time and money to scope out your complete packaging needs. In the case of single-serve items, such as chewing gum, tea bags, or instant oatmeal packs, you may need both a product package and a display case to hold several small packages. Your packages may also have decorative or protective elements, such as peel-back heat-seal films (for plastic tubs of dips or hummus), cellophane shrink wrap, hangtags, or cardboard supports to avoid breakage.

Each of your product sizes needs its own packaging and design. Often, each of those packages has a minimum production run, meaning the smallest number of units your packaging company is willing to make for a set price. (Your designer or packaging broker may have ideas to combine, or "gang up," the designs into one run.) Each size may also need to be filled in a different way, further complicating production. If you're on a tight budget, prioritize the sizes strategically: The products 80 percent of shoppers will buy? Or that contribute to 80 percent of your revenue? It all goes back to your mission.

Beyond the packaging that holds your food, food sold in retail stores often needs a few more packaging containers, kind of like Russian nesting dolls.

Case packs. These packages commonly hold six to twelve units of product, such as beverage four-packs, pasta sauce eight-packs, or energy bar twelve-packs. Display sleeves are another sort of case pack, those branded boxes you see filled with twelve or more units either sold by box often at a discount (such as energy bars) and mint tins or snack-size bags by the cash register.

Master cases. These large cartons, or shipper cases, hold multiple case packs for transporting on pallets and delivery to retailers. These are the boxes you see distributor reps unloading onto store shelves. If your target retailers might stack your master cases, and you have the budget, you might eventually design branded cases.

For example, Rooibee Red Tea ships a branded outer master case that contains three four-packs. In addition to telling the product's story, the master case includes a perforated window that opens up to show-case the featured-flavor four-pack. Such packaging is a selling point for retailers, as it creates an instant, effortless display and is ideal to stack on endcaps, the coveted spot at the end of store aisles.

Be sure to optimize the number of case packs per master case to appeal to your target stores. If you deliver too many case packs in your master case, small stores won't want to risk selling all of that product, and they may not have enough shelf space anyway. When packing for "free fills"—the product some retailers require new businesses to pro-vide for free to prove your market potential—packing fewer case packs in a master case minimizes your cost. The optimal quantity might vary depending on the product category.

POCO DOLCE PACKS FOR THE OCCASION

Sweet-toothed San Franciscans are no stranger to the allure of Poco Dolce Confections, a candy maker that's won awards and kudos from retailers and customers alike.

Because she runs her own production kitchen, Kathy Wiley and her nine-person team can package the crave-worthy confections a number of ways, easily experimenting with new packaging formats (often a struggle when outsourcing to co-packers). The diverse and growing product line includes bonbons, hot chocolate, chocolate bars, and bittersweet chocolate "tiles." The range of Poco Dolce packaging spans metal tins, cardboard boxes, plastic boxes, translucent paper envelopes for single-serve bites, all-occasion gift boxes, and chocolate bars in resealable cardboard sleeves.

With this diverse product line, Wiley's chocolates can be placed in candy store–style display cases, at checkout counters, and in the candy-bar aisle of the supermarket. Customers can meet all their chocolate-buying needs too: a quick pop-in-the-mouth snack, more committed chocolate-bar munching, and the beautifully packaged thank-you gift. Kathy's commitment to deliciousness above all led the Specialty Food Association to award Poco Dolce the coveted Sofi Gold Award for Outstanding Chocolate in 2010 and made her a Good Food Awards finalist.

BALANCE PACKAGING SUSTAINABILITY AND FUNCTION

Look to your value proposition and competitive analysis to project what will catch a customer's eye, differentiate your product and brand, and lead to a sale. California's Saint Benoit Yogurt started by imprinting custom-made ceramic cups with the company's name, for which it charged a refundable fee. Customers would often keep the cute cups to reuse as rustic coffee mugs—a boon for Saint Benoit. As the company grew, they switched to cute, but plain, glass jars. What's the probable trade-off here?

Evaluate Sustainable Packaging Trade-offs

The packaging industry is quickly innovating planet-friendly packaging that's indistinguishable from its bad-for-the-planet brethren.

Packaging	Pros	Cons	Good for . . .
Glass jars	Airtight, reusable (with a cute label on the lid, it can also be an ad for your brand), continual engagement with customers, especially if returnable	Heavy and expensive to ship, breakable, not standard for many retail categories, not acceptable in some food-service venues	The usual items sold in glass jars (e.g., jam), a nice alternative to plastic for locally sold products
Compostable cellophane bag with tie	Low cost, looks cute and "artisan," giftable	Short shelf life, crushable	Small packs of food to be eaten soon
Resealable lined paper bag with roll top and closure	Relatively cheap	Informal looking, but can be gussied up with a nice label or rubber stamp	Baked goods; granola, coffee, other quickly consumed items
Heat-sealed plastic wrapper	Low cost, simple	Not resealable, a burden to keep closed after opening	Food to be munched on the spot (e.g., cookie two-packs, single-serve bags of peanuts)
Resealable flexible plastic pouch	Low cost, simple; various finish/color options, customizable closure options (pour spouts, zip locks)	Informal, opens easily (spillage), hard to keep upright on store shelves sometimes	Snack mixes, muesli and granola, nuts, jerky, superfood ingredients
Plastic tub	Simple to pack, good for storage, convenient for snacking, minimal breakage, light to ship	Looks cheap	Larger quantities of crackers or delicate cookies best laid flat, some candy
Plastic tray in printed wrapper or cardboard box	Sturdy and easy to ship in cartons, convenient storage, lots of brand messaging space, long shelf life	Expensive/complicated to produce, using several pieces and different materials; could be perceived as wasteful	Large-volume, delicate snacks and baked goods best stacked on their sides

Packaging	Pros	Cons	Good for . . .
Potato chip–style bag	Familiar, lots of branding space	Not resealable	Snack foods, popcorn
Tin	Can be imprinted with brand messaging, keepsake/eco-friendly	High up-front cost to produce, may not be airtight	Gifts of snacks, candy, and desserts

GOOD IDEA: CAN IT!

Hiball had the best of intentions when it chose glass bottles for its energy drinks. Brand designer Alyssa Warnock shares the company's lessons from the beverage aisle. "We originally thought glass would differentiate the product—so that the product seemed more unique and premium," she says. "This led to issues in inventory, breakage, shipping costs, and profit margins." The clincher—consumers often didn't realize Hiball was an energy drink. The switch to cans had numerous benefits: more real estate for graphics, easier shipping, a wider choice of co-packers that could work with cans, and easier recycling. Sales immediately increased once the cans hit the shelves.

PLAN AND WRITE YOUR PACKAGING INFORMATION

Once your ingredients, name, and brand identity are nearly final, you can start sketching out the information you want printed on the package or label. Since you have limited space, prioritize your messages in what's called an "information hierarchy." The most important information is the most eye-catching, and the less important details smaller, down to the itsy-bitsy legalese. Information hierarchy helps you keep your design simple. Check out Larabar's boldly colored wrappers. They state their ingredients with very little other text, with theater marquee–like simplicity.

As you start jotting down ideas for your copy (or you hire someone to do it for you), think about the different areas on the package that can display info. What should be on the front, top, side, back, or bottom? Approach this task strategically.

Focus on the 80 percent of facts that will make the sale and inspire repurchase. Could you get away with fewer than ten, or even five, key words on the front of the package? Maybe use graphics or photos to get the message across? Direct buyers to your website to learn more, such as which farmers you source ingredients from. Then you can shorten your message on the package to "farm direct," for example. An exception: When your farmer partners have strong brand recognition, their name or logo on the package could give you instant cred with buyers.

What the FDA Requires

The good news: If you aren't making nutrition claims (e.g., fat-free) and are selling fewer than 100,000 units per year to consumers in the United States, the FDA Small Business Nutrition Labeling Exemption may let you off the hook from having a nutrition-facts label outlining calories and nutrients. The bad news: When sharing shelf space with competing products that reveal nutritional details, consumers may pass your food by for a product that includes that information. (See "Analyze Nutrient Profiles and Shelf Stability," page 130, for the scoop on making nutrition facts labels.)

Also be aware that labeling requirements for products differ based on their destination (direct to consumers vs. wholesale vs. food service). The FDA spells out exact font sizes and which packages need what information. Each required item has all sorts of nuances. On www.FDA .gov, you'll get answers to questions such as "Should water be listed as an ingredient?" as well as naming rules for certain products. For example, the FDA's jerky fact sheet (yes, there is one) specifies the terms allowed to describe processed jerky products, which include beef jerky, beef jerky chunked and formed, beef jerky ground and formed, etc. Tasty, eh?

In brief, the FDA-required items for consumer packaging as of press time include:

- **Name of the food.**

- **Net quantity of the contents in ounces and grams.**

- **Name and address of the manufacturer.**

- **Statement of ingredients, in descending order of weight. If one of the ingredients is itself made up of several ingredients, as** chocolate is, you also need to list those in parentheses next to the primary ingredient's name. A candy bar's ingredients might read: bittersweet chocolate (cacao beans, sugar, cocoa butter, soya lecithin, vanilla beans), unrefined coconut palm sugar, cream, butter, puffed brown rice (rice flour, rice bran, raisin juice concentrate, honey, salt). Now is a good time to grab a candy bar for further research purposes.

- Nutrition information. Nutrient-content claims such as "light" or "excellent source of fiber" have strict guidelines.

- Refrigeration statement, if applicable, which varies depending on the rate of deterioration if the item is not refrigerated.

- Allergen statements. Products containing certain potential allergens need a statement starting with "contains." You can add more specifics in parentheses, such as "contains tree nuts (almonds)." The allergens that should be disclosed are milk, eggs, peanuts, tree nuts (such as almonds, cashews, or walnuts), fish (such as bass, cod, or flounder), shellfish (such as crab, lobster, or shrimp), soy, and wheat.
    - You've probably seen a related disclosure: "processed in a facility that also processes nuts." More important is "processed using equipment also used for [insert allergens]." Before making gluten-free claims, see the FDA's guidelines, which went into effect in 2014. Visit www.FDA.gov/Food/GuidanceRegulation/default.htm.

Consider Optional Label Elements and Logos

As the minimalist package you dreamed of gets cluttered up with type, just wait—there's more.

Universal Product Code. Most commonly referred to as UPCs, these bar codes have unique numbers that identify your company and products. The codes capture and share important data with distributors and retailers. They also help trace products in case of recall. Consider adding UPCs to your labels from the start if you think you may ever sell through retail channels, so you'll be ready should the opportunity arise. Every stock-keeping unit (known as a SKU, pronounced "skew") that is scannable for purchase or inventory needs its own UPC. A can of garlic tomato sauce is a SKU. A six-pack of the same sauce is another SKU.

A tiny snack-size mint-chocolate bite sold on its own is a SKU distinct from the three-ounce version of the same chocolate. You also need a UPC for your master case.

You can buy UPCs in several ways. An organization called GS1 US is the official source. Securing codes from GS1us.org poises you for growth, since you need to buy a minimum of one hundred codes, which costs about $800. Another option is to buy previously used codes from a code reseller (think eBay for UPCs). This method costs less than buying new codes, but you risk potential conflict with products that previously used the codes.

Quick Response code. The QR is short for "Quick Response," an apt name for these bar code–like squares that consumers can "snap" with a smartphone QR code app, much like a photo. The app redirects to a Web page—no typing necessary! You can easily generate a QR code through several different free websites, such as Kaywa.com, and input the destination URL, whether an online product page, special offer, or video. Kaywa generates the QR code as an image that you can download. This cool technology helps you inform consumers (who have the technology) without the clutter. Creminelli Fine Meats includes a QR code on its salami wrapper, which links smartphone users to a video about how to best enjoy the salami. If you are printing your labels yourself, you might consider offering an option for high-volume gift orders (such as wedding favors or corporate gifts), which can include a customized QR code that links anywhere the customer wants— perhaps to an e-greeting card or even a video. This is a fun way to add more oomph to your customer's experience, especially for the smartphone-obsessed generations. Before going QR-happy, consider how likely your target is to use a QR code reader.

Certification logos. The logos stating your product attributes (such as organic or gluten-free), certifications, affiliations, and charitable causes can quickly take up all the space on your packaging, leaving little room for design. You'll find any third-party certification logos come with placement and size rules. Highlight the logos that are most likely to appeal to your target customers. See "Identify Product Certifications That Support Your Promise," page 104, for information on how to evaluate the various certification options.

Social media icons. Pretty much every company is on social media these days, so I'd skip the icons—unless they are coupled with a call to action like "Get recipes" or "Join the movement." Do include your website address and ideally a phone number and e-mail address.

GOOD FOOD **GREAT BUSINESS**

GOOD IDEA:
DIY PACKAGING EXPERIMENT

Start making your vision real. Use everything you've learned in this chapter so far to mock up a package for your product. Buy products from successful companies using packaging similar to what you're thinking about. They might be competitors in your category or products from other categories (e.g., a slender juice bottle for a pasta sauce). Shortcut your experiment by pasting your design over the bottles or boxes or bags. When mocking up your package, you'll need to cover a few bases:

- Determine the amount of product per package.

- Find examples of packages with similar usage instructions or ideas. Will the food be eaten directly from the package, poured out, used as an ingredient, or grabbed in handfuls?

- Know the required FDA regulations for what the label must include.

- Write the text that will appear on the packet. Make a dummy nutrition-facts label and grab any certification logo images you'll want to include from the various certification websites.

- Print out the text and glue or tape your labels onto the package. Voila!

TEST YOUR PACKAGING

When designing your labeling and packaging, think about its visibility when sold at retail. One snack-food company clearly had convenience and anti-crumbling in mind when it selected a plastic "clamshell" box for its raw vegetable snacks. The eater could easily tote the box, flip the top open, and then snap it closed after eating. A single label wrapped around the box branded the product with a lively design along with all the product details. There was just one flaw: When stacked on a shelf, only the ingredients list and a product warning were visible. To make the product name or company name visible, a retailer would be forced to stack the products on a table (not a very realistic scenario). The company soon redesigned its packaging.

With your packaging mock-up in hand, visit a store that you hope might sell your product one day. Clandestinely place your mock-up alongside its competitors on the shelf. Sail down the aisle at the speed of a busy shopper to see how well your package stands out. In the spirit of audaciousness, you could even try to get the store's buyer to give you feedback, perhaps wrangling some team members to chime in as well. (For your sales calls, though, you want to bring in the final product.) Absorb any negative reactions as a valuable learning experience—appreciate the money and face you saved.

If your DIY skills aren't stellar, a professionally made prototype may be the way to go. A few companies, such as Virtual Packaging, can put together a simulated package that looks stunningly like the real thing at a reasonably low rate.

Be your packaging's best tester. Use it in real-life situations and test it with friends to catch issues early on. The goal is to avoid feedback like this from my mother: "This mustard comes in a tall glass bottle with an opening so small there's practically no way to get that mustard out. No spoon will fit into it, nor is the mustard pourable. The best you can do is find a knife that's narrow enough to fit in the bottle but wide enough to hold mustard." Not a feel-good customer experience!

Test ship your product, even if you're adamant about selling only locally. Hopefully, lots of fans will be shipping your goods as gifts. Altitude can break seals on bags of chips and wreak havoc on jars and bottles. Bottle or jar lids perfectly sealed at sea level might unscrew or break during shipping. Some say that this occurs when a bottle or jar is too full. Others fix the problem by trying out different caps and lids, which gets expensive. Ship a number of packages to a friend or business partner across the country to learn what does and does not work.

PRODUCE YOUR PACKAGING

Before you spend a dime on package production, confirm how you, or your co-packer, will be filling the packages. When your food products call for cellophane bags, jars, or little boxes, turn to packaging companies such as Nashville Wraps, or Tenka Flexible Packaging, or others whom you can meet at the Fancy Food Show or Natural Product Expos. Many Good Food producers buy shipping supplies such as cartons from Uline, which offers quick delivery and a doorstop-size catalog.

Call packaging and labeling companies to explore your options. These folks regularly get calls from hapless entrepreneurs and will kindly educate you on what they offer, or suggest other vendors if they're not a match with your needs, and vice versa. If a packaging company sounds like a good fit, the sales rep will likely supply samples to help you with design and testing.

Get packaging quotes from at least three vendors. The prices may shock you. Shop around. Or tap a packaging broker to help you find the right printing and packaging companies. Be sure to ask the packaging brokers for references for packaging companies that look promising.

Plenty of Good Food makers reluctantly end up printing their packaging abroad because of the tremendous cost savings. Though importing packaging may go against your promise, weigh it against your costs and projected profits. Given the choice to be competitive in the marketplace or go out of business, well . . . the choice becomes clear. Or, if you're dead set on doing everything locally, what other changes to your 5 Staples mix could overcome sky-high packaging estimates?

TAKE 5:
TIPS FOR PRINTING PACKAGING

(1) Build all of the packaging, design, and associated shipping costs into your packaging budget.

(2) Order a low quantity of packaging initially. Chances are that you are going to have to make changes. Plus, you've got to store any extra packaging you're not using right away. Calculate the cost and convenience trade-offs.

(3) Combine several print jobs if you have several flavors of the same product with the same packaging—ordering a higher quantity of packaging will get you savings. For example, Paleo People achieves a 100,000-quantity price break by printing 33,333 packages each for three flavors. Even when printing labels, ask the printer if you can combine your front, back, and side labels into "one" label run, drastically reducing the cost.

(4) Plan to conduct press checks at the printer to be sure everything is perfect.

(5) Get everything in writing, including if you require the packaging made in the United States. Even U.S.-based printers may have printing plants abroad they may choose to use, unbeknownst to you.

GREAT BUSINESS ACTION PLAN

☐ Contact companies whose packaging you admire to ask who designed and/or produced it. If the company's products are in your same category, see if they'll reveal the optimal number of units per case pack—a serious shortcut for your research.

☐ Define your packaging requirements and hire a professional packaging designer. Project ahead to determine how your packaging might evolve, and if you want to intentionally plan a short-term packaging strategy.

☐ Determine how you or your co-packer will fill the packaging you're thinking about, or if you'll need to work with a third-party food-packaging company. Calculate how much the packaging process will cost.

☐ Decide how you're making your nutrition-facts labels: Are you doing it yourself or through a vendor? Peruse TheDieline.com for packaging redesign and strategy ideas. DIY labeling? Check out *Packaging World* magazine's *Labeling Playbook* at Packworld.com/playbook.

☐ Learn labeling rules to feel in control, even if someone else is doing the work for you. Talk to a packaging designer, visit www.FDA.gov/Food, and check out the useful resources on LabelCalc.com as well as FoodLabels.com.

☐ Test, test, test your packaging and usage as if you were the real consumer, from the time of purchase through usage in various scenarios.

ON *GOODFOODGREATBUSINESS.COM*

Get a quick start with the Research Template and Checklists template along with links to packaging planning, design, and production resources.

CHAPTER

FIND THE BEST INGREDIENTS

BURNING QUESTION:
WHEN DO I FINALIZE MY INGREDIENT SOURCES?

Taste, texture, and composition of natural ingredients can vary wildly depending on age, storage, and growing conditions. Your recipe relies on the exact ingredients you use, so the sooner you decide on your sources, the better. On the other hand, you can't finalize your sources until your recipe is finalized (in case something you planned on changes in taste or texture when used in a large batch.) This conundrum illustrates a classic challenge of any large-scale food preparation. It ain't over till it's over.

THE GOALS: TRACEABILITY, TRUST, AND TRANSPARENCY

Good Food starts with superlative ingredients. Sourcing those ingredients is where you put your research and connecting skills to the test. A good rule of thumb is to let these three Ts guide your sourcing efforts:

- **TRACEABILITY.** Ensure that you and your customers know exactly where your ingredients come from and how they were produced. Ideally, directly source from farmers or form close connections with those who globetrot to source direct. Second best, buy certified ingredients through a traceable supply chain, such as the fair-trade system, to better guarantee that your products support good producing and labor practices.

- **TRUST.** You want to work with suppliers whose business practices you can trust. And you also want to interact with your own customers and other suppliers in ways that develop trusting relationships. Trust and authenticity go hand in hand. Good Food has no sleaze factor.

- **TRANSPARENCY.** Be forthcoming with your sourcing (as much as you want to reveal) and what's going on with your business. The more transparency you offer, the more your customers have reason to trust you. It also means sourcing from producers who are transparent about their own practices.

When you embark on selling your product, store buyers may grill you—for good reason. "Responsible sourcing is knowing everything you can about the food you sell," says Sam Mogannam of San Francisco's wildly popular Bi-Rite Market. His team members seek background information on the source of each product they sell so that they can share the story of those products and be transparent with customers.

Buying local and direct adds to your story, allows for freshness, and provides an amazing community feeling. Variations by season may also add to your value proposition and story. One candy maker warned on its package: "Each piece may vary as we hand stir our caramel in small pots using organic European-style butter made with grass-fed cow milk with flavor that varies by season." That is one decidedly appealing disclaimer. Buying local can also earn you certification from your state, as it did for Nuts About Granola, which has the "PA Preferred" seal for its products from the Pennsylvania Department of Agriculture. Certifications like these are a huge asset when focusing on local sales. Sourcing U.S.–grown ingredients also can reap rewards if you plan to export, thanks to support from the USDA. (See "Phase 3: Going International—Massive Reach and Volume," page 156).

Whether you want to sell at Whole Foods or not, its Unacceptable Ingredients for Food list is an educational read. The lengthy list includes ingredients often found in "mainstream" foods, such as vanillin and aspartame. While formulating your production recipe, cross-check any non-natural-sounding ingredients with this list (or with guidelines from other stores at which you would like to sell). Leslie Horne of Aurelia's Chorizo sought out Berkshire pork from a small farm to comply with Whole Foods' 5-Step Animal Welfare Rating Standards. She also developed a chorizo line using a lower-priced, noncertified organic, yet still antibiotic-free, pork, targeting lower-income consumers. With this two-pronged product strategy, Leslie serves a broad base of consumers, opening up more distribution opportunities. She also keeps production simple by focusing on similar meat products.

IDENTIFY PRODUCT CERTIFICATIONS
THAT SUPPORT YOUR PROMISE

Around twenty-five third-party product certifications exist to assure eaters that their food is what the manufacturer says it is. Keep in mind when testing recipes that product quality and taste comes first. Most consumers won't buy "just because" of your certifications. In addition, getting these certifications can get expensive. Some of the best specialty shops feel that if something is unique or made traditionally, certifications are less important, especially if their costs or requirements aren't feasible for the producer (think wood-smoked sea salt or 100 percent maple syrup tapped from family-owned maple tree farms). As with life's 80-20 rule (see "Understand the 80-20 Rule (The Quick Way to Make the Right Decisions)," page 31), about 20 percent of the certifications are the most common. Read on for some examples.

Certified Organic

For a product to display a certified organic seal, you need to apply through one of the organic certification agencies, such as California Certified Organic Farmers and Oregon Tilth. (Your business does not need to be located in one of those states to apply, which is a bit confusing.) If your product is 100 percent organic, it's probably worth pursuing certification, especially with foods that are targeted to kids and health-conscious consumers, that might otherwise have genetically modified ingredients (such as corn or soybeans) or that contain ingredients such as strawberries that may be pesticide-laden if conventionally grown.

You can shortcut this process by sourcing from well-known and respected organic farms. Name those farms or brands in your promotion and packaging, and you've instantly created a value proposition.

Gluten-Free (GFCO.org)

Gluten-free products are enjoying jaw-dropping growth, at around $10.5 billion in U.S. sales in 2013—44 percent annual growth since 2011. The market is expected to reach around $15 billion by 2015. The National Institutes of Health has estimated that more than two million people in the United States (1 in every 133 people) have celiac disease. The National Foundation for Celiac Awareness believes that 95 percent of those remain undiagnosed, meaning they have yet to adopt a gluten-free diet. Then there's the "nonceliac gluten-sensitive" folks, a phenomenon that describes eaters whose health improves by eliminating gluten from their diet.

When you're making gluten-free food, and especially when you go the extra mile for a fully gluten-free facility, take the pains to seek out certification. Certification from the Gluten-Free Certification Organization (GFCO) or the Celiac Sprue Association (CSA) will not only reassure buyers and differentiate your product but will also help you comply with some retailers that now require certification. You'll also increase appeal with GF customers and influencers such as "Gluten-Free Girl" blogger Shauna James Ahern.

Fair Trade (FairTradeUSA.org)

For a food manufacturer to include that familiar "Fair Trade certified" label on its products, the maker must source ingredients from certified farms and organizations, pay Fair Trade prices and premiums, and submit to supply-chain audits to be sure the actual ingredients came from the certified farms. Certification by Fair Trade USA helps get the "good" value proposition across, while helping consumers choose products that have ingredients with guaranteed traceability and transparency. Some small food companies—such as craft coffee and bean-to-bar chocolate makers—question the value of certification and may opt to source directly from growers and intimately know the suppliers' practices. (If you love traveling to distant climes, this is your chance to integrate fun with work.) Food companies sourcing directly might use the phrase "fairly traded" or "better than fair trade," which requires transparency on their end and trust on the consumer's end. The direct approach also avoids the licensing fees related to Fair Trade USA certification.

Kosher (OUKosher.org, OK.org, and more)

Certifier OU Kosher reports that more than $150 billion in kosher-certified products are consumed annually, and that spending continues to rise dramatically. Good kosher food can fill a need for those following Jewish dietary laws, as has Holy Cow!, a kosher beef jerky. When approved by your chosen kosher certification agency, you receive permission to add the agency's kosher mark to your package along with an indication that your product contains meat or dairy, or is *pareve* (which means free of meat and dairy). The certification process involves an application, reviewing the ingredients, a supervisor inspection, fees, and ongoing monitoring from one of several organizations. Using a kosher-certified co-packer can expedite your certification but won't necessarily cost you less.

Non-GMO Project Verified (NonGMOProject.org)

According to the Non-GMO Project, as much as 80 percent of conventionally processed food in the United States contains genetically modified organisms (GMOs). Anti-GMO sentiment is gaining steam. In the first nine months of 2013, sales of 14,000 Non-GMO Project Verified products had topped $5 billion. Trader Joe's is said to enforce a non-GMO policy for its private-label products, and, as of this writing, many of Whole Foods' 365 Everyday Value products are Non-GMO Project Verified. Additionally, around fifty countries ban products containing GMOs—good to remember when choosing ingredients if you might export. The "easy" way to assure buyers your ingredients are GM-free is to achieve organic certification, which by default prevents GM ingredients from being used.

HOW TO SOURCE GOOD INGREDIENTS

Finding ingredients is easy. Finding sources you'll stick with for the long haul is not.

If you're handling manufacturing, you're in control of ingredients. But co-packers often want to supply the ingredients, whether to simplify their own operations or to know the ingredients' origins, or to make a little profit by buying large quantities at low cost and using them for various products for different companies. For example, after healthful frozen-food company Peas of Mind signs a co-packer agreement, the co-packer purchases common ingredients, such as salt and black beans, within Peas of Mind's guidelines (i.e., organic and U.S. grown). Founder Jill Litwin does not require that her co-packer purchase ingredients from any one specific source, knowing the co-packer might get better prices from another supplier with whom it already does business. The co-packer provides the Peas of Mind team with ingredient samples from several different suppliers, so they can approve them before the co-packer purchases them.

When ordering a measly few thousand pounds of an ingredient (which sounds like a lot, but isn't) you might have to rely on brokers, unless you can buy directly from a small producer or cooperative. As your production grows, you can go straight to the larger farmers or food importers instead of through brokers. Mary Waldner of Mary's Gone Crackers buys more than two million pounds of rice yearly direct from California family farmers. High volume means good relationships. So when a bad year for rice reduced supply, the farmers made sure that Mary's Gone Crackers had enough. The cracker team has also visited and formed relationships with their quinoa growers in Ecuador and Bolivia. Putting the faces behind the grains makes business more fulfilling. Plus, you'll be more likely to hear about crop-quality variances that might affect your product consistency.

Here are a few ways to track down great ingredients:

- Join Food-Hub.org or CropMobster.com, which connect ingredients producers with buyers like you.

- Search online, using very detailed phrases such as "organic farm direct macadamia nuts," "United States sunflower seed organic farm," or "pesticide-free vanilla grower Tahiti."

- Check the certification websites, such as FairTradeUSA.org and Tilth.org, which often promote the brands and farms they certify.

- Ask other local producers of similar products about their sources. Be understanding if they don't want to tell you.

- Contact specialty food companies whose consumer products interest you to see if they sell in bulk. For example, you might choose to work with vanilla specialists such as the family-owned Nielsen-Massey company. Or you could reach out to specialty food companies that manufacture vanilla on a smaller scale, such as Sonoma Syrup. Just Tomatoes packages freeze-dried veggies and fruits for consumers but can also sell by the container load.

- Meet ingredients producers at trade shows such as the biannual New Hope 360 Natural Products Expo, the Fancy Food Show, or Produce Expo, where suppliers from around the world come to promote their vanillas (connecting the dots to those folks mentioned previously), oils and vinegars, nuts and nut milks, flours from almond to wheat, superfood ingredients, fruits in every permutation—preserved, dehydrated, pureed—sugars and all manner of substitutes, and whatever else you can think of.

- Check warehouse clubs, which increasingly offer more fairly traded and organic products.

- Contact commodities marketing boards when experimenting. Most fruit, vegetable, and nut types are represented by a marketing group that lists producer members on the association websites. The associations might also send you various samples to help with your product-development explorations; they're helping member producers when you buy their ingredients.

- Once you launch your business, contact them again to see how they might promote your products—again, helping their member producers. I was delighted to see Valley Fig Growers featuring Quince & Apple's fig and black tea preserve in its Fancy Food Show booth. A win-win for the fig growers and for the Madison, Wisconsin–based artisaneurs, who achieved unparalleled exposure without even having a booth at the show.

GOOD IDEA:
GROW YOUR OWN

If the idea of producing your own ingredients piques your interest, investigate your state's agricultural-producer laws. Janet Brown and Marty Jacobsen discovered that California's agricultural-food-processor law allows farms to make value-added packaged products using food that they grow. After planting a small herb and flower farm in Lagunitas, California, they developed a line of herbal salts, sugars, and hydrosols—and Allstar Organics was born. Foodies naturally gravitate to these so-called farmstead products, where the ingredients producer also makes the packaged product.

TAKE 5:
TIPS TO MANAGE INGREDIENT COSTS

High ingredient prices plague all small producers. Pure ingredients from small or organic sources simply cost more to produce than large commercial farm products. Here's how to manage the high price challenge:

1. **Buy cheap.** Don't pay retail prices for ingredients even when experimenting. When buying locally, let the farmer or grocery store manager know that you're starting a business and ask for a discount to help with your product development, saying

that you'll be happy to get early feedback and collaborate in the future. (You can also obtain a wholesale license, which will allow you to buy ingredients in larger quantities at reduced costs. You may want to wait until you are sure your business is a go before committing to this.)

(2) **Get bulk discounts.** Explore buying cooperatively with other companies to achieve volume discounts, from ingredients to packaging. Craft coffee roasters around the United States have banded together to buy directly from growers around the world, taking turns visiting the various farms. When buying in bulk, be sure to account for any warehousing expenses.

(3) **Anticipate shortages.** Watch trends, like the explosion of coconut-everything and the bee colony collapse disorder. As demand goes up, so do prices. Commodities prices generally rise over time. In recent years, skyrocketing sugar prices have taxed food manufacturers of all sizes. Weather or bee-pollination issues can drastically cut a year's crop yield. Some manufacturers raise their prices, while others choose to eat the extra costs rather than risk lowering their sales volume.

(4) **Consider proximity.** When your product depends on Vidalia onions from Georgia or on Wisconsin cheese, could the cost you save by avoiding shipping justify that big life-changing move? I once discussed starting a food business that would involve buying citrus direct from a friend's farm in California's Central Valley. The cost of delivering the lemons versus the cost of processing locally was astonishing. The team at Happy Girl Kitchen knew what it was doing when it located on a major coastal farm belt, minimizing the journey from farm to jar.

(5) **Buy rather than make it all.** You may start out making or preparing an ingredient, such as nut butter that goes into a meal bar, yourself. Over time, you may realize a company that dedicates itself to nut roasting can deliver the nuts the way you need them for perhaps even less than your raw materials cost. In that case, outsourcing production could be the way to go—unless some principles or promise within your brand compels you to "make" your own. This particular theory dates back centuries to economist Adam Smith, whom Adam Davidson alluded to in his *New York Times* article "Don't Mock the

CONTINUE ▶

Artisanal-Pickle Makers." The article parallels observations from this late-eighteenth-century economist to today's craft-food movement: "When everyone does everything—sews their own clothes, harvests their own crops, bakes their own bread—each act becomes inefficient, because generalists are rarely as quick or able as specialists." Many food brands and retailers worked with Sunland, the country's biggest organic peanut butter processor, located in New Mexico. Things got sticky when the company issued a massive product recall due to salmonella. Then Sunland declared bankruptcy. While the company's ultimate fate is to be determined, this saga offers a useful lesson: Think twice before putting all your chocolate-covered peanut butter eggs in one basket.

TAKEAWAYS

- Traceability, trust, and transparency are important when it comes to your ingredients and production methods.

- Product certifications (such as organic, gluten-free, etc.) cost money but may be worth it in the long run, as you start to depend on the product selling itself; when you're personally selling at a farmers' market or other event, you can explain your sourcing more readily.

- There are a variety of ways to source the best ingredients. The availability of consistent, quality ingredients will change, and possibly become more challenging, as you grow and need to tap in to multiple sources or look beyond U.S. suppliers.

- The high cost of ingredients is one of the top challenges for small producers.

GREAT BUSINESS ACTION PLAN

☐ Identify five people you can ask about ingredient sources that match your value proposition. Write up a must-have ingredients list. Ask for references to any sources, and gauge long-term reliability and partnership potential. Dig in to how they're sourcing.

☐ Plan an ingredients- and label-reading session to learn how your competitors and the brands you admire make their products.

☐ Learn about the certifications you're considering, including how much consumers know and respect those certifications.

☐ Sign up and connect with suppliers at Food-Hub.org.

☐ Investigate trends and their effect on commodity supply and prices, as well as other risks, such as weather.

☐ If your product uses one specific commodity, start mulling over whether you'd want to locate manufacturing close to the ingredients producers.

☐ Stay informed about new developments in the natural foods space by subscribing to the very useful newsletter from NewHope360.com.

ON *GOODFOODGREATBUSINESS.COM*

Get a quick start with links to the certification agencies and ingredients suppliers.

CHAPTER

8

GET INTO PRODUCTION

BURNING QUESTION:
WHERE IS THE BEST PLACE TO
START MY FOOD BUSINESS?

Before plunking down fees for local permits and licenses, signing a lease, or committing to a local co-packer, you need to know for sure that you've chosen the right location.

Consider these tips before settling down:

- *Know how closely tied your location is to your strategy. Had Lee Mathis launched his Decadence Gourmet Cheesecakes in an urban area rather than a small Colorado town, his cheesecakes-in-a-jar business would have looked completely different, with local rather than online customers. He overcame the limitation of expensive shipping costs (and his location) by setting up additional production in a California commercial kitchen. The Bay Area became his oyster.*

- *Tax breaks or grants to support redevelopment efforts may benefit community builders crafting foods in a "hip and upcoming" retail location.*

- *Food-truck entrepreneurs will find that some cities love their businesses while others ban them.*

- *For meat-based products, if exporting is key to your distribution strategy, manufacturing outside of the United States (i.e., in Canada) might help you avoid various import-export embargoes between the United States and other countries.*

- *Use the vision you wrote as a checklist as you evaluate possible production setups and business locations.*

THINGS ALL FOOD ENTREPRENEURS GO THROUGH

Some rules of thumb apply to production, whether making food yourself or contracting with a co-packer. For example, when making three flavors of one product, each flavor counts as a new batch. Cleaning up after each production run takes time; time is money. So if you were to make only 100 of an item, the per-unit cost would generally be prohibitive. This is why a deep product strategy, with you making, say, popcorn in cheese, barbecue, and herb flavors, is less costly and easier to streamline than a broad product line made up of popcorns, crackers, and potato chips. Here are two more very important things to know as you approach food production.

You Need to Scale Your Recipe for Production

What is delicious in a small batch in your kitchen can taste very different when you start making it in bulk. Depending on your food craftiness and food science know-how, there are a few paths to recipe development for large-scale production:

- Independent recipe developers offer expertise in product taste, smell, appearance, and how ingredients interact. Search phrases such as "culinary consultant" and "food scientist" to land on consultants such as Rachel Zemser, who couples degrees in food science and culinary arts. Also tap in to universities with entrepreneurship programs, food professional institutes, cookbook authors and chefs, and ex-employees of food-product-development companies.

- Many co-packers offer product development or consulting services, often for an hourly fee. Some co-packers include large-batch recipe testing in the overall manufacturing fee; others charge separately for the testing process.

- Large product-development companies such as CCD Innovation, Mattson, and ABC Research Laboratories are there to serve well-funded entrepreneurs.

- Do it yourself. Experiment with recipes, study the differences, and adapt your own twist to come up with your small-scale proof of concept. Measure each step and each recipe element down to the penny. Focus more on cutting variable production costs, such as hand-sprinkling cupcake toppings, that add up with each run over small one-time expenditures.

Simulate the real equipment and batch sizes as closely as possible when working on the larger batches. The result may very well morph into a food far from your vision, especially when heating and multistage cooking are involved. For mixes such as dried spices, cookie mixes, and snack-mix blends, scaling up batch sizes is relatively easy—no chemistry involved. Your shelf-life tests may reveal flavor shifts, however. Then it's back to the kitchen to tweak the recipe. You may face that moment of truth: How far can you go in changing your recipe to maintain your ideal texture, flavor, shelf life, and cost without botching your value proposition?

Even after paying hundreds or thousands of dollars to a co-packer, recipe developer, or product development company to verify your scaled-up recipe, you still may not be happy. At that stage, you face searching for another co-packer or manufacturing the food yourself. Whichever path you choose, you'll write a batch-process recipe, which acts as step-by-step, ounce-by-ounce, second-by-second instructions, so the production person can deliver consistency and quality with every batch.

You Need to Practice Licensed, Safe, and Sanitary Production

When setting out to manufacture on your own, the required permits may vary depending on the type of food you make and how you make it. Contact your local Department of Health or Small Business Administration office for more information. In addition, all food entrepreneurs need to know about the FDA's Good Manufacturing Practices (GMP), which specify safe and sanitary food production and facility maintenance. Whoever actually manages production (you or a co-packer) needs a Hazard Analysis and Critical Control Points (HACCP) plan. The FDA defines HACCP as a management system in which food safety is addressed through the analysis and control of biological, chemical, and physical hazards from raw material production, procurement, and handling to manufacturing, distribution, and consumption of the finished product. For HACCP to effectively prevent food safety hazards, your facility must be operating in accordance with the GMP, or risk being shut down by the FDA. 'Nuff said.

Certain food categories have their own rules and regulations. Meat products such as jerky and dairy products such as ice cream need to be produced in a USDA-approved facility when sold interstate, which is often a "tipping point" for artisaneurs to either put a stake in the ground and set up their own facilities or to go out and find an approved co-packer. And jam and jelly makers using other than the standardized recipes available on the website for the National Center for Home Food

Preservation (nchfp.uga.edu) must have process reviews on each of their products to ensure that the final product is safe and shelf stable. Understand the rules before finalizing your recipe, in case a small tweak might save loads of money and hassle. For example, Green Mountain Mustard in Vermont made a slight change to its recipe, which contains eggs, to control costs. The team had to retest and submit a revised scheduled process to the Cornell Food Lab—part of the Northeast Center for Food Entrepreneurship—for approval before going to market.

GOOD IDEA:
MULTIPLY YOUR GOOD WITH NONPROFIT PARTNERS

Nothing says or feels "good" like collaborating with organizations that train people who might otherwise be unemployable. Arnon Oren set out to explore affordable ways to grow his Oren's Kitchen artisan nut business. He stumbled upon a local nonprofit that helps developmentally disabled people learn job skills and improve their self-esteem through work. These people fill the nut packages in an inspected, licensed facility. It's a win for everyone.

Nuts About Granola, along with natural bakery Shiloh Farms, was chosen by the Pennsylvania Association for the Blind and Vision Impaired from among hundreds of entries to produce its natural foods in a 19,000-square-foot facility employing blind and vision-impaired workers. This triple bottom-line arrangement allows the mother-and-daughter granola-making team to pursue its growth goals (such as offering co-packing services to other granola companies) and fulfill its social missions.

While—or before—you investigate production options, consider how you might thread together cause-related production.

INSIDE SCOOP:
NEO COCOA ENVISIONS LOCAL CHOCOLATY GOODNESS

Culinary-school graduate Christine Doerr envisioned a confection business that provided the sensual experience of a cocoa-covered traditional French truffle in all the cool, exotic flavors of hard-shelled truffles. Christine chose to use all local ingredients

CONTINUE ▶

and coined the tagline "hearts of the truffles" to advertise her unique twist.

As a novice entrepreneur, Christine looked to San Francisco's La Cocina kitchen incubator to help her plan and launch the business, as well as give her business and production support. Widespread promotion from multiple awards and placement at the La Cocina kiosk in San Francisco's Ferry Building attracted wholesale buyers from around the country to Neo Cocoa. Christine also decided to sell selectively to stores outside of California—a nice way to increase exposure with new consumers and further boost online sales.

Christine outgrew her hourly kitchen rental and asked around about other facilities, finding another nearby fine-chocolate confectioner who was seeking someone to share her space. Christine signed on with her, and watched her business transform in some basic yet important ways:

- She eliminated the pressure of working in an hourly kitchen.
- She streamlined production, saving time and money. "Now I can have all my production, packaging, and shipping supplies in one location with a dedicated table area," she says.
- The new kitchen provided space for new services, such as classes.

Christine began offering chocolate tastings and events at companies such as Twitter, Google, and Pixar (a testament to both luck and strategy in locating your company near your ideal target customer base). "Most of my revenue is from wholesale accounts that have 30-day pay cycles. These event services, where they pay immediately, keeps the income diverse." Plus, she gets exposure among a chocolate-loving group of potential customers and has fun getting out of the kitchen. Neo Cocoa exemplifies the journey from artisaneur to community builder, and shows how your vision and 5 Staples can remix over time, if you so desire.

CHOOSE YOUR PRODUCTION METHOD AND REALITY CHECK THE PLAN

One day you're in your home kitchen, the next you're in a rental. Your business is growing and suddenly you find yourself overwhelmed, on the hunt for a co-packer, and reminiscing about the days of eight-hour sleeps. The tasks and challenges you will face will vary depending on whether you make your food yourself or contract out your manufacturing. Here are some considerations to help you choose how to proceed.

The Joys of Making Food Yourself (for Artisaneurs and Community Builders)

After starting out in a rental kitchen or home kitchen (if their state allows), artisaneurs tend to grow into their own production facilities (whether they rent or buy) or transition to a co-packer while they continue developing new products and engaging with customers.

Pinpoint the Right Facility

Spend plenty of time evaluating the short- and long-term pros and cons of spaces before signing a contract—particularly keeping in mind the potential to expand into new product lines and potentially to offer tours, tastings, classes, and other events. For example, Brooklyn-based Mast Brothers Chocolate moved to a warehouse and put its chocolate-making operation in a glassed-in area, leaving the remaining space open for visitors and events. When Dafna Kory's INNA Jam outgrew its rental kitchen, she raised $25,000 on Kickstarter to fund a dedicated kitchen. Space for classes topped her kitchen requirements list. (Classes = smart. You can charge to share your knowledge and offset any seasonal ups and downs in product sales.)

Location, location, location remains critical when customers will be coming to you. The risks of up-and-coming neighborhoods decline when a number of artisans and your city are behind a revitalization effort—or if you have built up a following elsewhere. For example, Blue Bottle Coffee located its roastery and café near Jack London Square in Oakland, California, in a light industrial area that seemed off the beaten path compared with its highly trafficked San Francisco locations. In this case, the perfect location was more luck than planning. Blue Bottle founder James Freeman says, "I just fell in love with the building and had no idea who was going to go to the café." The answer again is loca-tion: Oakland-based fans who'd enjoyed Blue Bottle in San Francisco are thrilled to now have a local destination.

When searching for facilities, also think about sharing a warehouse space or production facility with other food businesses. Sharing usually reduces costs. Also, much like having roommates share chores, you can support one another with those dreaded tasks. A shared catering kitchen in Princeton, New Jersey, offered Nicole Bergman much more than she'd bargained for when getting her Simply Nic's shortbread cookies and mixes business off the ground. She ended up collaborating closely with fellow renters on kids' baking classes, farmers' market tables, and even customer leads.

TAKE 5:
TIPS FOR LANDING THE RIGHT SPACE

Finding the perfect production space can be tricky.

(1) Think ahead: What production conditions do you need? Air conditioning, storage space for packaging or raw ingredients, a gluten-free environment? Based on your planned sales and promotion, how quickly will you outgrow your space?

(2) Save time: Focus on spaces previously used for the same type of production that you are planning to do.

(3) Plan for success: For retail spaces, visit the location every day of the week at every time of day to check out foot traffic and get a *feel for the block's dynamic*.

(4) Read the fine print: Make sure that multiple businesses can legally operate out of one kitchen if you plan to rent (or sub-lease) out any of your space. Some areas don't allow this.

(5) Come up with a "don't want" list. This will help you work out any negatives before they happen. Perhaps you don't want to share space with a barbecue sauce maker whose smoke will seep its way into your sponge cakes.

As you plan your production, think about other help you may need. Flip to "Build Your Support System: Commune, Contract, and Hire," page 209, for ideas on hiring, artisan collaborations, and contracting out to social enterprises.

Renting Versus Owning

Renting a kitchen versus owning one parallels the epic debate of renting versus buying a home. Renting leaves you relatively carefree and debt free, yet you must operate by the owner's rules. (A gluten-free baker once contacted me in desperation after losing her kitchen rental, which forced her to cease operation.) With owning, you can make whatever you like, whenever and however you like (within zoning guidines). You also take on the burden of higher up-front and fixed operational costs, in the high tens or hundreds of thousands of dollars. You have to pay for your mortgage, the insurance, building and equipment upkeep, and utilities. Anyone running a kitchen will also likely pay for annual licensing, health permits and inspections, and taxes; certifications (organic, gluten-free, kosher, etc.); insurance, including workers' compensation; and staff salaries or wages. To open your own kitchen, you must also register online with the FDA to comply with the Bioterrorism Act of 2002, to help with tracing food in the case of recalls or other food-safety concerns.

Getting the Equipment You Need

New is nice, but cheap is smart. Check Craigslist or local restaurant-auction companies for used production equipment. Consider what's "plug and play" (wheel it in, plug it in) versus what requires elaborate installation, which could rack up labor costs. And start small. Anticipate how quickly you'll grow so you don't end up with a hodgepodge of equipment or spend all your time replacing small-scale gear. Always try equipment before buying—even if you need to travel to test it. This was a costly lesson one entrepreneur learned the hard way.

Also think about automating repetitive tasks. Carpal tunnel syndrome has ruined more than one artisaneur's life. You can find machinery and equipment to wrap candy, fill packages, and do other tedious work, and using machines does not necessarily mean you have to lose your "handmade" designation. If expense is the problem, propose sharing machinery with other artisaneurs.

INSIDE SCOOP:
RUSTIC BAKERY EVOLVES ORGANICALLY

In 2005, after years of running a clothing design and manufacturing company with her husband, Carol LeValley felt a calling to apply her experience to something more uplifting: baking. Her husband, Josh Harris, advised against fresh bread, because of all the great loaves available locally and because it was not a shelf-stable product.

CONTINUE ▶

Crackers seemed like a great idea. They have a longer shelf life, fill a void in the market, and draw on Carol's cracker-making hobby.

Carol's first thought was to connect with Cowgirl Creamery to get the opinions of owners Peg Smith and Sue Connelly. Carol reached out to them and brought in a batch of several flatbread flavors for them to taste. Coincidentally, Cowgirl Creamery had been searching for a handmade cracker to pair with its cheeses. Rustic Bakery landed a standing order on the spot for fifty cases a week. This instant success just goes to show that timing is everything. Carol and Josh took the plunge and shut down the clothing business.

Since their first sale was through Tomales Bay Foods, which is Cowgirl Creamery's distribution arm, Rustic Bakery had to establish distributor prices from the get-go. This bit of luck helped them avoid the common pitfall of setting suggested retail prices so low that they wouldn't make a profit. "Being in Cowgirl Creamery was a stamp of recognition that we had a quality product. Everyone started calling us," Carol says.

At first, the couple was just going to build a wholesale bakery, but then synchronicity took hold. They came across a sixty-year-old bakery for sale at a great price, with all the equipment needed to bake crackers. They quickly formed a corporation, bought the bakery, and went into production. "In the beginning, all I wanted to do was make the crackers and pay the bills," says Carol. "But the bakery had a café in front of it. Our lease required that we have a retail presence." The retail space inspired experimentation, and little by little, the café proved to be a huge asset. Rustic Bakery soon expanded its offerings to include organic baked goods and soups, salads, desserts, and sandwiches. The café also presented the opportunity for a wholesale business. In 2008, Rustic Bakery launched an eight-cookie line in retail stores, some of them in collaboration with popular cheese makers such as Point Reyes Farmstead Cheese. (The two companies later shared a booth at the Fancy Food Show.)

Their vision soon led to several more café locations. "What I love about the cafés," Carol reflects, "is they're the heart and soul of the business. It's a gathering spot." Visit their Larkspur Landing location at the Marin Country Mart, and I think you will agree.

The Joys of Good Co-Packers Making Your Food (for Business Builders)

You've already learned a bit about co-packers, or contract manufacturers, who help companies of all sizes and in all categories. Co-packers take responsibility for manufacturing with consistency and quality, following FDA regulations, local sanitation guidelines, and, most important, your specifications. With a co-packer, you need less up-front investment, compared with setting up machinery at your own manufacturing facility. And you don't incur costs when production slows down.

A co-packer might be a one-person bakery making cookies for you, a spice shop to blend and package for you alongside working on its own products, or a large company with massive equipment and hundreds of employees. Artisaneurs who have maxed out their capacity may choose to transition to a co-packer so that they can spend their time developing future products, as does San Francisco–based granola and bar company 18 Rabbits.

Even back in 1912, the inventor of Life Savers found a pill manufacturer to press his little imprinted candy rings. Much as with Life Savers, relationships with co-packers come in many flavors. Some examples:

- You may manufacture on their equipment or on equipment you own, if you have very specialized requirements for your recipe.

- You may source all or some of your ingredients, or use ingredients the co-packer procures at a lower price than you could, due to their higher-volume purchasing power.

- You may contract for a few short product runs or establish a long-term relationship.

The Downsides of Working with Co-Packers

On the surface, finding someone to make your food seems like a dream. But as with any outsourcing, you depend on someone else to accomplish your goals. You don't control manufacturing and capacity, something to consider in urgent production situations. You also don't control the quality (and care) of the production workers. And sometimes you can't even get on a busy co-packer's schedule. Specifying the ingredients is not a foolproof way to ensure that those same ingredients end up in your product. You really need to oversee all production runs to watch the ingredients and to troubleshoot variations in time, temperature, and numerous other factors.

One co-packer, who chose to speak anonymously, shares his perspective. "When making sauces, we find the most success with customers who realize that when you're going through the manufacturing process in a 250-gallon batch, things change. Food science is not an exact science. Ingredients like sugar, salt, vinegar, and flavorings vary between a test-batch size and larger quantities. We can't assure you that the product you make in a jar will be the exact same product you make in your kitchen." (Got the heebie-jeebies? See "Inside Scoop: Tessemae's All Natural Becomes an Accidental Manufacturer," page 45.)

INSIDE SCOOP:
PEAS OF MIND REALIZES ITS VISION
FOR HEALTHFUL KIDS' MEALS

Jill Litwin is the founder and CEO of Peas of Mind, a kid-friendly healthful frozen-foods company that sells in grocery stores and military commissaries, and also appears on school-lunch menus. Jill had no idea she'd be able to make such a statement about herself back in 2004, when she was working in the snowboard industry in Vermont.

The company started innocently enough. Jill began helping a coworker make healthful meals for her young son. Word spread, and Jill's one customer blossomed into fifteen. "I started to walk the grocery store aisles and realized there wasn't anything out there at the time besides baby food and chicken fingers," says Jill. "I was born with that entrepreneur computer chip inside me . . . I just didn't know which direction to go." Peas of Mind was the business opportunity Jill was looking for.

Knowing about California's bountiful organic food and the health consciousness of its people, Jill headed west. Upon arrival in San Francisco, she threw herself into a business-planning class at an entrepreneur support organization called the Renaissance Center. They pointed her to La Cocina, which was, at the time, a new nonprofit business incubator with the mission to help lower-income individuals, mostly women, pursue food entrepreneurship. Jill was La Cocina's first program participant and graduate. She also found a mentor at the government-funded Small Business Development Center who consulted with Jill over the years—at no charge.

With an eye on growth, Jill funded the business with loans, an equity round from two angel investors (see "Investors: Giving a Piece of the Pie (Angels, Venture Capital)," page 226) and a line of credit—all lingo and financial choices she learned about through her entrepreneurial courses.

From 2005 to 2007, Jill handled everything herself. Life was a blur. Jill would go to the produce terminal to buy ingredients. Monday was production day in La Cocina's commercial kitchen. On Tuesday, she would cook and package what she made on Monday. Wednesday and Thursday would look just like Tuesday. On Friday, she'd pack in the morning, then process the ingredients in the afternoon. The late afternoons were for opening new local accounts, evenings for e-mail catch-up. After her first year, she began working with a local distributor who would take care of warehousing and delivering the food to stores. "I met with Whole Foods as I was moving production to a co-packer," she explains—just in time to handle a big jump in sales.

All along, Jill had envisioned widespread distribution to make a huge impact on how kids eat, as well as to build a thriving business. She designed some recipes that would be gluten-free, dairy-free, vegan, low in sodium, soy-free, and with zero grams of fat. Brain-childs such as Veggie Wedgies (baked version of fries) would then appeal to parents and meet school allergen guidelines. Jill foresaw the day when schools would implement healthful food mandates (while giving kids the fries they crave) and grocery stores would increase the shelf space they dedicated to gluten-free products.

With her manufacturing capacity poised for nationwide growth, Jill tapped into connections to find staff sales reps. She hired two seasoned, retired grocery executives with deep industry ties as regional sales VPs. Both quickly landed big accounts. Jill also set up relationships with various sales brokers and distributors for different channels, from natural chains to box stores to conventional supermarkets. Her sales team manages the brokers. A product manager is Jill's right hand, and a publicist handles press and marketing.

Frozen foods stand alongside fresh perishables in complexity and risk. Space in a supermarket freezer is hard to come by; you need to sell, sell, sell to keep that space. Challenges include getting shoppers to the frozen-food aisle, competition for space in the

CONTINUE ▶

frozen-food cases, frosty glass making it hard for buyers to spot your products, shipping costs requiring dry ice, and all the things that can go wrong with the temperature between the time it leaves the production facility to when it gets to the grocery. If you guessed that the company spends most of its promotional budget putting the products on sale, running ads, and doing in-store promotions, you would be right.

Over time, Peas of Mind repositioned itself as "reinventing the classics," such as fries and pizza. "Kids want those unhealthy classic dishes. We have created a much healthier version of them." Parents can surely appreciate her value proposition. Today, Jill's products span the nation in supermarkets, natural food stores, schools, and commissaries—fulfilling her mission to bring kids healthful food and parents convenience.

Search for Co-Packers

There are as many types of co-packers as there are product categories. Sauce and preserves companies work with co-packers specializing in "wet" materials that need jar-filling equipment. Some co-packers subspecialize in foods such as barbecue sauces and soups. "Dry" co-packers cover mixes, spices, and teas, and also may handle a wide variety of other products. Beverage makers can tap into bottling plants. If a co-packer you like doesn't have the equipment you need, securing the equipment and training the co-packer staff may also be an option.

Products requiring unusual cooking techniques, allergen-free environments, or off-the-beaten-path ingredients face the greatest challenges. Frozen-meal company Saffron Road specifically sought out a co-packer skilled in multipart cooking processes; its halal meals use about 15 different ingredients cooked in two stages, with rice, sauce, and meat cooked separately—no small feat for an inexperienced manufacturer. Artisaneur Susie Hojel, owner of Chile Crunch, did not anticipate how few companies would be able to make her fried spicy garlic condiment the right way. She also encountered the "minimum batch" conundrum. On her own, Susie could make Chile Crunch batches of any size, but large co-packer production runs would mean not only big bucks for paying to make the food but an additional storage cost. The gap between expenses and revenue confounds many entrepreneurs.

Your packaging may also limit your co-packer options, especially when automating the process of filling packaging with your food comes into play. Many co-packers will want to use the packaging sizes and styles for which they have filling machines and established processes. Remember the ugly story of the hermetically sealed plastic spice bottles? (See "Define Your Packaging Elements," page 88.)

As with much in life, begin your quest for a co-packer by searching online for your specific need, such as "organic tea co-packer." Consider synonyms or more general terms a co-packer might use, such as "dry mix co-packer," which could potentially also handle blending and packing teas. Contract manufacturers can be hard to find online. Some choose to operate under the radar, focused on serving their existing customers. And many are simply too busy to care if they're found by another underfunded start-up. Try a search on www.contractpackaging.org to explore possible co-packers in your area. And don't judge a co-packer by its website, especially the smaller and older companies.

> ## GOOD IDEA:
> ## TRAIN THE MAKERS
>
> The team at Effie's Homemade wrote a quality-control manual to guide their co-packer's production team. The instructions include how to make, package, and palletize their product down to the level of how to stack the cases onto wooden pallets and shrink-wrap them for shipping.

What to Ask Co-Packers—and What to Watch Out For

Here's a short list of topics to discuss with prospective co-packers:

- **TRANSPARENCY.** Will the co-packer answer all your questions and allow you to visit any time, especially during production runs?

- **MINIMUMS.** What is the minimum production per flavor or product line?

- **INGREDIENTS.** If you want to source ingredients on your own, mention this to the co-packer early on. A co-packer might say no to non-FDA-certified ingredients to protect its own operations.

- **QUALITY CONTROL.** What measures are in place for quality control?

- **WAREHOUSING AND DISTRIBUTION.** What services does the co-packer offer?

- **PRICING AND COSTS.** How does the co-packer make money? Find out where responsibilities lie as far as ingredients issues such as spoilage, how refunds are handled, and what future cost increases you can expect. Learn how rent, utilities, storage, and labor rates will impact you. Set up co-packer contracts that let you benefit from cost decreases and limit your exposure to increases, and any other contracts for services in which rates may vary.

- **CAPACITY.** Ask how quickly and in what quantities they can make your products not only today but in the future, especially if you have a rush situation.

- **CERTIFICATIONS.** Ask what certifications they have that can help you (including if Costco has certified them, if you might want to sell there). If, say, your product is gluten-free, can the co-packer keep it separate from products that contain gluten?

Good co-packers will ask you plenty of questions too. One respected co-packer shares her perspective: "People are starting their lives out and depending on us. We want to manufacture your dream, what you want to make. You're going to be the one going out and marketing it. We're going to make it the way you like it, not how we want it." Still, you need to be vigilant and get everything in writing. One preserves and sauce maker shared her horror upon tasting one of her sauce batches. Turned out the worker making the batch saw no reason that distilled vinegar wouldn't do just fine instead of balsamic. Even though the co-packer funded the redo, the company had to explain to its customers why its product was out of stock.

And sadly, some Good Food businesses have had even worse experiences. One entrepreneur visited her co-packer, incurring costs for travel and lodging. She then spent a full day at the co-packer for research and development on various recipes she'd provided (she also gave the co-packer clear instructions and samples). Three separate batches were totally unusable due to the staff not reading the recipes correctly or not listening to instructions. The co-packer agreed to waive the charge for that day. In the following weeks, the co-packer made three or four more batches. The result still did not match the samples. It turned out they had substituted ingredients that were not comparable—e.g., white wine instead of red wine. The co-packer agreed to waive most of the bill but shortly thereafter presented an "overdue" invoice, broke the contract, and raised prices 30 percent—which essentially put the company out of business.

Lessons learned: (1) Get every agreement in writing, (2) follow up promptly, and (3) befriend a lawyer skilled in the art of threat letters. (For more horror stories—and the fortification to persevere—read Oregon Chai founder Tedde Mcmillen's story in her book *Million Dollar Cup of Tea*.)

Don't let the horrors scare you away, though—just know the right partner is critical to your business. For her Peas of Mind foods, Jill Litwin ended up contracting several co-packers that specialized in different food types (e.g., some are set up to make fried food, others to bake). Here's how she goes about getting started with co-packers:

① An initial call with several potential co-packers screens the companies to make sure they have interest, the capabilities, and that the company sounds like a good fit.

② When a relationship looks promising, the co-packer signs a nondisclosure agreement.

③ Jill gives the co-packers formulas and gets preliminary pricing.

④ The co-packers run a small test batch in their research and development (R&D) kitchen.

⑤ Peas of Mind then signs agreements with just one co-packer and conducts a larger test run on the production line.

⑥ The recipe either gets adjusted or, Jill says, "We're in business."

Start with the Co-packer Evaluation Questions and Research templates on GoodFoodGreatBusiness.com.

Write a Rock-Solid Contract

Protect yourself by investing in a lawyer well versed with co-packing contracts. You want to make sure that the contract has your interest in mind. Here are some good tips to know and/or include in your contract:

- **Don't send the recipe ingredient list or formula until you have a signed, lawyer-authored nondisclosure agreement. You don't want a co-packer to adjust the recipe to make it work in large volume,** not tell you how they modified it, and then claim to own it. (Better yet, try to get ballpark pricing from the co-packer before sending your formula to decide if working with them is even feasible.)

- When sourcing ingredients through your co-packer, try to cover liability for spoilage. The more the co-packer purchases, the more carefully they'll take care of the goods. Buy as little as possible, because if it gets ruined at its facility (such as 5,000 pounds of wheat flour damaged by a flood), you may have no recourse. Ask your co-packer about all of the available purchasing options. For example, can you lock in a corn price for the year? Will the price fluctuate if you choose to purchase per production run?

- Specify when and how the co-packer may raise its rates. One producer explained that his margin is very small due to three price increases from his co-packer in one year. "He adds a 30 percent margin on top of ingredients and labor, so the more ingredient prices go up, the better it is for him." The margin should be adjustable so it's a fixed amount on top of ingredients.

- For canned acidified foods, ask for proof that the processor has registered with the FDA. The FDA requires registration to ensure safe manufacturing, processing, and packing and to verify the processes are being followed.

- Specify that if machinery breaks down, your production will still be covered, so you don't run out of inventory.

- Require a monthly packaging inventory count, if storing packaging at the co-packer's facility. Include in your agreement: "for every run, you're allowed to damage X percent of packaging." Anything over that amount should be deducted from your invoice.

- In your termination clause, spell out what happens with any paid-for ingredients, product, and packaging so it cannot be held hostage. Have a bulletproof exit clause in case you need to cancel your relationship for whatever reason.

TEST YOUR PRODUCTS

A recipe can change quite a bit during production development. Whether making the food yourself or with a co-packer, be sure to get feedback on the final formula. You also want to see how eaters react to the finished product and your proposed packaging with the food in it.

A tasting at this point should be more analytical than your early "Should I do this?" tests. You want to gather specific data to understand small changes that could have a big impact on desirability. For the best insight, plan to collect quantitative data (by tallying up responses to a survey) as well as qualitative data (descriptive, essay-style feedback). Ask customers and wholesale buyers to help you test. Their involvement and personal input increases the chance they will support you later. If you plan to distribute nationwide, tap in to friends of friends who might be more likely than friends to dish out honest opinions. Set up an online survey and ship your product to testers around the country.

Dave's Gourmet has an in-house taste panel that gives the thumbs-up on a new product before external testing. After customer testing with online survey tools (such as SurveyMonkey and Zoomerang), founder Dave Hirschkop asks a trusted circle of people to taste further. Then the products debut at a trade show. If the products continue to get the thumbs-up, they are ready to go to market. Katie Das of Das Foods also employs an online survey tool to test consumer acceptance of her products, as well as get feedback on changes to her 5 Staples mix, on things like promotions or packaging.

You could also make testing part of your customer experience. TCHO Chocolate made its name with "beta bars," using a software analogy that paid homage to the founders' techie backgrounds. The chocolate makers started by making small batches, which they tweaked based on "user" feedback. The playful "Lab Tech Initiative" at Xocolatl de David in Portland, Oregon, looks to chocolate lovers for input on David Briggs's upcoming products. This Good Food Award winner makes recruiting testers almost as fun as eating the chocolate itself. He chooses three or four "lab techs" at random, who receive test chocolates in return for honest feedback.

ANALYZE NUTRIENT PROFILES AND SHELF STABILITY

When striving for a particular nutrient profile, such as allergen-free or 100-calorie cookies, analyze your foods while you're still in product development. After finessing your production recipe, you will analyze one final time. You have a couple of options for analysis:

- Database analysis uses the statistical average for commodity products, which can vary with growing conditions and other factors. Food Consulting Company, a Southern California–based food analysis service, says most clients choose the database method because: (1) the FDA actually encourages the use of nutrient databases as a low-cost alternative to laboratory analysis, and (2) this method is typically a better predictor of the nutritional analysis than lab analysis. For around $300, Food Consulting Company analyzes products to determine the 100-gram data and generate a package-ready nutrition-facts panel. Using do-it-yourself food analysis and labeling tools such as nutraCoster software or FoodCalc.com are also common ways to learn a products' nutrient profiles, adjust the production recipe if needed, and generate the nutrition-facts labels.

- Laboratory analysis uses scientific tests to determine the composition of a food as well as test for certain nutritional properties or microbial organisms like bacteria, which usually costs extra. For unusual products for which nutrient data is not available or for foods that undergo processing in which the nutrient changes cannot be confidently predicted, a chemical analysis makes sense.

If your product is shelf stable, you might start by tucking date-marked samples in a cupboard or in the refrigerator to visually examine and taste daily or weekly. This is not scientific but is an inexpensive way to get early data. Plan to invest in lab tests if you're selling to retailers or your food is prone to mold or other problems. At Food Consulting Company, a scientist tests your product for pH, water activity, moisture, solids, and other components. Those findings are then used along with specifics about the product ingredients, processing methods, and packaging to determine the product's shelf life. They also note that voluntary inclusion of a freshness date ("best before" or "use by") on labels encourages retailers to rotate product inventory.

As you can guess, food-testing costs add up quickly. When manufacturing yourself, you might eventually get your own testing equipment for more flexible analysis on the spot.

GREAT BUSINESS ACTION PLAN

☐ Figure out if where you live is the best place to set up your business. If you have the flexibility and inspiration to either move or manufacture elsewhere, peruse the "best places for small business" lists you'll find online. Or start by finding the ideal co-packers, wherever they may be. Prospective home-based food makers should make sure any place you move has a cottage-food law and that your foods will qualify. (A whole new and exciting research to-do list arises if you do start to consider moving.)

☐ Search for space or co-packers, depending on how you're producing (consider using a commercial realtor to help look for a space). Fully understand your production and packaging process when evaluating spaces, to know what machinery and space you'll need even if a co-packer is manufacturing for you.

☐ See if you can test-drive a space, such as renting hourly, before committing for the long term.

☐ Learn any rules and regulations related to producing the type(s) of food you're making. Check with your state and local government for licensing, zoning, and inspection guidelines.

☐ Look for food testing labs early, to budget in the costs.

☐ Familiarize yourself with the FDA website (www.FDA.gov) and the USDA website (www.USDA.gov), which offers templates for recall plans as well as an interactive nutrient-profile database at Ndb.nal.usda.gov.

☐ Investigate production and inventory management software. Some industries, such as baking, have industry-specific programs to help avoid spoilage and control costs.

☐ Write a production manual to help you think through your production flow, from start through packaging. You'll ultimately hand this off to your helpers.

ON *GOODFOODGREATBUSINESS.COM*

Get a quick start with the Co-Packer Evaluation Questions
and Research template along with links to labs, production,
and testing resources.

STEP
4

GET YOUR
FOOD
PRODUCTS
TO
MARKET

CHAPTER

WHERE WILL YOU SELL?

BURNING QUESTION:
DO I REALLY NEED TO SELL IN STORES?

No? Yes? Maybe! The answer goes back to your vision. For many product categories, big growth goals mean selling through "channels," including retailers. (Coffee roasters often end up selling beans, in addition to running their own cafés.) But, but, but... direct-to-consumer sales through farmers' markets and online sales, or sales to food service chefs, could equal the profit you could make from selling in many retail stores, especially if your product category has lots of competition within specialty and natural stores.

PLOT YOUR SALES AND DISTRIBUTION PHASES

In this chapter, you'll learn strategies for getting your product to the right places to reach your customers. Specialty food businesses follow the following common path to growth.

- **PHASE 1: Selling Direct—Higher Profits, Closer Connections**

- **PHASE 2: Selling Wholesale—Higher Volume, Lower Profits, Greater Impact**

- **PHASE 3: Going International—Massive Reach and Volume, (Ideally) Highest Net Revenue**

Your company mission, vision, and target customer should guide your distribution; that is, the "place" part of your 5 Staples mix. With your customer persona in mind, don your research hat for the answer of where to sell your Good Food. Expect to find juicy tidbits, such as that millennials (born between 1982 and 2001) are 23 percent less likely to value food brands (that is, they are more likely to buy unknown brands) and 18 percent less likely to shop at traditional grocers than baby boomers (born between 1946 and 1964). The same 2012 Jeffries/Alix Partners study reveals that millennials value convenience and are much more willing to shop across different brands and channels (mass merchants, club stores, drugstores, convenience stores, online, etc.) as well as shop online, via smartphone, and with delivery services.

Even if you're only planning to sell locally, read through this entire chapter, in case a nugget of information sparks a new plan.

Maite Zubia started selling her chocolate-covered *alfajores* cookies at the Ann Arbor, Michigan, farmers' market. I saw her mentioned in a story and invited her to sell through Foodzie.com's online artisan food marketplace. Her business snowballed, a lesson in going with the flow as opportunities present themselves. *People* magazine mentioned a celebrity's tweet about "one of the best cookies I've ever eaten." Retailers came knocking. She learned the hard way what happens when you sell a perishable good to stores whose customers don't know who you are (slow sales and aging product). So Maite decided to focus on the farmers' market and direct-to-consumer mail order, realizing that profit margins would be higher and her product would be fresher. But then Zingerman's Mail Order—also based in Ann Arbor—approached her about joining its popular mail-order catalog. Despite making less money per order than with direct sales, Maite knew the exposure through Zingerman's would be invaluable in building a fan base. She said yes. And so the nation discovered the joy of American-made chocolate-covered *alfajores*.

PHASE 1: SELLING DIRECT—HIGHER PROFITS, CLOSER CONNECTIONS

Selling direct to your end consumers, sans middlemen, usually gives you the highest profit—plus you enjoy those fulfilling interactions that make your long days and nights worthwhile. Direct selling may be online, at farmers' markets, or good old-fashioned person to person.

Learn Your Online Selling Options

Selling online helps you reach a world of people and simplifies taking local orders. We'll cover setting up your own store in "Define Your

Digital Marketing Strategy," page 173. As you plan all the places you might want to sell, consider your other online options:

- Craft-centric Etsy makes it easy for artisaneurs to set up a store in just a few minutes. Etsy brought Brooklyn-based Whimsy & Spice to the attention of a huge online community of craft lovers, who appreciate their sweets. The selling cost is low, as are the options for expressing your brand. Most of you will want to also set up your own online store to build a strong brand identity.

- For local selling, GoodEggs.com (available in a few cities, with plans to expand) helps artisans take orders online that customers can pick up from you, or that you or GoodEggs can deliver.

- Amazon also gives you an easy way to start selling. Shoppers may stumble upon your products by accident or while searching for foods like yours. You usually ship the products directly to the customer (called "drop shipping"), or you might be able to set up fulfillment through Amazon (in which case you need to carefully evaluate your products' shelf stability, as well as the cost and benefit of doing so).

- Online food marketplaces such as Abe's Market, Food52, Buyer's Best Friend, Fooducopia, and Eat Boutique carefully choose and promote products appealing to artisan-food-obsessed shoppers. You usually pay a fee or commission to sell, then drop ship the products directly to the customer, although the arrangement may vary.

- Brick-and-mortar retailers with mail-order businesses, such as Williams-Sonoma, Zingerman's, and Dean & DeLuca, are tough to get into but can "make" your business. They usually purchase at wholesale or lower, if they're offering a deal. They might want you to drop ship the products, or they may choose to warehouse the goods and handle shipping.

- Tasting boxes get samples of interesting artisanal foods in front of adventurous eaters around the country. Models vary as far as if you get paid for your samples or if you need to consider inclusion as a marketing expense. If you are invited to be part of a box, ask what kind of follow-up the company does to continue your connection with its customers.

Selling on Your Own Website versus on Other Online Food Sites

You'll find yourself weighing visibility and sales versus maintenance and cost when choosing how (and if!) to sell online. Here are some pros and cons of various options:

Opportunity	Selling on Your Own Site	Selling on Other Online Food Sites
Promotion	You control how your brand is presented; can offer special promotions.	Visibility among new customers.
Placement	Your products stand alone; you have full control of messaging, product offerings and presentation, fulfillment, and policies for returns and shipping. (Plus if you take some time off, you can easily hang up a virtual "gone fishin'" sign.)	Displayed alongside possible competitors and nonfoods; may get lost among other products on the site; quality of fulfillment and customer service may be out of your hands.
Price	Although you get 100 percent of the profit, you also incur the costs to develop and maintain the website. You control any promotions.	Fees to sell vary but it can get expensive; your partner may control pricing as well as discounts.
Promise	You can offer deals and control shipping to align more with eco-friendly practices; you earn more money to donate to causes if you so desire.	Fulfills your mission to get Good Food to more people than you could do on your own.
The bottom line	You control everything about the website, from the look to the functionality, which means there is more technology to manage.	A great way to get sales going and build awareness. Your branding comes through less, but you can get great visibility and connections.

For any of these options, double-check to make sure you'll make a profit, and if you probably won't, ask yourself if the visibility is worthwhile.

Selling at Markets

If you can weather the weather, farmers' markets epitomize Good Food and the joy of community connections. Markets are downright mainstream these days—75 percent of folks surveyed for the Mintel/Specialty Food Association 2012 Specialty Food Consumers Annual Report had shopped at a farmers' market at least once in the past year. Likewise, I've met quite a few food entrepreneurs who gave up on retail sales to join multiple farmers' markets in pursuit of higher profit potential and the rewards of interacting with local fans. Markets are also great for testing new flavors and getting feedback. You can sell irregular products and small batches, which keeps things interesting for both you and your customers. Plus, each farmers' market has a different character. Management ranges from nonprofits to cities to private companies. After you target markets in your area, Step 1 is to ask for the vendor guidelines from the market manager, learn about the application process, and find out if you qualify.

Much as with dating, you need to put yourself out there. And with dating, you never know who's out there. A writer from the UK's *Guardian* sampled Happy Girl Kitchen's spicy tomato juice at the San Francisco Ferry Plaza and dubbed it one of the "best 50 foods in the world." Stonewall Kitchen got its big break when vacationing Whole Foods staff stumbled upon Jonathan King and Jim Stott's jam at their Maine farmers' market stand. Twenty or so years later, the company had more than 6,000 wholesale accounts.

Before committing to sell at a farmers' market, ask vendors who currently sell there for the full scoop on the pros and cons of that market. The easier it is to get in, the more you need to confirm how much food traffic and sales other vendors are seeing.

Mastering the Market
To sell at a market, you'll need some equipment. Plan your setup to account for weather variations as well as the movement of the sun. At the very least, you must have a tent (if the market is outdoors) or a booth, tables upon which to place your wares, and signage that attracts customers to your booth and explains your offerings once they get there. Different markets require different kinds of permits as well.

Have a couple of extra hands on call should the flu fell you or if you need to be out of town on market day. These needn't be employees; they can be reliable friends or passionate fans. Offer them commissions only or a small fee plus commissions, so they are motivated to sell rather than check their cell phones. Sell alongside your new teammate for a couple of weeks to be sure she or he represents you well.

Consider how the market's target customer matches your own. Do you need to cater to vacationers coming to your area? Make it easy to pack up your goodies for picnicking, gift giving, or shipping back home.

And at the end of the day, revel in the time-honored merchandise swap with other vendors. It's a win for everyone.

TAKE 5:
TIPS FOR SELLING DIRECT
BEYOND THE FARMERS' MARKET

Popular markets are hard to get into. So if you're rejected, don't despair. Ask if you can do anything to change their minds, such as sourcing produce from another market vendor or adding a unique twist to your foods. No? Consider some alternatives:

1. Allow for local pickup from your production facility along with tastings, like June Taylor does at her Berkeley, California, kitchen. People can walk in while she stirs up batches right there in the kitchen. Visitors can taste her jams, fruit preserves, and candies; learn about the fruit growers and her methods; and then buy her foods. A bit old-fashioned? Just how she likes it.

2. Collaborate with a friendly retailer or farmers' market vendor to let you drop off customers' prepaid items for pickup. You might limit such options to larger purchases, such as a case. Offer a small commission to the vendor who helped you out.

3. Join (or launch) pop-up markets and local fairs both to make money and build your local fan base. Neighborhoods seeking to revitalize, such as downtowns and warehouse districts, are converting both open and indoor spaces into multivendor markets. Brooklyn's warm-season Smorgasburg attracts thousands who come to shop in their two locations for artisanal products, prepared foods, and well-crafted housewares from up to 100 vendors.

4. Branch out to farmers' markets a little farther away from your home turf.

5. Community Supported Agriculture (CSA) boxes gather local farm produce for easy pick up or delivery to eaters. CSA services are increasingly expanding to include artisan products. Look into options for getting your food into CSA boxes, especially if what you're making complements fresh fruits and vegetables (ask at your local farmers' market, or do a Web search for CSAs in your area).

Weddings, Parties, and Corporate Gifts

Imagine receiving an order for 500 or 1,000 of the same thing, and getting paid all at once at near your direct-to-consumer price. Pretty dreamy, eh? Whether selling $2 party favors or $200 gift baskets, you can earn a great living catering to the gift market, even when you give a volume discount. As an added bonus, you reach lots of potential customers.

Before you agree to a deal like this, time how long packing each gift takes. Account in advance for hired help; after tying 237 bows, you'll be ready to move on to more pressing things. Be sure to factor in all the packing-material expenses. Even if you've accepted a job for more exposure than profits (e.g., an awards-show goodie bag), you want to know how much you're investing.

Seasonal Gift Fairs, Festivals, and Craft Shows

How would you like to work yourself to death seasonally and relax in the off months? For many Good Food makers, garden fairs, craft fairs such as Renegade and Patchwork, food and wine events, and home decor shows all present opportunities to connect with people who set out that day to discover and buy. Plus, there's less competition from other food vendors than at markets that sell only food. The time and money you put into shows can add up. Before committing to a show, know what you're in for, who will staff the booth, and what you stand to gain. (And if your area has a lack of gift fairs and craft shows, connect with indie-minded entrepreneurs (of food and beyond) to get a new one going.

Kelly Davis discovered how efficient a well-targeted event can be for sales and awareness. She had been driving from state to state doing in-store Lusty Monk Mustard demos when suddenly gas prices started going through the roof and the price of mustard seed tripled. She had heard about an upcoming beer festival that would gather 8,000 hungry people in one place. Kelly connected the dots: "They're the right people, because they like spicy, they like gusto, they're likely to think the logo is funny," she says. (See "Inside Scoop: Lusty Monk Spreads Itself," page 146.) Rachel Flores and Bill Waiste were lucky enough to get their P.O.P. Candy nut butter crunch into one of the early Renegade Craft Fairs, where their prime position near the entrance and exit brought in lots of sales. At a different show that charged shoppers $10 to get in and located the P.O.P. booth in a back corner, sales limped along, however. In this second case, connecting the dots from the eyes of a shopper clearly forecasts slow sales: a family of four will have spent $40 just getting in to shop.

PICK YOUR PLACES: DISTRIBUTION OPTIONS AT A GLANCE

Each distribution choice has its upsides and challenges.

Distribution Method	Benefits	Challenges and Solutions
Your own Web store	Direct customer connections with potential for future promotion and engagement; most control in design, offers, and messaging; highest profits	Packing and shipping, potentially lots of small packages; need to generate interest and traffic

CONTINUE ▶

Distribution Method	Benefits	Challenges and Solutions
Drop-ship market-places that feature your products, which you ship out	Exposure to potential custom-ers; direct customer connec-tions with potential for future promotion and engagement; relatively high profits	Packing and shipping, poten-tially lots of small packages; less control in presentation
Your own retail location	Direct customer connections with potential for future pro-motion and engagement; be part of the fabric of the local economy	Expensive to set up and main-tain; need a great location, which can get expensive; need to figure out how to drive traffic into store
Farmers' markets and local fairs	In-person customer connec-tions with potential for future promotion and engagement; high revenue; low risk in terms of costs	Sometimes slow days, weather challenges; a need to be there regularly or hire someone to be "you"
Events, parties, and weddings	Potentially lucrative; great if you love variety; reach poten-tial future customers—perfect!	Need to excel in perfect pre-sentation; party favors often get the short end of the budget, so market to corporate or affluent customers
CSAs (local food-box subscriptions) and direct local sales	Very high revenue, potentially in volume and in profit margin; reaches new customers; con-nects you with local farmers	Most CSAs are produce-centric, although many are starting to include artisan food products.

PHASE 2: SELLING WHOLESALE—HIGHER VOLUME, LOWER PROFITS, GREATER IMPACT

Wholesale refers to selling at a volume discount to a reseller who then marks up and sells your products to the end consumer. The wholesale buyer may be a retail store, an online seller, or someone using your products as part of another product, such as a prepared food or gift basket. Learning from the early days of selling your product wholesale could radically change your 5 Staples mix for a few reasons:

- Your product and packaging need to be just as desirable to whole-sale buyers as it is to your end consumers.

- Your pricing needs to work for all buyers and still be profitable for you.

- **Your promotion should inspire people to seek out your products, especially if you're selling in stores . . . gotta "move the merch!"**

The wholesale journey for many growth-minded entrepreneurs follows a typical path:

1. You or your co-packer manufactures your Good Food.

2. You sell to retailers at a wholesale price (most easily described as 50 percent of the retail price; see chapter 10 for the long story). You'll most likely start by personally delivering to local stores. Buyers at smaller stores love this direct contact, getting a feel for you and having something new to offer. Absorb any feedback and keep an eye on how your products are merchandised. Be prepared to demo early and often!

3. You soon realize that spending your days driving all over making deliveries is not the best use of your time. You're feeling confident your product is pretty darn good, and it's perhaps selling in ten or more local stores. You think you can expand, so you look into selling to local or regional distributors. The color drains from your face as you realize your price to distributors is 20 percent to 30 percent off your wholesale price, plus potentially giving volume discounts. On top of this, you'll probably hire and pay another 5 percent to a commissioned sales rep, known as a broker, to help you sell to bigger stores and chains. Even though it's costly, selling through a distributor will likely increase your reach. And anyway, some larger stores will buy only through distributors as they combine many small orders into single big deliveries. Retailers can then receive and process hundreds of small deliveries like clockwork. As you expand to large stores, such as Whole Foods and other major supermarkets, you may switch to a nationwide distributor, such as United Natural Foods ("UNFI") or KeHE Distributors. Not only will you be making less money per item, but distributors have no obligation to tell you where your product is selling.

To deliver to distributors, you (or your co-packer) will deliver shrink-wrapped pallets of product. Perishable food distributors will require more frequent deliveries. If you're using a co-packer, the distributor may pick up product while delivering ingredients or doing a general pickup from the factory.

Another option is for your company to skip selling to and warehousing with a distributor to instead directly deliver large orders to stores. This is ever-so-logically called "direct-to-store delivery," or DSD. To deliver directly to retail stores, you'll need a dedicated sales team to get the product shelved and merchandised. Stonewall Kitchen does just that, so it can better control quality and where the product is sold, which supports its high-end branding.

(4) However you choose to distribute your products, your number-one job is to make sure they sell, referred to as "selling through." You, a sales rep, and/or a broker might take on the task of generating orders. Consumers can also supplement your sales and marketing efforts. Many of Stonewall Kitchen's new accounts arise through customers requesting that a store carry its line. This is ideal. Consider how you feel when a store responds to your request to carry a product: Listened to. Happy. Loyal. Good for everyone!

Selling to Local Stores Yourself (a.k.a. Pounding the Pavement)

Small specialty stores are hungry for something new and something to captivate their customers—all the time. In fact, once you're not new, you need to either have a good stream of demand from customers or keep the magic alive through demos, new products, or other involvement, lest you be banished to a shelf's nether regions. Choose your early retail stores strategically. Be sure they're the stores you love, who you would love to say they "made" you. These are the same stores you should connect with for feedback while developing your products and packaging.

You need not be 100 percent buttoned up with your packaging to start pitching to stores (though you should have your conviction, story, and pricing down pat). When Greg Vetter started Tessemae's All Natural, he channeled his inner sales guy, packed a plastic container full of salad greens tossed with his dressing, and showed up at the Annapolis, Maryland, Whole Foods store. His questionable offering met with doubtful glances. One taste later, Whole Foods agreed to host Tessemae's All Natural—at this point just a guy with homemade dressing—at one of their store's upcoming grand openings, provided he meet its guidelines. Greg filled out Whole Foods' paperwork, rented a commercial kitchen, and produced batches of dressing. At the event, Greg's gamble paid off, as he sold five cases in forty-five minutes. Notice his low-risk approach of waiting until he had validation before investing in his food production. (For more on Tessemae's story, see page 45.)

GOOD FOOD **GREAT BUSINESS**

Sell in multiple channels to level out trends and reach a broader audience—and have more fun, if you like variety. Ian Kelleher pinpointed customers of yoga studios, gyms, corporate cafeterias, convenience stores, and airports as likely cravers of his Peeled Snacks dried fruits. His 2012 *Inc. 5000* ranking as one of the country's fast-growing small businesses confirms the wisdom of this strategy.

Along with your on-the-ground sales efforts, look into listing your products on Buyer's Best Friend (BBF), a vast online wholesale-products marketplace. Adam Sah (a former Google employee) and Joyce Guan (a former food broker) created BBFdirect.com to help wholesale buyers easily discover and purchase from small companies (versus fielding sales pitches by phone calls, fax, and carrier pigeon). Buyer's Best Friend helps you easily start taking wholesale orders, which you or your distributor ship. You'll then be part of an account's order history, increasing the chance of a reorder. On your own website, you can ask buyers to contact you and/or link to your BBF store.

You may find there's a delicate balance between appealing to small stores while trying to make it in larger retailers. One anonymous condiment maker bemoaned how as the company grew, big stores said her company was too tiny. The small guys said "too huge." "We had developments and trials with big companies telling us we'd be the next big thing on their shelf," she explains. "We'd be in R&D with them for nine months. Then they'd turn around and not return my calls." So goes the risks of dealing with people, no matter how well-laid your plans.

TAKE 5:
TIPS FOR SELLING TO RETAILERS

You're competing with scarce shelf space and even scarcer attention from retailers. A little preparation (including printed pricing and marketing materials) will help you make the sale:

(1) Call the store and ask to speak to a buyer; better yet, get the buyer's name and direct number. If you can't reach a buyer after numerous attempts, call another department and ask to be transferred.

(2) Once you reach a buyer, make an appointment to bring in your product for tasting. Then show up on time, dressed as if you care.

CONTINUE ▶

(3) Know each store's guidelines, style, and merchandise, and have a solid list of reasons why your product would be an asset to each particular store (your reasons may vary based on the store).

(4) Establish your policies in advance. For your first order, require up-front payment via cash, check, or credit card, to establish that the retailer will be a good business partner.

(5) Be flexible and adapt to the retailer's policies, or go elsewhere if a deal is truly not right for you.

INSIDE SCOOP:
LUSTY MONK SPREADS ITSELF

The name Lusty Monk epitomizes Kelly Davis's approach to business: iconoclastic and individualistic. A die-hard history buff, Kelly became intrigued by a mustard recipe while thumbing through a Victorian cookbook. She made a few batches of the recipe, then tested it by giving it out as gifts and handing it out with pretzels at the Asheville, North Carolina, microbrewery where she worked. Kelly's brother realized she had something when he panicked as his personal mustard stash ran out. He decided to invest, and Lusty Monk came to be—the ironic name poking fun at a strict order of monks that avoided mustard due to its purported aphrodisiacal qualities. A graphic designer with a sense of humor came up with the logo, a "Spread the Lust" bumper sticker, and an "Indulge. Repent. Repeat." T-shirt. Another friend designed the Lusty Monk website.

Food-business incubator Blue Ridge Food Ventures helped Kelly with business planning. Kelly also appreciated the chance to decide if she truly liked making mustard and to verify that the product would work in the marketplace. "And you can do it without investing in all that kitchen equipment right off the bat," she notes.

Kelly needed a production facility, but also wanted flexibility to be with her kids. With that goal in mind, she came upon a house with an old beauty salon on the property. To comply with FDA regulations, she redid the floor and got a three-compartment sink and some stainless-steel tables. Making cold-process mustard doesn't take that much equipment: buckets, grinders, a big immersion blender, and a couple of refrigerators. Goal accomplished!

Whole Foods decided to put Lusty Monk mustard in its seven North Carolina stores as a start, to see how sales would go. Kelly alternates production runs with delivery road trips during which she listens to audiobooks, which she loves. She says "They generally give me a week's lead time for out-of-town stores. When one store orders, I'll call the other stores in the area who carry the mustard to see if they need restocking." The stores appreciate Kelly's do-it-yourself hard work. "You're not supposed to show up with a delivery after receiving hours," she says, "but most of them know I'm doing it on my own, driving a 600-mile loop, so they cut me some slack."

She has thought about hiring employees, but her answer to "What do I want to do all day?" includes avoiding employer issues. For now, a few entrepreneur friends who are delivering to the same stores take Kelly's wares as well, and they get a 10 percent cut. "This works out a lot better than a full distributor discount. They get help paying for gas; I save time and travel," she says.

In the meantime, Kelly's sister Kris took some mustard to her favorite brewpub in Albuquerque, New Mexico. After seeing the positive response, Kris decided to learn how to make it, and now she's producing and selling in Albuquerque and the Rocky Mountain states.

One thing better than filling hundreds of individual jars is selling mustard by the gallon. Kelly does so through the specialty distributor Southern Foods, which sells to high-end restaurants focused on meat and seafood. A key benefit of food service: No waiting for jars of mustard to sell. "People get to taste it and they can buy it there too. It's like having a demo all the time."

Despite her small scale, Kelly has been able to quit her other jobs. She loves her life, including when she walks through a crowded festival and hears people saying, "Hey, isn't that the mustard lady?"

Engage Food Brokers as Your Sales Team

As you start selling to larger stores like regional chains, the hard-core sales negotiations might push you well beyond your comfort level. For example, the ultimate retail coup is to land on a store's "planogram"—a visual diagram of the products a store always tries to keep in stock, shelf by shelf. Food brokers, essentially freelance sales representatives, can help you land such prime real estate. Great food brokers have excellent sales skills and know your local retailers intimately: what they sell, what they think is new and exciting, store guidelines, and who at the store will be evaluating your products.

What Brokers Cost

You will likely pay 10 percent to the broker for sales in which you deliver the product to the store, or 5 percent if distributors warehouse and deliver your product. Some brokers require a retainer fee to "pioneer" a line—in other words, to be the first to introduce it to the marketplace. When agreeing to pay a monthly broker fee, consider limiting the agreement to six months, and specify that this fee is a "draw," or advance, against commission in case a rep fails your expectations (or you fail hers). You may also want to build in a sales guarantee or other performance goal as motivation. Such goals might relate to total sales dollars, numbers of accounts, and reorders. Be sure to follow the S.M.A.R.T. goal methodology (see page 25).

In addition to its online wholesale buying system, the Buyer's Best Friend team works with many of the industry's regional and national chains, corporate campuses, airlines, and hotels, and can get you on the radar with these large, hard to reach buyers. They can work with you or your broker for a reasonable fee.

What to Ask For—and What to Watch Out For

Contact brokers early on to get feedback on your plans and sales ambitions. (You can find them by searching online or at food trade shows.)

- **Evaluate a willingness to collaborate. Will your broker share tips (and reality checks) on how to get, say, your natural vegan jerky into convenience stores?**

- **Start with a broker whose market matches yours. Buyer's Best Friend cofounder Joyce Guan suggests if, say, you're looking for twenty to forty new accounts in your first year, you should find a regional broker who covers a certain territory, presenting and selling multiple brands to stores.**

- Brokers should (1) have a track record of success in your food category and (2) focus on the venues in which you'd like to sell, such as mainstream supermarkets, natural food stores, Trader Joe's, Costco, convenience stores, or universities. Brokers may work on their own or as part of a larger brokerage firm.

- Before signing a contract, ask how many brands the broker reps, if any are competitors to your product, and how much time they have to dedicate to you.

Working With Your Broker(s)

Here's an easy success tip: Remove the guesswork. Simply tell your brokers exactly how and to which businesses you want the brokers to sell. You might go so far as sharing the types of accounts that have already been successful. Brokers helped Nick Kelley quickly grow his Alive & Radiant raw foods sales. He provided early sales data from Whole Foods Northern California to expand his products into other regions.

Your broker can only get in front of larger chain stores when the store has a "category review" scheduled. A "category" represents types of foods, such as frozen meals or candy. Brokers present product lines at these meetings, which typically happen once or twice a year. They often hear that a store doesn't have shelf space. Your broker may be more focused on higher-volume product lines. Be patient, and keep pushing your broker to present to your target stores until the buyers say yes. Keep in mind that hiring a broker does not mean you should pull back on your marketing efforts. The more awareness and interest you build, the easier the selling job.

Let me reiterate, you want a broker with a proven track record, one who has the time and energy to dedicate to your brand, has squirm-inducing persistence, and gets a thrill out of closing deals. I speak from experience: Several food entrepreneurs hired me to act as their broker, with only my enthusiasm and knowledge to recommend me. I faced the challenge of getting unknown products purchased, placed in a visible position, and eventually selling through in retail stores. An unknown brand, no matter how great the packaging, doesn't sell itself. Unfortunately, I lacked the time and focus to keep the sales coming, ultimately recommending they go with other brokers.

He knew that to grow his business, he would need partners to help develop the company and drive sales. Cuong happened to meet Betsy Fox in New York and Robert Bergstrom in San Francisco. The trio realized they shared common interests—Vietnam, fish sauce, culinary authenticity, and Asian cooking—and had complementary business skills and experience.

As a truly artisanal product, made from about five pounds of black anchovies per bottle, Red Boat commands a premium price. Cuong, Betsy, and Robert devised a strategy to package the fish sauce for three different target customers: specialty grocers (with a bottle tailored to a high-end customer and that could fit neatly on small shop shelves), Asian independent stores, and food-service chefs. Soon after entering the marketplace, the partners realized that while the biggest sales volume would come from the Asian channel, mainstream specialty distribution was essential to create buzz around the product.

Three factors led to Red Boat's success in the key mom-and-pop, Southeast Asian–owned shops, which cater to customers for whom fish sauce is a staple:

(1) They knew that store owners would understand "real" fish sauce and would be likely to purchase it, as would their customers.

(2) They explained how Red Boat's product would allow for greater margins than would lower-priced fish sauces.

(3) They effectively trained smaller stores on how to create a sampling program and sell to different types of customers.

The sales speak for the product quality too. People come back to buy cases, thinking they might not ever find this delicacy from the "old country" again. Smart thinking, because despite its limited availability, Red Boat quickly grew to become the super-premium market leader. And well before the *Today* show listed Red Boat on its Top 10 pantry-staples list, some of America's best chefs had fallen for the product. I've sampled the sauce with many a friend. Praise is unanimous (including from one of my Airbnb guests who revealed a fish sauce obsession). Simply good.

HOW TO SELL TO ZINGERMAN'S COMMUNITY OF BUSINESSES

Zingerman's is legendary for its irresistible selection of artisanal products from around the world, sold in its Ann Arbor retail locations as well as online. Brad Hedeman of Zingerman's Mail Order shares the company's sourcing process (which you can likely apply to selling to other mail-order businesses):

First, before contacting Zingerman's, know how (and if) your product is a good fit. Calculate your shipping costs to the company, the costs for warehousing, and Zingerman's own markup. Then figure out if the retail price will appeal to customers and is high enough that Zingerman's can make their expected margins. Otherwise, no matter how much buyers like your food, they simply can't buy it.

Zingerman's wholesale buyers might choose to sell your product in its stores, in the printed catalogs, or online. To begin with, they might bring on a small quantity of your product, write a feature about it in their newsletter, and then see how the product sells. But before they do, the team may do shelf-life tests and, if applicable, freezer tests on your products. So be sure you've done your own tests ahead of time.

Most important, reach out to Zingerman's while you have limited distribution. Brad confirms that when a product gets wider distribution, he usually can't compete with the prices. He says, "It's the difference between me buying five cases and a larger store buying five containers or pallets. They're going to get a better price and don't have to work with the same margins we do, so they can often sell a product retail for only a few dollars more than I can buy it for."

Good Food and Chains Can Mix

Each supermarket chain you might wish to sell to has its nuances and benefits. Here are just a few examples.

Whole Foods

Whole Foods' sixth core value is "Creating win-win partnerships with our suppliers." If you've got the right product and can do demos, Whole Foods is a great place to reach lots of customers.

First, check Whole Foods' website to familiarize yourself with its product guidelines and Unacceptable Ingredients for Food. Then, be bold! Your start may simply entail walking into a store with your products, asking for the specialty buyer or manager, and offering samples on the spot. (See "Inside Scoop: Back to the Roots Sprouts DIY Success," page 180, and "Inside Scoop: Tessemae's All Natural Becomes an Accidental Manufacturer," page 45.) Early on, you generally have to present to each store in the region for evaluation, but you can eventually apply for regional approval, which allows any store in the area to order from you via the Whole Foods ordering system. If your product is a top seller, it may also get approved for national sales.

Occasionally, Whole Foods has a vendor fair where you can meet local team members. Nicole Bergman debuted her Simply Nic's shortbread at one such fair, called a "localpalooza," in Princeton, New Jersey. The buying team brought her briskly selling shortbread into the store, positioning her goodies at the well-trafficked coffee bar. The company's Local Producer Loan Program has helped many a farmer and food artisan develop their businesses, with the company's teams and stores engaged in your business success.

Costco

Selling to warehouse stores such as Costco can be an efficient way to make a living. Selling those big pallets piled high with large-size products to fewer stores is a lot easier than selling many small packs to many small stores. Dave Hirschkop of Dave's Gourmet, a longtime pasta and hot sauce maker, calls Costco simply fantastic: "They really are focused on value to their members, combining the highest quality with the best price."

In addition to mainstream staples, Costco seeks out products that will appeal to local customers' tastes—great for food entrepreneurs like you. In fact, Costco's December 2012 magazine highlighted a series of specialty food makers in a multipage article, along with insight into the company's buying process. You will be required to meet all the Costco criteria, such as creating a special size for them and offering multipacks (e.g., two 48-ounce jars to a pack) as well as constructing a display that sits on a pallet, which is how most merchandise is presented in the store. You must be able to produce in volume, have a consistent product, and work within Costco's time frames. How's this for good: Costco wants to ensure selling there is profitable for suppliers. Plus, they manage your risk, requiring that suppliers not rely on Costco for more than 25 percent of their overall sales. The stores like variety, and they don't repeat products very often.

The more familiar you are with Costco, the more you'll know where your product might fit in, in terms of department, product mix, and competition. Learn more and contact its buyers by clicking on "Vendors & Suppliers" at the bottom of Costco.com. You might also reach out to Costco's in-house broker, Anderson Daymon Worldwide (ADWW.com), or another food broker that specializes in selling to Costco.

Trader Joe's

Trader Joe's offers great deals, which means it gets great deals from its suppliers. Selling under the TJ's private-label brand can be a good thing if your products are non-GMO (kudos to that policy) and you can produce them at a low enough cost—which may only be possible if you're manufacturing the food yourself.

The company will likely want to label the foods as Trader Joe, José, Giotto, or the like. You'll find an online application on the TraderJoes.com Contact page.

Strategize to Sell through Distributors

Time your foray into distribution for when you have committed retail accounts. Why? For one thing, if you make a mistake in just a few stores, righting the boat is easier than when hundreds of stores are selling your food. For another, if your products don't sell and you're not moving your minimum, a distributor will likely give you the boot after just a few months. For this reason, you're better off selling more products through one distributor, because they stand to make more money than if you spread your product line around. If your chosen distributor doesn't sell to all your target stores, you may end up needing to work with a second distributor.

Try to work with distributors and brokers that already have relationships with the stores and departments in which you want to sell. You might enjoy working with smaller, regional distributors, at least to begin with. Often family run, these smaller distributors may, after you train them, sell and pitch products, giving you a little more control than with large distributors, which usually dictate pricing and terms. Taza Chocolate co-founder Larry Slotnick sells his chocolate through a dozen smaller gourmet food distributors, all located near major urban areas. Larry tries to "protect" the distributors' territories so that they aren't competing with each other.

TAKE 5:
TIPS FOR SELLING THROUGH DISTRIBUTORS

Distributors can spread your product far and wide, but it's a whole different ballgame than your direct sales. Consider these tips to maximize your knowledge and profit:

1. Find ways to gain insight. Once selling through larger distributors, you may be hard-pressed to get reports and know where your product is sold. When distributors ask for a discount for particular customers, you might get a chance to peek at sales reports. Take it.

2. Calculate your benefit when a distributor or large customer asks for extra product to run a promotion. How much you can afford to provide? How does the promotion benefit you? Feel free to say no!

3. Think creatively to cut costs. For example, distributors might charge a "pick fee" to assemble a pallet made of a few flavors. To avoid the pick fee, you could offer a standard mixed-pallet option made up of, say, eight cartons of apple juice, eight of grape, and eight of peach. Wholesale buyers can then offer variety, seeing what sells best to their customers.

4. Mind your own expiration dates. Outside of bakery items, retailers rarely monitor short expirations on things such as fresh marshmallows (and the distributors will be no help here either). Clarine Hardesty chooses to sell her Clarine's Florentines in fewer stores. Customers know where to find her cookies, and the stores reorder frequently, keeping the product fresh.

5. Know when to quit. If you find your products aging and losing the quality you wish to deliver to customers, consider that your Good Food may not be suited for widespread distribution. One cookie maker pulled her products from a popular store for that very reason, not to mention she realized the arms-length selling model simply did not fit with her vision.

If, in time, you find that wholesale simply does not fit with your vision, connect the dots to develop a new strategy. That's what Sondra Bernstein did after learning a classic lesson while selling her Girl & the Fig preserves through distributors. While product sales were growing, the more products she sold, the more money she lost. Sondra, also owner of the Girl & the Fig restaurant in Sonoma, California, explains how she shifted course. "We didn't want to increase prices. And we realized if we stopped selling through distributors and just continued to sell direct and to the end user in our restaurants, our sales would be lower, but the bottom line would show a profit," she says. "Within six months we were able to go in that direction." The company had its best year to date.

PHASE 3: GOING INTERNATIONAL— MASSIVE REACH AND VOLUME

Artisaneurs may discover that an international market for their products has unexpectedly taken flight. June Taylor's preserves developed a cult following in Japan after a friend introduced her products in Tokyo, long after June had established her Northern California business. "The Japanese customers love our preserves and understand the nature of hand-making food," says June. Her success in multiple Japanese stores attracted the press, which wrote several extensive magazine articles about her company. And her San Francisco farmers' market booth became a must-visit for Japanese tourists.

The prospect of exporting may seem as far away as profitability. Still, think through your international policies and plans early on. For example, some businesses will let an international wholesale buyer place an order only after confirming that the buyer will store, handle, and sell their food properly. That conversation is also a great chance to learn both about the buyer's needs and their customers' cultural preferences. Starting out selling through a U.S.–based company that has stores abroad may simplify the prospect of exporting, with the stores handling the nitty-gritty details.

Is Exporting Right for You?

Not all products are ripe for long rides to distant lands. The best candidates for export tend to be lightweight (with lower shipping costs), superlative or unique in taste (intriguing to buyers), and have a shelf life of more than one year (leaving time for the products to be discovered and to travel through the distribution channels). Besides produce, which is appealing because it can fill gaps in seasonality, most food products that the United States imports fit the same criteria.

The USDA offers an online self-evaluation that asks about your domestic sales record, international marketing plan, production capacity, financial resources for marketing and sales, commitment to and resources for successful sales and service, and more. Visit www.FAS.usda.gov.

Know where exporting falls in your priorities. Early on, Justin Gold turned down many requests to export his nut butters, choosing to keep focus on his U.S. expansion goals. With an "abundance" mind-set, he assumed that the export opportunities would always be there; no need to say yes out of fear. When he did decide to export, he put the burden on the buyer to pay in advance and handle all aspects of shipping— rightly assuming that if the buyer really wanted his products, they would be able to do so. Remember, business is about relationships. We know how appealing "hard to get" can be.

Get Export Support and Offset Your Costs

For information on available export support, contact the USDA State Regional Trading Group near you:

- **Western companies work with the Western United States Agricultural Trade Association (WUSATA).**

- **Midwest and Northeast companies work with FoodExport.**

- **Southern companies work with the Southern United States Trade Association (SUSTA).**

These groups provide a broad range of programs and services, such as subsidizing domestic and international trade show costs (a surprising number are included!) and helping you meet new foreign buyers, form new distributor relationships, conduct market research, and sell products for the first time in a new market to stores and restaurants. You can also learn about shipping products overseas, export payment mechanisms, and how to track expenses to apply for government refunds.

The USDA also runs the Branded Program, two words you will want to remember as your company grows. The Branded Program serves "small" food manufacturers whose products contain at least 50 percent U.S.–produced agricultural ingredients. What's "small?" According to the Small Business Administration: Independently owned and operated, organized for profit, not dominant in its field, and with 500 to 1,500 employees.

The program might also reimburse up to half of certain international marketing and promotional activities. Yes, finally, your tax dollars at work!

Reach out to your State Regional Trading Group early. Karin Campion of Sonoma Syrup got started with help from WUSATA on label translations and expanding the company's export markets, with a little bit of paperwork and expense tracking. Justin's Nut Butter also tapped into WUSATA early on, helping offset trade show costs and getting access to programs and business-development opportunities. Be sure to connect those dots using your observational skills too. While still planning her Slather Brand Sauces, Robin Rhea heard about another sauce company that was exporting to fifty-two countries. She called SUSTA, which guided her toward signing up. Soon thereafter, she found herself at the London IFE food trade show investigating whether Europeans would be interested in her Slather Brand Sauces. They were. At the East Coast Fancy Food Show, one of the largest brokers in Europe came to set up meetings with her. She made the sale. Now, this broker picks up product from Robin and handles all the logistics of getting it overseas.

Buyers may also come from other countries to the United States on government-hosted trade missions, visiting specialty food stores to discover intriguing products. Ask your regional trade group if they can help you to get your products in front of these buyers—once you're ready. You might meet folks such as the importers from Kuwait and the United Arab Emirates who went on a shopping trip to the 2013 Summer Fancy Food Show and expressed interest in nearly $800,000 worth of products.

Quiz International Buyers

When an international buyer approaches you, put your research hat on and learn. Ask if your label would be acceptable (concerns about the ingredients or nutritional claims, even "gluten-free" claim guidelines, vary by country, and as of 2013, stevia cannot be called "natural" in the EU), the right price point for customers, and what most appeals to buyers in the particular country. Find out what wholesale and retail price points might work as well.

GREAT BUSINESS ACTION PLAN

- ☐ Map out short-term and long-term sales and distribution plans.

- ☐ Make a short list of people to reach out to, whether to apply to sell at a farmers' market or to contact retailers for feedback.

- ☐ Talk to other producers selling in stores and markets where you'd like to sell, for the inside scoop and to ask for introductions to market managers, buyers, and brokers.

- ☐ Learn your target customers' buying criteria before finalizing your product, packaging, and pricing.

- ☐ Think about how you could approach test marketing your products in another country.

- ☐ Evaluate your desire to export against your products' suitability for export.

ON *GOODFOODGREATBUSINESS.COM*

Get a quick start with the Digital Marketing Strategy template for your online selling planning. You'll find links to various places you can sell along with sales planning resources and consultants.

PRICE YOUR PRODUCTS

> **BURNING QUESTION:**
> **CAN'T I JUST MAKE UP GOOD PRICES?**
>
> *No. No and no. Incorrect pricing is many an entrepreneur's Achilles heel. The Specialty Food Association's Ron Tanner lays it out straight: "One of the biggest mistakes people make is in their pricing. When you start your business, you have to look at where you want to be in three years and five years. You almost have to start selling your product at a higher price than you think you should and have the margin built into your product. People almost feel guilty doing this. But if you don't, two years down the road you may not be in business as you can't easily raise your prices."*

DON YOUR POINTY-HEADED ACCOUNTING HAT

To price most accurately, you need to set aside any aversion to math, or enlist a finance-minded friend, and really dig in to your expenses while simultaneously making sure your value proposition makes your prices palatable to your target customers. In this chapter, we'll look at ways to estimate sales and figure out how to price your products in a way that's good for everyone.

HOW TO PROJECT SALES WITHOUT ANY SALES HISTORY

To set your prices and plan production, you need to estimate future sales. That's easier said than done. Lots of factors can throw off your calculations. Publicity might spike sales. A competitor or new buyer at one of your accounts could bring sales to a screeching halt. But you've got to start somewhere.

Joyce Guan of Buyer's Best Friend shares a three-step method for estimating sales, based on her experience as a specialty food broker:

 Talk to other producers who seem to be a couple of steps ahead of you with their sales and see if they are willing to share their sales numbers. Or look at similar brands' websites to see price points and retail locations.

2 Contact retailers to ask how much they are buying of similar products monthly. Talk to a small store, then a medium one, and finally a larger one.

3 Project sales for your own products based on the approximate volume other products are doing per month at these stores.

New food categories have no track record of sales or what people will pay, making price setting a challenge. For example, not so long ago, raw snack foods were a brand-new category. Nick Kelley put a small army of dehydrators to work, experimenting with what would become Alive & Radiant (formerly Kaia Foods). He hit the kale chip phenomenon just as it was on the upswing—with only a rough idea of what he could charge. Nick got started by walking into local retailers, offering samples, and making sales. After landing twenty-five store accounts, Nick decided his crunchy kale chips and other raw snacks had real market appeal. Based on the initial sales, he projected future sales and expenses as he grew the company. He decided to build his own production facility in Oakland, California, giving him flexibility to evolve the product line and grow his business. Plus, there weren't really co-packers specializing in his type of dehydration-heavy operation. After learning from a year's worth of income and expenses, Nick was finally able to accurately determine production costs.

DETERMINE HOW MUCH YOU CAN CHARGE

Your prices need to fall within a range that's palatable to your target audience. The prices you set will position you as low-end (accessible to many), high-end (scarce and accessible to few), or somewhere in the middle. When your price is higher than your competition's, your value proposition really needs to pay off. Think about natural Greek yogurt versus the old pectin-thickened kind. Or margarita mix made with fresh lime juice versus artificial flavoring or concentrate.

People told Mary Waldner to simply charge as much as she possibly could for her Mary's Gone Crackers products, before she knew what her actual cost would be. So she looked at other crackers, and then set a price that made hers the most expensive. "We weren't profitable at first, until we learned to make them more efficiently," says Mary. "Since then, we've only had two price increases. The demand goes up, the cost of ingredients goes down, and production gets more efficient."

Though Mary was successful, you might try a slightly more scientific method for setting retail prices:

1 Check online and at your target retail stores to learn the competition's pricing. Most likely you will not be able to make an apples-to-apples comparison with similar products—try and factor in how your packaging, ingredient sources, branding, and other factors will add to or detract from your price.

2 With your prototype and proposed retail price, ask several target customers (ideally not your family) what they might pay. If the response doesn't match the price you had in mind, reevaluate your 5 Staples mix. Changing your product, promotion, or perhaps the place you sell could suddenly make your pricing work. (Also, now would be the time to make a go or no-go decision as far as moving ahead with your business.) Your proposed retail price also needs to allow you enough margin to make a profit when you sell at wholesale costs to retailers.

3 Once you get to a price that works and you've been selling for a while, test a few temporary price reductions or increases at the farmers' market, online, or at retail to see the effect on demand. Evaluate customer responses and any possible negative fallout.

Understand How Your Price Communicates Your Value

Outside of the foodie bubble, you may run into the reality of buyers comparing your seasonal salsa to preservative-laden brands. One entrepreneur tells how they were invited to join a mini craft market. "We're sitting up onstage, and the first person asked, 'Why would I buy your products when I can go into a market, and they're so much cheaper?'" The bottom line is that a $20 bottle of wine is a hard sell to the $2 drinking crowd—unless you can make a value proposition for the extra $18. Perhaps scarcity, the handmade methods, a trendiness factor, or the unusual grape quality that year would do the trick.

What Goes into Your Pricing

Your prices need to cover all your costs and let you and any sales partners profit, plain and simple. This holds true both when selling direct to the consumer and at lower wholesale prices to a retailer or distributor. Start with a big-picture look at your category. What is the "expected price" for similar products, taking into account your special 5 Staples mix? Will customers expect your food to sell at a premium? Will a lower price bring your brand quality into question? Or is your mission to bring Good Food to lower-income people? In the case of too-good-to-be-true low prices, you'll want to explain how you're able to charge so little.

With your big-picture idea of what your prices should be, it's time to see how many products you need to sell to make a profit. One important concept to master is "breaking even." This means selling enough SKUs, or units, to cover your costs. Your price multiplied by the quantity of product you sell is called *revenue*, and, ideally, it will be more than your costs. And you will have many costs:

- **VARIABLE COSTS. Expenses that generally go up and down based on the number of products made, and that relate to production, storage, and delivery of your products are variable. These include hourly labor, hourly kitchen rental, co-packer fee, ingredients, packaging, labeling, gas, water, and electricity. *Cost of goods sold* (*COGS*) is an accounting term that is meant to encompass all of these costs. There are a few other variable costs. *Chargebacks*, or fees retailers deduct from payments, may appear as another cost, should your products not be sellable or the retailer decides you've somehow not delivered what you promised. *Sales expenses* are usually variable, unless you employ a sales team.**

- **FIXED COSTS. Monthly and yearly costs incurred regardless of how much you produce, such as insurance, monthly rent, and salaries, including your own salary, are fixed. If you stop producing for a month, you still incur the fixed costs. Fixed costs are oftentimes collectively called *overhead*.**

The first step is to calculate your *gross margins*. Gross margins are revenue minus variable costs. A good gross margin is 60 percent (this means that your variable costs do not exceed 60 percent of your revenues.) But if you can make a profit at a gross margin below that, that's fine too. However, some experts suggest you should never go below a 25 percent gross margin, even after promotional discounts.

Profit is your gross margin minus any fixed costs. Another way to look at it is your revenues minus all costs. Typical profit margins (the percentage of your sales that are profit) differ by product category. Shoot for at least 10 percent profit, unless a particular customer provides some other long-term business value, such as exposure.

Account for Your Donations

Next, if part of your 5 Staples mix includes a promise to donate a percentage of your profits, you'll need to plan for this as well.

Be careful if you do choose to state you will give "a percentage of . . . " on your packaging. Here are some interpretations:

When you say . . .	You're really saying . . .	And you're committing to . . .
1 percent of sales goes to . . .	We're donating 1 percent of sales to X cause. We're generous and committed.	If you take in $1,000, you're giving out $10—risky, before you've subtracted business costs.
XX percent of profits goes to . . .	We're generous but not really committing until we are profitable.	Not much. Many companies go for years before turning a profit, during which technically you don't need to give any money away.

Rather than promising a percentage of profits or sales on your packaging, you might keep it simple, occasionally donating chunks of money to various causes and offering matching grants. In addition, you could tie donations to marketing activities, like "$1 donated for everyone who 'Likes' our Facebook page," particularly around certain holidays or other events. Or give back with food donations, volunteering, or education. For example, Two Degrees states it will give a meal pack to a child for every energy bar sold. Another bar company, KIND, inspires consumers to engage in acts of kindness, extending their brand—and goodness—throughout the world.

GOOD IDEA:
DECONSTRUCT GOOD PRICING EXAMPLES

Picture this: A coffee chain prices a generously sized, elegantly wrapped chocolate caramel two-pack at $1.75, a pittance for gourmet candy. The sweets fly off the shelf as fast as the café can stock them. Perhaps the maker is achieving a profit. Or perhaps the café is not making any money on the products. They may price without profit to draw in customers, using the caramels as what's called a "loss leader."

Take into Account How Retailers Really Price

You'll hear a general rule of thumb that retailers double the wholesale price to get to their retail price. The truth is that retailer markup over the wholesale price might range from 33 percent to 50 percent. A great example comes from Maggie Bayless, of Zingerman's ZingTrain training group. Here she shares the technique her buyers use to derive their retail prices.

A retailer's total product cost includes the wholesale price you or your distributor charges and the cost of freight to the store, plus the retailer's costs. In math terms:

Total cost = raw cost + freight cost x yield percentage + peripheral costs. For more explanation of these terms, keep reading.

- RAW COST. This is your wholesale price plus the markup that your distributor (if you have one) will charge. For products sold by the pound, this is simply the wholesale cost per pound. For packaged products, it is the per-item price (case price divided by number of items in the case).

- FREIGHT. If you didn't charge "delivered prices" (with freight built into product pricing), the retailer adds it into their costs. Retailers prefer that suppliers or distributors quote simple delivered prices; it's less work on their end.

- YIELD. The difference in weight or quantity of what the retailer received and can sell (raw versus cooked foods, or food trimmed before selling). The retailer may subtract product for sampling in that calculation (reducing their yield), so a case of 24 actually yields only 23 sellable items.

- PERIPHERAL COSTS. When buying in bulk, the retailer may add in the cost of repackaging materials into individual units.

Retailer total cost example: A carton of 24 chocolate bars, at the wholesale price of $2 each, including shipping, costs $48. One bar is used for sampling, leaving 23 to sell. The cost per unit (assuming no other selling costs are incurred) comes to $2.09 ($48 divided by 23) because the cost of the sample is amortized, or spread, across the other bars.

Retailers often price products by estimating how many units they will sell at a certain retail price, subtracting all of their costs for that product, and then figuring out how much they need to charge to make a profit on each unit. Many retailers also use their gut feeling for how much customers will pay when deciding on a retail price. For widely available products, retailers may be forced to set prices on par with other stores, even if they don't receive volume discounts as a larger store might. Offering exclusivity helps the retailer set a profitable price as well as giving consumers a reason to visit that store.

Why does a retailer's price matter to you? Well, if a retailer feels it can charge customers only a certain price, this may mean that they will only pay you a certain (i.e., lower) wholesale price to make sure they will get the margins they would like. You need to be able to profit at this price.

How to Quote All-Inclusive Prices for Direct Wholesaling
In addition to your wholesale price, you may need to create a price list that includes shipping and handling costs to the wholesale customer, called a delivered price. The delivered price helps a buyer quickly calculate the per-unit cost: total quantity divided by the number of units or weight.

Shipping costs that vary during the year and by geography make for tricky estimating. If you're confident that the account will be a long-term, year-round deal, calculating an average price may make sense. Or you might create various rate schedules to address delivery to different regions of the country. For example, fuel costs tend to be higher on the West Coast (Alaska, Arizona, California, Hawaii, Nevada, Oregon, and Washington), so you might want to charge more for delivery there.

Delivering by car? Many new food producers deliver at no charge to their local accounts or offer free local delivery when the purchase exceeds a certain dollar amount.

> **GOOD IDEA:**
> **MAKING IT WORK TO SPEND MORE AND CHARGE LESS**
>
> Since its early days, Clif Bar & Company has shaped itself around the triple bottom line, taking care to serve people—its employees, customers seeking healthful foods, and suppliers—and the planet through eco-friendly practices. The company also looked after its own profits to build a sustainable business. Yet for many years, it had sourced conventionally produced ingredients in order to

achieve a price that would be accessible to more consumers. As time went on, however, Clif Bar realized that going organic was essential to fulfilling its mission. Shockingly, the company decided to keep the retail price the same and not pass the significantly higher production costs to consumers. The dare paid off. Consumers loved the switch to organic, and sales took off. Clif Bar has since grown its sales each year by double-digit percentages, on average, for the last 10 years.

A FEW MORE PRICING TIPS AND COSTING TRICKS

- When calculating the product yield from your ingredients, account for loss in the manufacturing/production process. For example, chocolate expert Clay Gordon notes that you likely won't get eight 1-ounce chocolate bars from an 8-ounce block of chocolate.

- Price consistently within a product line by averaging your cost across flavors. If you offer four cracker flavors all at the same retail price, shoppers have one less factor to consider when choosing which flavors to buy.

- Time the tasks involved in your production. Eventually you will have employees, and you may pay them by the hour. Knowing how long production takes will help you estimate your employee costs.

- Avoid "channel conflict" by setting your direct-to-customer prices as the same or higher than retailer prices to avoid taking away their sales opportunities.

- When expanding your product line, you may incur many of your original product-development costs and time, especially when entering a completely new product category. For example, you may need to reapply with the FDA, undertake new health inspectors, and plan a new recall system. Take this into account when setting pricing.

- Promotional and free product requests from stores, called "free fills," can really add up. Pack fewer products per case to take a smaller bite from your promotion budget. Or ask the store if it can cover the cost of samples.

I'll leave the complexities of managing your P&L (profit and loss) statement, final pricing calculations, and other financials to the experts you should tap into for accurate guidance. Also look into software programs or books designed to forecast and manage food production.

GREAT BUSINESS ACTION PLAN

☐ Analyze prices of your closest competitors as compared to your brand and target customer. Do the math and start to calculate the prices you need to charge, both wholesale and retail. (Commit to pricing only after you know your costs.)

☐ Seriously consider hiring a finance or sales consultant to work with you on pricing as an investment in your future profits.

☐ Make a plan to estimate your sales in the main places you're thinking of selling. If the number seems low, look at what might you adjust in your 5 Staples mix.

☐ Track every little labor and materials cost, to make sure that the ways you think you're saving money on materials aren't, in reality, eating up your time—costing you more.

ON *GOODFOODGREATBUSINESS.COM*
Find links to pricing and sales forecasting resources.

CHAPTER

PROMOTE YOUR PRODUCTS

BURNING QUESTION:
HOW DO I GET THE BUZZ STARTED?

If your story is a good one, put yourself out there to get the marketing buzz started. Frozen-treat-on-a-stick company Little Bee Pops had barely hit the Mountain View, California, farmers' market when the story-hungry media started coming out of the woodwork. Liz Snyder drew upon her experience as a sustainable-food advocate and purposely let this "earned media" (unsolicited coverage by news outlets and magazines) run its course. At the height of a buzz lifecycle, she explained, paid-for advertising could actually detract from the company buzz.

UNDERSTAND MARKETING: LEARN YOUR AIDAES

Promotion, or marketing, gets your messages out to your target customers, and the people who influence them. Every time you expose your brand you're marketing: on packages, in social media, through customer service interactions, in ads, on T-shirts, on your website and blog, during your farmers' market chats, and with in-store demos.

Marketing is where your customer relationships begin. The marketing cycle generally follows this pattern:

- AWARENESS. A prospective customer realizes that a brand and its products exist.

- INTEREST. The offering piques the prospect's curiosity. She begins investigating and evaluating the products against other alternatives.

- DESIRE. The prospect really wants what the company is offering.

- ACTION. The prospect responds to your call to buy, share, give feedback, etc.

Sound oddly familiar? You've surely been the object of this cycle for many a marketer. This concept, abbreviated as AIDA, has guided marketers' promotional activities since the early 1900s. We'll add an E for *engagement*, a 21st-century addition for today's social world. Particularly relevant to Good Food entrepreneurs, engagement builds close relationships with customers to a point where they feel connected to and invested in your company. You might look at engaging as a return to old-fashioned personal connections, much as food crafting takes us back to slower times.

Amazon shoppers can observe this entire cycle occurring on each product page, with product details, reviews, products other people looked at, and, of course, the "buy" button . . . followed by a request for you to review the product and related products displayed upon your next visit.

PLAN YOUR MARKETING STRATEGY

If you are starting small and selling locally, simple community connections, social media, and demos may fulfill your promotion needs. But when you're on the hook to generate lots of sales quickly (maybe you've raised money from an investor, are doing a big production run, or are setting up a retail space), you'll need a well-thought-out marketing plan.

Going through a planning exercise—even if you plan to not follow your plan—can help you focus your time and energy. When times get busy, prioritized goals will focus you. Luckily, marketing strategy makes up a big chunk of business planning (covered in "Sketch Out Your Business Plan," page 234).

First you'll come up with your big goals, and then break them down into an action plan, using a spreadsheet or to-do list app. Be sure your marketing goals are S.M.A.R.T.: specific, measurable, actionable, realistic, and time-based. A marketing strategy generally includes these sections:

- Background or overview. If you'll be handing the plan over to a marketing vendor, start by summarizing where you are with the business.

- Business goals. What do you ultimately want to achieve through your marketing? For example:
    - Increase sales 50 percent by XX date.
    - Land five new independent natural food retailer accounts by XX date.
    - Donate $25,000 to XX nonprofit by year's end.

- Marketing goals. Spell out what the marketing activities should accomplish to bring the business goals to fruition.
    - Attract 5,000 customers to sample new flavors by end of Q3.
    - Build awareness among 10,000 new customers by March 31.
    - Establish us as the most innovative, community-involved XX company in the region in the next year.

- Target audience. These are people you want to reach, either the customers you identified in chapter 4 or other people with whom you want to build AIDAE, such as sales channels and influencers. Get specific, because your audience will have a bearing on the type of marketing you do.
    - Health-conscious parents with children ages seven to fourteen in the Chicago metropolitan area.
    - Dessert-centric food bloggers with more than 1,000 Twitter followers.
    - Friends of customers who purchased online from us at least once in the last quarter.

- Tactics. What you will do to achieve the marketing goals, such as:
    - Run Facebook ads in five versions, targeted to parents based in Western states who are interested in hiking and gluten-free diets.
    - Sponsor a Back to School tweet-up (Twitter chat) with mommy bloggers to give away 100 free product coupons in a five-hour period; promote for a two-week period preceding.
    - Run a Kickstarter campaign to build awareness and raise $10,000.

- Measurement, or metrics. Set realistic goals to define success for each tactic—this will help you evaluate your return on time and money spent.
    - Five percent purchase rate.
    - Ten reviews by food bloggers including photo(s).
    - Twenty-five retweets from locals promoting our community giving.

- Key messages. These messages will draw upon the value proposition, features, and benefits from your business plan. Any writers will start with these messages, which should all be in sync, from PR to packaging.

- **Call to action.** Always include your "ask," what you want the prospect or customer to do. For example: buy now, follow you on social media, spread the word, request a sample, or give feedback.

- **Desired response.** Ever get gussied up thinking, "I want people to tell me I look hot!" Same idea here. What do you want your target audience to say or do? For example: "I'm totally addicted! I eat these every day!" Or "It's the perfect, easy dessert. I serve it at every party."

- **Assumptions.** Such as that you'll be using existing creative components (logos, videos, etc.) or that a certain online-contest software service will be used.

- **Timeline and team.** Jot down the schedule with tasks, due dates, and who'll do what if you're not doing it all.

When you're ready to plan, get a quick start with the Marketing Plan template on GoodFoodGreatBusiness.com. Refresh the plan as needed.

Your marketing activities will, of course, vary depending on what you're creating. A logical progression for food start-ups might go something like this:

Phase 1: Get Online—Plan. Shoot. Build.

Phase 2: Launch and Ride the Word-of-Mouth Wave

Phase 3: Keep the Buzz Alive with Promotion and Marketing Support

The lucky few who nail their 5 Staples mix and build a big fan base can avoid Phase 3 for years as fans keep your brand buzz going.

PHASE 1: GET ONLINE—PLAN. SHOOT. BUILD.

Whether or not you're selling online, plan to make the Internet your always-on marketing machine. You need to control your brand online. A Facebook page is not enough.

Set Up Your Domain and Social Media Accounts

The second you settle on a company name, jump online and reserve your website's domain name, also called the URL or Web address. Domain names are cheap, around $10. Don't worry if your domain name doesn't match your business name. If MarysCookies.com is taken, try a similar twist, like EatMarysCookies.com or ShopMarysCookies.com. You might also reserve names with misspellings, such as ShopMariesCookies .com. For long company names, like the World's Best Damn Pickles, consider a shorter domain, like killerpickles.com. Domain taken? If you've trademarked your brand, the domain owner may be legally required to hand over the URL to you.

If you're in a hurry to launch, you can easily post a placeholder Web page with your logo and contact information, which most domain hosts (such as GoDaddy) include at no charge. Or, you could do a temporary redirect of your domain to your Facebook page. Best yet, launch a simple website, which you'll read about in the next section.

It's never too early to post your company on various Internet directory and review sites. In addition to any local directory websites, consider listing on sites such as Yelp, Citysearch, and Google Places. Specialty food directories such as BBFdirect.com, Food-Hub.org, and LocalHarvest.com will get the awareness and interest going as well.

Next, register all your social media accounts: Facebook, Twitter, Pinterest, Instagram, Google, YouTube, Flickr, etc. Match your social media user names as closely as possible to your company name. Set up your business accounts separately from your personal accounts so you can easily hand your business's social media and e-mail reins to a helper.

Define Your Digital Marketing Strategy

Figuring out exactly what you want to say and do online will help you clarify exactly which systems will do the trick. A little upfront planning will save you lots of time and money in the long run.

As a rule of thumb, the less important that online sales are to your business strategy, the less you want to spend on technology. Some companies, such as Late July Organic Snacks, have grown just fine with a simple blog as a website, even well into life as a nationwide snack maker. Within an hour or so you can "go live" with a basic website using nontechnical tools like Wix.com, Squarespace, or ready-to-use themes from Wordpress.com or Blogger.com.

Running your own Wordpress system (easier than it may sound, thanks to one-click installs from various Web hosts) is perhaps the most popular way to run a low-cost website. Your own system—versus the more limited system hosted on Wordpress.com—gives you room to grow and change. In addition to pages with basic information, you can run an online store, a blog, and all sorts of fancy features. Plus, you can run ads on your site (which Wordpress frowns upon), if this strategy is key to your business. Whatever you envision is probably doable at a very low cost, thanks to free "plugins" that tack on to the basic system the way you add options to a car.

When an online store is key to your strategy, you'll want to look at the user-friendly hosted e-commerce systems out there, which usually include features such as flavor options, gift messages, and shipping options. Shopify, Volusion, or Bigcommerce are just a few. Before you sign up, figure out how and if you'll recover the monthly hosting fees. When your big differentiator includes a customized ordering option (like Chocomize.com) or fun delivery service (like Chicago's Foiled Cupcakes), that's when you need to brace yourself for an investment. I'll admit, though, that I was impressed that Foiled Cupcakes designed and built its fun and sophisticated website by customizing their own Wordpress system for about $15,000.

Within five minutes of reading this sentence, you can be set up to take credit cards too. Services such as PayPal Here, Google Wallet, or Square are familiar to consumers, and they charge based on transactions. Both PayPal and Square let you accept cards at farmers' markets or events with a card-swiping device you plug in to a tablet or smartphone.

You'll find a lot more about digital marketing strategy on GoodFoodGreatBusiness.com.

GOOD IDEA:
TURN YOUR PERSONAL E-MAILS INTO PROMOTION

E-mail back-and-forths with customers and influencers make it easy to get little nuggets about your company across, using the "signature" below your text. Every e-mail program has a feature to set up a signature. Along with your contact information, you can include a press quote, recent award win, or mention of a new product line, such as Donna Sky's bold, orange-colored one-liner (matching her brand colors): "Local, organic, handmade, sustainably packaged, and fabulous flavor—just a few of the many reasons to Love the Love & Hummus Co." On Julie Nirvelli's White Girl Salsa e-mail signature, she trumpets: "Now available at all 50 Whole Foods Markets in CO, KS, UT, NM, and TX."

Bring Your Online Presence to Life

Visuals and words tell your story online. Look at other websites you admire, whether they are in the food space or not, and see what kinds of information they include. Write up your content (or hire a writer), and then it's up to your Web designer or team to do the rest (unless you're a tech whiz). Your Web team will do its best work if you've got photos, logos, and your overall brand locked down before you pass everything off to them. Consider featuring any press mentions on the home page. If you have well-known corporate customers, ask if they will give permission to feature their logos or names on the home page.

At a minimum, food-company websites typically have the following sections. Test yourself and see which result in awareness, interest, desire, action, and/or engagement.

- ABOUT US page, similar to the "boilerplate" text you see at the bottom of a press release or website. Optionally, have a separate *Our Story* page with details about you, your team, how you came to launch the business, and stories of your suppliers and partners.

- NEWS/PRESS/TESTIMONIALS, highlighting stories and mentions. Add a "press kit" with a company fact sheet and photos to your website as well. This should include logos, photos, reprintable blurbs, and PR contact info, even if it's just your e-mail address.

- PRODUCTS, with an index page showing all products, and then individual product pages. Peruse other websites in similar categories to get ideas for interesting content, such as usage ideas.

- CONTACT US, with an e-mail or form to send e-mail directly to you—and ideally a phone number for personal connections and to get to know your customers. Include social media as contact options, but trust me, my mom won't be tweeting you to ask about shipping timeframes. If you've got a retail location, include your address and hours.

- FAQs, including shipping and rate information, help smart shoppers get quick answers, increasing the chance they will purchase. Flip to "Master Order Fulfillment," page 197, for other ideas of what information to include.

- **PRIVACY POLICY and TERMS OF SERVICE** pages outline the legalese for ordering and shopping online. You can combine the two.

- **BLOG** to post news and updates; don't rely only on Facebook posts (although you should post links to blog posts in your status updates). Blog posts are easier to read, attract new customers as they come up in Internet search results, and help build your brand. Let your blog reflect your personality, like Katrina Markoff's "Peace, Love & Chocolate" blog, which links to her Vosges Haut-Chocolat website. Katrina writes about yoga, travel, and the inspiration for her chocolate flavors.

Bring your brand voice into your policies and FAQ to build rapport with even the most disgruntled customer. See how the couple behind Black Dinah Chocolatiers, whose Maine island sees plenty of "weathah," does just that: "Well, the peepers are loud enough to wake us in the middle of the night now, which means summer is just around the corner. Thus, we will start using insulated boxes and coldpacks to ensure that your order arrives the way it looked when it left the island...." Friendly yet effective.

TAKE 5:
TIPS FOR ROCKING THE WEB

Your website is the front door to your brand. Engage your visitors from the get-go:

1. Keep it simple. Don't feel pressured to fill up the site with a ton of information or features. You can expand it over time.

2. Design and write your site to fit with your brand identity.

3. Test, test, test. Test the "Pin It" button to make sure your photos work correctly on Pinterest. See how the site looks on smartphones and in a few browsers. Ask friends to visit the site and watch how they navigate. Be sure your shopping cart works.

4. Update your content weekly or more often. Search engines rank frequently updated pages higher. Freshness inspires sharing too.

---

⑤ Respond to customers who contact you through your site. Whether from your phone or computer, get back to them quickly—particularly to answer questions and say thank you.

Shoot Pinteresting Photos

Luscious food photos are worth a bazillion words—especially for people new to your brand. For giftable items, include shots of packaging and gift-wrapped products to ease a purchase decision. Take some photos against white backgrounds, which is the typical style for online and print magazines. After all, you want to be ready with a photo when they discover and select your creations for their gift guides.

Set aside at least a few hundred dollars for gorgeous professional photos. You might request photographer info from companies whose photos you admire. Or, hire food bloggers to take your photos, make videos, develop recipes, or write your Web content. They often need the paid work to support their writing passions and will likely promote you as a result. Your written contract should give you photo ownership, also known as unlimited usage, so you can use the photos on other marketing materials besides your website.

Be sure photos on your site are set up in a way that Pinterest can display them. Upload photos to Flickr as well, with meaningful names like "Michigan Cherry Jam"—this way the photos will turn up in Google search results when people search for that phase.

Get Your Story on Video

Video can be as easy as using a mobile phone, with you or a fan chatting about your product along with luscious product visuals. You can also embed videos posted on YouTube and/or Vimeo within your website. It's best to upload to those services, versus "hosting" the video yourself, so more people stumble upon your video . . . hence your brand. Videos also help you get more visitors from Google searches. Say you're selling a special sauce for pizza and you have a cute video called "Gluten-Free Pizza Disappears in 10 Seconds." Or even "How to Make Gluten-Free Pizza." Your video will likely appear alongside a bevy of recipe website results when someone searches for "gluten-free pizza recipe."

Punk Rawk Labs is so into video it created an online TV program. Early videos featured its kitchen-in-the-making and interviews with their plumbers and other contractors. Charming, feel-good, and personable.

Create Search Engine–Optimized Content

Good writing not only sells but also makes a website easily discoverable by search engines, a technique known as search engine optimization (SEO). SEO is the best "advertising," and it costs you nothing—if you plan for it up front.

Don't hire a company to "SEOize your website" or "increase your ranking in search" after the fact. (Any reputable Web agency or contractor should tell you the same.) Simply write informative copy (called "content"), and link to other highly respected websites on your website's press page or, when blogging, integrate phrases and keywords people might use to find foods like yours naturally within your content. Search engines tend to weigh content in headlines and higher up as more "important" when deciding which sites to rank higher. Luckily, that approach echoes good writing practices. For SEO and ease of reading, write meaningful headlines, and make sure the "title tags" that appear at the top of your browser on each page relate to the page's content. This is important: Your Pecan Fudge Brownie page shouldn't say *Products* at the top of the Web browser, but Pecan Fudge Brownie Gifts, or Susie's Sickly Sweet Treats Online Store, or something similar that includes specific words for which people might search.

In addition to your awesome writing, most software services, such as Wordpress, and e-commerce systems come with tools to help you optimize your website for better ranking on Search Engine Results Pages (the pros refer to these as SERPs).

> **GOOD IDEA:**
> **WELCOME NEW CONNECTIONS**
>
> Include your phone number, e-mail, and social-media icons on each page of your website so people have multiple ways to connect with you. Be sure your number is clickable from a smartphone.

Test Your Content

Have a good editor give your Web content a run-through. Verify with a couple of impartial people that the content reflects your brand and makes them want to buy or share.

Integrate Social Media for Content Marketing

Strive for your content to double as your marketing engine; this is called "content marketing." It's simple: sharability. Integrate tools into your website so that people can share and follow any blog posts, promotions, and product info. You'll do so in three ways:

- SOCIAL-MEDIA-SHARING WIDGETS. These let visitors spread the word about you. Make sure every product page has sharing buttons, and test them to be sure they work.

- "FOLLOW" BUTTONS. This button links to your social media accounts.

- STATUS-FEED WIDGETS. These help display your latest social-media activity right from your site; the longer they stay on your website, the better. The "Developer" sections on the various social media sites walk you through how to get the code and set it up.

For the first two, you or your developer gets the sharing code from ShareThis or AddThis and can select the social-media services you wish to include in the sharing widget.

Add E-mail Sign-Up (Because Spam Isn't Always Bad)

While lots of people bemoan e-mail overload, the direct nature of e-mail marketing still works, provided you do it right. A 2012 ExactTarget survey revealed that 91 percent of online consumers check their e-mail at least once a day. Your e-mail list is gold: permission for you to contact interested people. Even before you have a newsletter plan, add a "sign up for news" box to your site. Then at every event, have an e-mail sign-up sheet on hand. Requesting permission is important due to CAN-SPAM. No, it's not a pink food; this U.S. law requires people to choose, or "opt in," to receive e-mail.

You might choose to twist your e-mail sign-up as building a community integral to your mission. That's what "cause-related marketing" is all about. See how bar company Two Degrees brilliantly turned an e-mail sign-up into a call to join the cause:

"I, [fill in your name], believe that together we can solve global childhood hunger. Please reach out to me at [e-mail address] and let me know how I can help."

The thank-you page engages consumers as well, stating:

"Purchases of Two Degrees bars have led to the donation of hundreds of thousands of meals to hungry children around the world. One bar = one meal. Together, we can make a serious impact on childhood hunger."

The company inspires action with an offer:

"To show our gratitude, please use the discount code XXXX for 10 percent off your next purchase!"

Most online e-mail marketing services are designed for nontechnical users. Check out MailChimp, Constant Contact, or Emma. These services make it easy to grab code to place on your site that creates the sign-up form and later set up newsletters. We'll delve into planning your e-mail campaigns in "E-mail Your Updates," page 186.

INSIDE SCOOP:
BACK TO THE ROOTS SPROUTS DIY SUCCESS

Two U.C. Berkeley college grads were on the corporate career track when a professor mentioned that mushrooms could grow in coffee grounds. From that offhand comment, Alex Velez and Nikhil Arora connected the dots to create Back to the Roots Mushroom Kits. For around $20, customers can give an affordable gift with a sustainable, educational story that yields multiple mushroom crops per kit.

After experimenting on their own, Alex and Nikhil walked into Whole Foods to demo their kit—at that point, merely mushrooms growing in an old paint bucket. Whole Foods saw the potential and signed the products up. The team arranged to pick up used coffee grounds from local coffeehouses such as Peet's Coffee and transform the refuse into Good Food that has an educational twist. Back to the Roots also focuses on educating kids in schools about sustainability and growing their own food.

Within a couple years of forming, they'd been invited to the White House and profiled on the White House "Champions of Change" website. Support from the Slow Money movement and Whole Foods' Local Producer Loan Program drove company growth faster than post-rain fungi. Funding helped the young team staff up, turn a warehouse in Oakland, California, into their "farm," and engage in extensive PR, advertising, and grassroots marketing campaigns (such as employing on-the-ground brand ambassadors). In 2013, Martha Stewart featured the kits in a Top 10 American Made holiday gift guide.

PHASE 2: LAUNCH AND RIDE THE WORD-OF-MOUTH WAVE

Once you're all set up online, it's back to the world of personal communications to spread the word and support your sales efforts.

Create Good Old-Fashioned Printed Materials

Leave a great impression in person or when shipping packages. Print up beautiful business cards (not those cheap-looking online freebies) as well as postcards or other pieces that tell your story and perhaps offer a discount on the next order. Include all of these in your mail-order shipments—and better yet, add a handwritten thank-you note. The nicer the materials, the more likely customers will keep them on hand and get the warm fuzzies.

For your wholesale business, you'll need to print a few pieces, which you should also have in PDF format to e-mail and can double as marketing:

- **SELL SHEETS.** These traditionally two-sided brochures showcase your product, the features and benefits, a blurb about your story, glorious photos of the food and packaging, and suggestions for how to merchandise the products. Ideally you'll have quotes and testimonials. SeaFarePacific albacore tuna producers invested in a heavy card stock piece that clearly checkmarks all of a wholesale buyer's hot buttons: American owned and operated, innovative, consumer tested and approved, verified shelf life, and easy shelving (along with the exact shelf dimensions). A prominent phone number and offer to "come visit your store, answer any questions, and get you started" shows that this company knows what's what.

- **PRICE LISTS/ORDER FORM.** Create a PDF price list that includes your item numbers (SKUs), the names, wholesale prices, and suggested retail prices. Highlight any price breaks you might offer at different volume levels as well as your pricing rules and other terms as far as returns. Include all of your contact information.

- **MERCHANDISING MATERIALS.** Especially with smaller stores, ask what you can provide. Recipes? Shelf-talkers (that mini-signage that attaches to a shelf)? Many stores have their own style and will say no. Still, including such information along with your delivery will increase the chance they know your story and will share it with customers.

Feed Bloggers and the Press

Bloggers and traditional media love to tell a great story. A new Good Food made with the perfect 5 Staples mix is great. As you learned from Little Bee Pops (see page 169), the best press comes when writers discover you themselves. How do you get discovered? Get your products out in the world—a good reason to sell, even selectively, in markets outside of your local area. That's how Punk Rawk Labs ended up in *VegNews* magazine—a writer found its Minnesota-made nut cheeses at the first store in New York that had picked up the product line.

Once you get more well known, the challenge reverses. Bloggers may deluge you with requests for samples. Choose wisely—you only have so much time and money. One food entrepreneur cleverly set up a Google form as an "application" for bloggers to fill out. The form guides bloggers on timing to taste, write, and circle back to the company to discuss their thoughts. Cookbook author and blogger Amy Sherman shares her insight on developing fruitful blogger connections:

- Start by finding blogs that do product reviews and look like a good fit for your product. Check their review policies. Review their links to other blogs, called "blogrolls," to find other, similar blogs.

- Get familiar with a blogger's work before making contact; don't send generic e-mails.

- Offer via e-mail to send samples, with no strings attached. You want an honest, enthusiastic review; don't require that the blogger write about the product (the law requires bloggers to state when they received samples or payments). Check that the blogger received the samples. Ask for feedback a few weeks later, even if the blogger has not reviewed your product. The many months it took me to finally buy a frozen pizza a PR guy asked me to review became a big joke between us. He continued to follow up, and the company name became ingrained in my mind.

- Consider inviting local bloggers to tour your facility or to interview you.

You may one day find yourself wanting more publicity. When your production can handle an onslaught of new business, consider your public relations options. Drawing upon many years of promoting fair trade and Good Food companies, media strategist Haven Bourque shares some useful tips for handling PR yourself or hiring a PR pro:

- When hiring a PR consultant to do it all, you need to be willing to make a three- to six-month investment, which may run several thousand dollars. For that investment, you're connected to the relationships that these media mavens have developed with the press. Plus, they know what will and won't work with the media in terms of messaging and timing. Find someone you admire and like, who is familiar with food business, and offers services you can't handle yourself.

- You might try handling public relations yourself if you are savvy about social media, great at telling your story, and have excellent writing skills. In tandem, you could hire a freelance PR consultant for occasional advice.

Write Your Introductory Press Release

Press releases tell the story you'd like to see written about you. Many outlets simply reprint press releases, and bloggers might grab content straight from a release.

When writing your release, draw from the story you wrote (see "Write Your Authentic Story," page 81). Include all the basic information in the context of a good article framed in a compelling story: who, what, where, when, why, how. Check out PRWeb.com for more tips on writing and ways to distribute your release. Subscribe to HelpAReporter.com to hear about reporter queries for entrepreneur stories and food experts.

After you get your press release out there, have your pitch ready for when the press calls. Haven suggests writing out three or four key points (or "sound bites") you want to get across in every interview. This should be a twelve-second statement about who you are and what you do that is short, sharp, and quotable.

Tailor your key points to the live-interview format and practice saying them out loud. TV and video are about how you look and sound. Radio should match the tone of the host and the pace of the show. Be proactive about reaching out. Check Twitter and Instagram to find the influencers whose work will spread your story the farthest. Monitor their feeds and read their work to determine whether they accept samples and whether they are realistic targets. Try pitching your product and your story to writers who write for the audiences you want to reach. For example, with senior citizens and people on the go, radio (the airwaves or Internet) and TV news could be your ticket. That way you have a shot at a feature piece and begin to build relationships with writers and reporters. When targeting the trade, ask the Specialty Food Association for a mention in its daily newsletter.

Lastly, always be professional and natural. Resist badgering writers and bloggers. They work hard, are under constant deadline pressure, and make very little money. Treat them like royalty. They are the megaphone to your audience.

What to Expect From Your National Press Mentions

What do you do when national magazines approach you about a feature? Breathe into a paper bag. Then drop everything, except your customers. Respond promptly. Send only your best product, packaged in the most lovely and professional manner. Then wait. After a week or two, follow up to make sure the package arrived. Refrain from obsessive calls no matter how eager you are (channel that nervous energy into making sales to your customers instead).

Major features may generate minor orders, as Liddabit Sweets discovered after an *O Magazine* feature, mainly because the article focused more on recipes than on its candy products. But the exposure was still invaluable. On the flip side, says co-founder Liz Gutman, a holiday *Good Housekeeping* gift-guide feature generated a slew of orders. Perhaps a magazine-reader discount code helped; the code also helped Liddabit track where customers were coming from. From what I've seen, national magazines' holiday gift guides seem to be a reliable winner, especially for new and different Good Foods.

Be sure to update your site with every kudo. KATZ Farm keeps a quote from the *Atlantic*'s revered food writer Corby Kummer front and center: "For my money, KATZ makes the best jams in the country."

PHASE 3: KEEP THE BUZZ ALIVE WITH PROMOTIONS AND MARKETING SUPPORT

So you've set up your online presence with your social-media accounts and your e-mail sign-up; it's time to get the word out and invite your followers in.

Master the Social-Media Ecosystem

As early as you feel comfortable, start connecting with fans, influencers, and the press to share updates through social media. Start by inviting friends, family, customers, and partners to connect with you on the various social media sites. You can also reach out to folks in industry trade groups, farmers, and nonprofits advocating causes related to your business.

Don't let the pressure of social media overwhelm you. No need to be online or respond 24 hours a day. Simply Instagram the new apple crop that's got you trapped at the stove. Or you can pre-write and schedule messages using tools such as HootSuite or Sprout Social (which work on all different kinds of social media) or TweetDeck (which only covers Twitter). You schedule the time the updates blast out. Set up Google Alerts to get notifications by e-mail when people mention you so you can thank them or otherwise start a conversation.

Write social-media updates with genuine conversation and enthusiasm, as if you're speaking to friends. And when you are selling, a little tongue-in-cheek humor never hurts. As far as topics, it's up to you whether you want to offer personal updates (e.g., your thoughts on being stuck at the airport) and/or your perspective on food-related news, or to focus solely on your business. Social media can help make customers feel like they are part of a bigger cause, and to understand that your food is not only delicious but meaningful. Of course, you can change your social media strategy at any point.

The more you inspire fans to spread the word, the more quickly your social network will buzz.

E-mail Your Updates

Commit to a regular update on what's new, your brand's progress, or specials. Your e-mails can be short, sharing information that will be interesting and valuable to customers. Keep your tone and voice genuine, as if you're speaking with customers at the farmers' market. The Nuts About Granola newsletter draws me in every time, with recipes, reminders of easy ways to buy local, personal updates such as founder Sarah Lanphier's love story, and blow-by-blow details of how they searched for their new facility. Sure, you can update Facebook with all of this or tweet out links to your blog posts—as well you should. But e-mails like those from Nuts About Granola and this one below from the KATZ Farm newsletter have an appeal that make readers more likely to buy when the need arises:

> *"Jacob and I are making a trip to Walker's Fruit Ranch in Sebastopol, California, to pick up the new crop of Gravenstein apples that are now ready to go. We will bring them back to our Napa River Kitchen to make the fresh pectin we use in the winter to produce our KATZ Meyer Lemon Marmalade."*

Increase E-mail and Ad Success with Landing Pages

A landing page is the website equivalent of a billboard. Rather than sending a reader to click through from an ad or e-mail to your website home page, you might create a clean and simple page, with minimal information and one or two links, to eliminate all distraction. The goal is to maximize the chance that readers will follow the call to action to buy, share, sign up, or whatever else you want them to do. And when they do, that's called "conversion." As a second best to a landing page, you could tailor your product page or other page to relate to the ad's message. An e-mail or tweet advertising a link to "Holiday Chipotle Popcorn Corporate Gifts" should click to a message specifically about that offering, rather than the general popcorn product page.

Promotions and Deals, Deals, Deals!

Promotions build excitement and an incentive to "buy now" when there's no holiday or season driving sales. Don't get hooked on discount promotions to create customer loyalty, however. You'll only attract deal hunters, in what is sometimes called "a race to the bottom."

Discount case sizes. For ingredient-type food, you could encourage throwing a potluck based around using your food, with people buying or taking home a product as a favor.

A "share with a friend" BOGO (buy one get one free) offer will bring you more customers.

Limited-time flavors not only engage customers, but help you plan future product changes.

Try out small discounts such as percentage off, dollars off, or free samples of other flavors. Highlight both the percentage off and the amount saved: "You'll get eight packages for the price of six. That's a 25 percent savings." A promotions expert advises repeating the phrase "save 10 percent off" (or whatever percent you're offering) because it sells more than just saying "save 10 percent" or "save 10 percent off," despite, or maybe because of, the redundancy.

When a company such as Groupon or LivingSocial approaches you to do a promotion, weigh the pros and cons of participating:

Pros

- You'll have the chance to reach new customers you couldn't reach on your own.
- Those new customers may turn into repeat customers, increasing your overall sales.

Cons

- Your profit margin may be slim, especially when considering your production and fulfillment costs.
- Offering your product at a discount may have a negative effect on your brand image.
- You might need to turn away loyal or local customers in order to scramble to fill the deal's less-profitable orders.

INSIDE SCOOP:
AMELLA CARAMELS REMIXES FOR MARKETING SUCCESS

Emir and Elena Kiamilev started Amella Caramels as a side business. They developed cake-inspired caramel recipes and then set up production with a co-packer. Momentum built as they sold their

CONTINUE ▶

caramels through various online marketplaces and their own website as well as at various Southern California shops. When they landed a specialty supermarket account, they rejoiced—it was a dream come true. One day, the specialty store announced it wanted to run a promotion to boost sales. "We, of course, said yes and borrowed money to fund the two-for-one promotion," says Emir. The company not only lost money on the deal, but sales dwindled after the promotion.

After the disappointment, the team reflected on the experience and connected the dots: The product and its beautiful packaging were better suited to high-end hotels, boutiques, clothing stores, and weddings than supermarkets. They completely changed their distribution strategy and found immediate demand along with profits, thanks to eliminating the commission and promotional costs tied to large retail accounts.

Yet the cake-themed caramels remained a niche item, not achieving the results the couple desired to grow the business. Back in product development, they devised a new line of sea salt caramels (all the rage) sweetened with agave nectar, appealing to natural foods shoppers. This time they designed an artsy, eye-catching cardboard package at a price point accessible for small gifts or small indulgences. They shrink wrapped the candy within, to extend the shelf life quite a bit longer than their earlier products. The company signed up with Buyer's Best Friend whose team, Fancy Food Show booth, and online system vastly expanded Amella's reach. Mission accomplished.

Along with this new strategy, Amella began to sell at several farmers' markets and local food fairs, as a form of marketing as well as to connect to the community. "It's hard to create a sustainable business online," Emir explains. "You can't get the volume a 200-store chain can get you." This rapidly changing strategy in an old-fashioned product category perfectly illustrates the dynamic nature of specialty food and the marketing mix.

Shortly after launching, the company's strategy was confirmed: The Taste Awards gave the new agave line the Top Caramel Award for 2013.

Paid Advertising

With the right 5 Staples mix, including a website optimized for high search ranking, you may be able to go years without paying for advertising. Still, you might choose to advertise locally to create goodwill in the community. Local *Edible Communities* magazines, newspapers and their websites, mobile ads on local sites, sponsorships on which your logo appears, and online ads represent just a few opportunities for paid advertising. Your donations to good local causes will go a long way too.

When you're aiming to distribute widely into retail, ads show buyers that you're making an effort to build awareness. They can be more confident your products will sell, so they will be more likely to buy. When investing in ads, research or ask what the expected reach is, in terms of the demographic and number of people, and request the most effective placement.

When I saw an Oregon cup-of-oatmeal in an Austin, Texas, café, I immediately contacted the café's food distributor to ask how in the world this obscure brand made its way to Texas. He'd seen it at a trade show. Then the same oatmeal popped up in a Northern California café. By then I'd clued in: This little oatmeal company had taken out a full-page ad in a trade magazine. When you're ready to advertise, you'll find niche magazines for coffee, produce, and all sorts of retail venues, such as convenience stores (and the more awareness you build, the more easily your sales team or broker can make the sales).

Advertising can quickly take a bite out of your budget. For online ads on Google, Facebook, LinkedIn (great for reaching a business audience), and blogs, target specific keywords for the most cost-effective "conversion" from idle browser to sales. Similar to homing in on specific words, also limit the ads to your local geography if you're selling only locally, to avoid wasting money. For example, "Bay Area artisan candy gifts" rather than "candy gifts." Corporate administrators often get assigned to pull together artisan-food corporate gifts, and they start with an online search. (I know, as they've often contacted me after that for help.) An online ad expert can help you research and plan the most effective keywords to use and advertising outlets to try out. I've learned the hard way: That $100 free-ads offer may rope you into trying an ad service. Be very careful to set up your maximum ad budget, lest that $100 quickly become $1,000 in clicks. Yes, we have no refunds.

The hot new thing eventually cools down or faces up-and-coming competition. And if you find sales dwindling, take a look at your 5 Staples mix in the new landscape.

GREAT BUSINESS ACTION PLAN

☐ Reach out to connections to ask publicity and marketing advice.

☐ Draft a three-, six-, and twelve-month marketing plan, and get feedback on it. A one-page plan for each timeframe can focus you and simplify writing the plan.

☐ Revisit your customer personas (see "Picture Your Customers," page 53) when conceiving of each marketing tactic.

☐ Set up your social-media accounts and domain along with a placeholder page. Or redirect the domain to your company's public Facebook page.

☐ Set yourself up on Internet directories and review sites.

☐ Find three websites/online stores that resemble what you'd like to create.

☐ Peruse the food photos on Etsy.com, Tastespotting.com, or any food catalog for photography ideas.

☐ Look up food videos on YouTube for inspiration (search terms such as *artisan food* or *farmers' market*).

☐ Write your pitch and press release, or hire a writer to do so.

☐ Follow up on all outreach and connections, especially with busy influencers.

ON *GOODFOODGREATBUSINESS.COM*

Get a quick start with the Marketing Plan template and Digital Marketing Strategy template. Find links to photography tips, Web development, and marketing services.

STEP
5

MAKE
IT
REAL!

NOW YOU'RE COOKIN':
SELL AND ENGAGE POST-LAUNCH

> ### BURNING QUESTION:
> ### WHAT IS "ENGAGEMENT" ANYWAY?
>
> *Unlike in romantic relationships, in a business you can engage a customer in an instant, with a sample and your story. (Okay, maybe it's not so different from a bar pickup.) That personal contact invites customers to join your journey. That engagement often can translate to instant loyalty, with customers looking out for your success and even helping you get there. Responding to messages from fans instantly engages, even if the answer is a simple "ha ha" or "thanks." Not responding puts your relationship into question: "Too busy?" "Doesn't care about me?"*

CULTIVATE A SERVICE CULTURE

From your first brand impression through post-sale follow-up, simple communication can make the biggest difference in whether a customer will spread the word and buy again. Customers enjoy giving feedback, so ask for it. When on the phone or e-mailing with clients, ask how they heard about you. Dole out gratitude to customers and the people spreading the word as liberally as you do samples.

The most beloved businesses take the perspective that they are "serving guests" versus "helping customers." That desire to please will naturally lead you to exuding a more service-oriented, friendly attitude.

When customer issues arise, tap into the power of three:

1 Thank the customer for informing you.

2 Offer a refund or replacement and something extra.

3 Explain how you will avoid the problem in the future (if it was your fault). Collaborate with the customer to make things right, especially if you messed up a gift situation.

This simple formula for customer satisfaction works just as well by phone, by e-mail, in person, or via social media. A proven rule of thumb is that a customer whose problem you've solved is more loyal than customers who haven't had problems. Why? You've taken care of your customer, and formed a relationship in the process. This is not to say you should create problems as a relationship-forming tactic. More that if a problem happens or the customer needs help above and beyond, such as a rush order, your heroism can pay off for years to come. On the flip side, a dissatisfied customer can cause lots of damage, especially in the online-review and social-media era.

YOUR NUMBER-ONE SELLING TOOL: SAMPLES

No matter how good your packaging and promotion, nothing equals the power of tasting and experiencing a food firsthand. Get your food to tasters early and often. This especially holds true for foods or flavors that are new to the American public. Vibrant Flavors introduced Portland, Oregon, farmers' market shoppers to its Oregon Dukkah, a twist on an ancient Egyptian spice-like snack made with Oregon hazelnuts. But Donna Dockins had to work hard to sample and educate consumers about her unfamiliar food . . . at least until Trader Joe's rolled out a dukkah product several years later.

This story about a demo I stumbled upon at Whole Foods shows how a 5 Staples choice may limit sales: From the first taste, I realized I'd discovered that perfect bar, a real meal substitute. The fellow regaled me with tales of how the company handcrafts the bars (which I didn't care about) and his father's long history in the health food industry (interesting). The price was right, with a freebie promotion to boot. The packaging didn't scream "buy me," however. In fact, if I hadn't tasted these and heard from the owner firsthand, I very well may have passed these bars by. But design didn't matter in this case, with product samples in my hand—or in my mouth, to be exact. Simply delicious. "When did you get started?" I asked. Seven years ago, was the answer. "Where have you been all my life (or at least the last seven years)?" I wondered. In the refrigerated section, it turns out. Not somewhere I would look for energy bars. I left the store, my wallet $17 lighter, with a box of bars at 10 percent off plus two freebies in hand—enough of a deal to stock up— all because of their sampling. The price, promotion, and product flavor was the perfect mix—except that I had to worry about refrigerating the bars. And since that time, despite my enthusiasm, they never come to mind when I'm browsing the store aisles.

As a longtime farmers' market shopper and worker (I've pitched peaches, oils, and breads), I've learned that there's a basic formula to moving product. Captivate people strolling by, then pay off with irresistible food. The family behind East & West Gourmet Afghan Food (popularly known in the San Francisco area as "the Bolani people") not only rope you in but also generously ply you with delicious low-calorie, vegan stuffed flatbreads and sauces. Their staff, usually relatives, greet you with a big smile, politely call women "miss" (not ma'am), and are empowered to offer deals. They proactively suggest deals on a product combo. Priced affordably, with very basic functional packaging, they hit on a perfect 5 Staples mix. The company expanded to selling at farmers' markets across California, online (with its food quality trumping expensive shipping costs), in food service such as school cafeterias, and into retail stores. Demo staffers at supermarkets and even Costco who offer that same big smile and friendly conversation get more people to sample their wares. Good people, great business.

TIPS FOR SAMPLING THAT SELLS

Pack away the cell phone, focus on the customer, and follow a few sampling tips from the trenches:

- **Staff well.** Tap into well-spoken, professional-acting fans, family, or store-provided demo staff, who may, for a fee or commission, be able to help you sell.

- **Plan for traffic.** For store demos, learn when your target customer will most likely be there (e.g., professional singles in the evening, parents with toddlers during the day) as well as the busiest times.

- **Make the food look tasty.** An appealing display is everything, from food presentation to cleanliness to your choice of sampling supplies, such as recyclable EcoTensil "EcoTaster" cardboard spoons versus plastic spoons. In What Women Want, Paco Underhill reports that women put cleanliness at the top of the list. I don't doubt most men agree.

CONTINUE ▶

- **Tailor your presentation.** Appeal to your potential customers' motivations and interests. For foods that serve as ingredients, will sampling finished recipes intrigue shoppers more than tasting the raw product?

- **Inspire.** Suggest uses and recipes for slower-consumption products with recipes and tips for unusual—and high volume—uses. A package of crumbled crackers might double as a crouton substitute. They'll be more quickly coming back for more!

- **Be transparent.** Tell interested customers about your challenges and joys, along with your promise to do good. The more you involve customers, the bigger your virtual cheering squad.

- **Sample smartly.** Hoard broken product for farmers' markets or in-store demos, whether for active sampling (where a demo person hands out samples) or passive sampling (where a customer helps herself to a sample). Effie's Homemade also packs up oatcake odds and ends to ship to distributors as part of demo kits, which are then passed on to retail stores.

- **Cross-promote.** Pair complementary food products, and ask fellow food companies to do the same. When Robin Rhea introduces her Slatherin' Sauce at retail, she asks to use products from the department in which she's doing the demo, say shrimp from the seafood counter. The collaboration helps the manager increase sales not only of her product but others that she's using in the demo.

- **Analyze.** Track the number of units sold at each demo or market, then analyze results to tailor your pitch for next time.

GOOD IDEA:
DONATE TO LOCAL FOOD BANKS

At the end of long, tiring days, re-energize with simple acts of giving. Set up a system to give any "irregular" yet edible product or daily unsold foods to local food banks or other causes. Consider other promotional "days of giving," when customers can buy food for you to donate.

MASTER ORDER FULFILLMENT

Be your own best (and worst) critic when it comes to fulfilling orders. You know how quickly late deliveries, package problems, and bad service can turn you against a company. Be sure any third parties you've contracted to handle your shipping care as much as you do and are prepared for any huge influxes of orders due to press mentions. Delight your "guests" by following a few shipping tips from the trenches:

- **PACK FOR THE DESTINATION.** You may be huddled for warmth in zero-degree flurries in Vermont while your customer swelters in an Austin heat wave, something to consider if your product needs to be kept below a certain temperature.

- **PACK WELL.** Dealing with and replacing a damaged package isn't good for anyone, especially when it comes to gifts. Environmentally friendly packing material is good, but intact arrival is more important. Use new shipping boxes, unless your customer asks you to recycle a box. U.S. Postal Service flat-rate boxes are free.

- **SHARE RESPONSIBILITY.** For perishables, remind customers to be on hand to receive the packages on the estimated ship date. Include your policy if the package perishes—particularly important when shipping to regions with warm weather. Provide a tracking number from your shipping service to help your customer plan to receive the package.

- **TURN HIGH SHIPPING COSTS INTO A POSITIVE.** Offer price breaks or suggest the best order quantity to minimize costs. Encourage customers to buy more to save on shipping, or to order early. If your product needs refrigeration in transit, explain that dry-ice limitations make it necessary to use ice packs, which are heavy and a bit expensive to ship. (Companies are developing cooling alternatives that producers say work with some products but not others.)

- **GIVE A HEADS-UP ABOUT YOUR SHIPPING SCHEDULE.** If you don't ship daily, or encounter delays because you're behind in production or in case of bad weather, let your customers know. Most customers will understand if the flu has foiled your production. Just hold off on the gory details, apologize for the delay, and include an extra treat and note when you do get back up and running.

TAKE 5:
TIPS FOR GREAT GIFTING

Gifts reflect directly on the giver. Try to overdeliver on expectations. It's easy!

1. Ensure arrival on or before the desired date.
2. Design your shipment to engage the recipient.
3. For corporate gifts, build in costs for any elves you may need to hire to help you.
4. Include ingredient and allergen information in every case.
5. If you can't deliver, suggest alternative vendors to your customers.

SELL WHOLESALE AND GET REPEAT ORDERS

You read about options for getting set up to sell wholesale using brokers and distributors, in "Phase 2: Selling Wholesale—Higher Volume, Lower Profits, Greater Impact," page 142. As you work on new accounts, be mindful that just as you treat your consumers as "guests," so should you serve wholesale buyers. There are plenty of artisan smoked salmons in the sea, and you need to be the favorite. These tips from the trenches will set you up for mutual success:

- Clearly state if your quoted prices are "delivered" (see "How to Quote All-Inclusive Prices for Direct Wholesaling," page 166). If you don't have accurate shipping costs handy, tell the buyer you will confirm total cost, as well as any handling fees, before finalizing the quote.

- Do the math, deal by deal. A large retailer wanted to buy direct from Effie's Homemade—a money-saving dream come true: higher margins than selling via a distributor. Or so Effie's thought. Between putting the order together and getting it to the retailer, the time quickly canceled out the money. Effie's pointed the buyer to order through the distributor.

- Weed out the not-so-serious sample requests by charging for samples for expensive products, offering a credit upon purchase.

- For new accounts that you're not sure are creditworthy, such as mom-and-pop stores, requiring credit card payment for the first purchase is standard and ensures you get the money, and quickly. If the buyer balks, take it as a red flag. As your trust level builds, you might extend terms to new accounts, allowing them to pay in thirty days, for example. Always check a customer's credit before extending terms, and that includes large stores.

- If you cannot fulfill an order, confirm in writing if a substitution or delay is acceptable.

- Follow the buyer's order, delivery, and invoicing to the letter or request an exception—in writing.

- Thank the buyer on your invoice, include extra samples, and provide marketing materials with cross-merchandising suggestions. Set a time limit for the buyer to notify you about problems such as damage or incorrect shipments (shortages, wrong products, etc.). Liability for shipping issues depends on who paid the freight.

- After delivery, respond to chargeback requests, in which the buyer may ask for a refund for unsellable products. Try to negotiate a mutually beneficial solution, no matter who was at fault.

- Follow up to keep your shelf space. Unless customers are clamoring for your goods, busy store buyers may forget to re-order. Buyers who purchase through Buyer's Best Friend have an order history for all the products they've ordered, another great reason to make sure you're part of the BBFdirect.com catalog. Only rarely will you get your coveted shelf space back. Call the store buyer two weeks or a month out to see how your products are selling. Before you do, be prepared to solve negative sales problems with ideas such as offering to do a demo in the store or handing out samples as customers walk into the store.

Stash Some Cash Before Selling Wholesale

Have ample cash on hand to fill the gap between manufacturing expenditures and income from getting paid. Work through the scenarios when a big order comes in to make sure you can handle a payment delay; large retailers will almost never do cash on delivery. Distributors typically will pay in sixty days or fewer, especially if you offer an incentive for faster payment. East Coast food sales consultant John Maggiore offers this example: On your invoices, you would write "2 percent 30 day; net 60 days." If you bill the distributor $10,000 on April 12, it would be allowed to deduct 2 percent ($200) from its payment if it pays before May 12; otherwise it owes the full payment within sixty days of April 12.

If stores are late in paying, be tenacious and start calling daily after thirty days. Collecting funds yourself nets you more than using a collections agency, although employing an agency makes sense if the amount is significant.

MEET WHOLESALE BUYERS AT TRADE SHOWS

Whatever planning stage you're in, travel to one or more food trade shows as soon as possible. This in-person experience may completely change or completely reaffirm your plans.

The famous Fancy Food Show is the ultimate industry event to which wholesale food buyers flock to discover new specialty foods. Specialty food companies and brand-new artisan producers from all over the world travel to the January show in San Francisco and the summer show in Washington, D.C., or New York. They set up booths to display their packages, offer samples of their foods, and meet with buyers, and they fend off food-obsessed consumers who sneak in to eat until they drop. Wait until you can fulfill large wholesale orders before investing the thousands of dollars exhibiting, however.

NewHope360's Natural Products Expo West and Expo East trade shows lean more toward granola and eco-friendly than fancy. These shows buzz with excitement, mingling new food purveyors with well-funded, old-time natural brands such as Stonyfield; aisles of housewares made with recycled plastics; and every kind of plant-based, cruelty-free health and beauty product you could dream of. These shows not only connect you with buyers from natural-product stores but with others seeking good food: Rumor has it that Starbucks' Howard Schultz discovered the Boulder, Colorado–based Two Moms in the Raw at one of these shows. Its raw snacks quickly became fixtures at Starbucks cafés.

Rooibee Red Tea handed out a sample to someone at Expo West who turned out to be a buyer for @Walmartlabs. Soon the buyer offered to include the tea in a new "tasting box" @Walmartlabs was testing. Rooibee jumped at the chance. (Read more about their rapid success in "Inside Scoop: Rooibee Red Tea Builds on Connections," page 218.)

Many niche trade shows can target buyers in specific product categories. For example, the National Fiery Foods & Barbecue Show in Albuquerque (FieryFoodsShow.com) celebrates everything hot. The Specialty Coffee Association Expo (SCAAevent.org) and World Tea Expo (WorldTeaMedia.com) bring visibility to beverage makers as well as makers of complementary foods and products: biscuits, blend-ins, equipment, and the like. These are all fabulous opportunities to connect with synergistic partners as well as buyers.

Beyond the United States, Anuga (Anuga.com), held in Cologne, Germany, stakes its claim as the world's largest food and beverage fair. (Hey, if you need a helper, I'm there!) SIAL (SialParis.com and SialCanada.com) is a longtime international food show that helps producers make deals and enter new markets. The International Food & Drink Event (IFE.co.uk), based in the United Kingdom, focuses on food and drinks. Candy makers and chocolatiers attend the ISM Candy Show (ISM-cologne.de) in Germany, which is the world's largest confectionary show. Artisans focused on traditional methods and dying traditions should definitely look into representing the United States at Slow Food's biannual Terra Madre event in Italy. When you're export ready, perhaps attending trade shows could be your tax-deductible golden ticket to see the world, should you so desire. (Need I repeat that offer to help out?)

TAKE 5:
TIPS FOR SUCCESSFUL TRADE SHOWS

Take time to plan the details of a trade show for the best return on investment:

1. Investigate a show's track record before committing. Look for testimonials on the show's website and reach out to past exhibitors for a firsthand account. Look at past exhibitor lists and attendee numbers to gauge a show's popularity and project how useful exhibiting, or just attending, might be for you versus the cost and effort.

2. Make your best, most professional impression and be prepared to sell on a large scale, at wholesale or distributor prices. Hold off on spending for a booth until you're ready to meet big demand from wholesale buyers. You might be able to test the

CONTINUE ▶

waters in a shared booth such as with a local association (California has Savor California) or Buyer's Best Friend, which packs in sellers and draws in big buyers, even supermarkets.

(3) Set up a Square or other card-swiping device on your smartphone, or provide another mechanism to accept credit card and debit card payments at the show.

(4) Think beyond the event. Plan to promote any show discounts (often called "show specials"), online ordering options, and gift-giving options; and by all means, sign up new customers to your e-mail list.

(5) Offer samples of your food amply and professionally, cleaning and tidying up your booth frequently. The more tasty, appealing, and gift-ready your products, the greater your chance of selling them.

WIN AWARDS

Awards translate directly to sales. Decide whether to enter a competition by weighing the benefits in terms of cost, exposure, your chances of winning, and personal fulfillment for daring to enter.

The Specialty Food Association's Sofi Award has proved time and again to launch food products into the spotlight and on to big sales. A team of judges and food buyers evaluate association member entries, after which winners are unveiled in a gala ceremony. In addition to the Sofi, many food categories have trade guilds or associations, along with award programs, such as those hosted by the Natural Products Expo, the Specialty Coffee Association of America, and American Cheese Society.

Be sure to check out the Good Food Awards, from which winners have consistently seen huge sales increases since the award's 2010 beginnings. The 2013 awards had more than 1,350 entries from beer, coffee, chocolate, cheese, spirits, preserves, pickles, and confections producers. I've happily been involved with the confections category for several years, and we've seen the award program's criteria serve as a useful guidepost for transparency, trust, and traceability.

TAKE 5:
TIPS FOR WINNING AWARDS

Increase your chances of winning by following some simple rules.

1. Read the rules and regulations carefully to be sure you qualify.

2. Package your food exactly as you do when you sell it. Even when packaging isn't judged, first impressions matter.

3. Label everything. A tasting may be blind, but your product should clearly state your company name and product name, lest it get lost in the shuffle.

4. Do what it takes so that your product arrives in perfect condition and on time. Understand what the storage conditions on site will be. Will your creamy cheese hold up?

5. To avoid confusion during judging, send the products you listed on your entry form. If you need to make a last-minute switch-eroo, explain clearly what product the awards team should expect.

MANAGE YOUR TIME AND MEASURE YOUR RESULTS

Once you are selling, you'll learn the new meaning of "busy." Keep it simple. Your priorities early on should be 4 of the 5 Staples.

1. **PRODUCT:** Make great food.

2. **PRICE:** Price it for enough profit to sustain the business.

3. **PLACE:** Get it to the right customers.

4. **PROMISE:** Make customers happy and do good.

Building and delivering on your reputation is a whole lot more important than spreading the word (promotion), which will happen naturally when you focus on mastering No. 1.

Most online systems include reporting, called "analytics." These tools let you analyze where people are clicking and what they're sharing. Then you can fine-tune your efforts. Google Analytics plugs into any website and gives you all sorts of insight, including keywords people searched for, how they landed on your site, the most frequently visited pages, and how much time they're spending on your site.

Most important, review your financials weekly, if not daily, to be sure you're on track with your projections. Periodically look at your sales reports to find your 10 percent of most valuable customers, and consider how to thank and survey them. In the next chapter, we'll cover systems, people, and funding to help you manage your business.

GREAT BUSINESS ACTION PLAN

☐ Chart out your customer sales experiences, both for wholesale, direct, and online, including policies and terms. Think about what help you'll need with managing your customer service, social media, and e-mail campaigns as well as other marketing. (You'll get tips for finding those folks in the next chapter.)

☐ Identify five upcoming events at which you can share samples. Include "guerilla marketing" ideas such as showing up at marathons or networking events with samples. Be sure to work the costs of sampling into your budget.

☐ Plan a tax-deductible trip to an upcoming Fancy Food Show and Natural Products Expo East or Expo West shows to walk the floor and take classes. Research retailers or other companies in the area you might want to visit or meet with. While there, collect printed literature and other marketing materials from other companies so you can analyze them later.

☐ Determine if you will enter the Good Food Awards and, if so, check early to see if your foods follow the guidelines.

☐ Follow up on all connections, soon and relentlessly. Let each connection blossom into many.

ON *GOODFOODGREATBUSINESS.COM*
Find links to resources to get started selling
and engaging post-launch.

CHAPTER

SET UP YOUR BUSINESS

BURNING QUESTION:
HOW MUCH MONEY DO I NEED?

To get licensed and produce a small batch of food in a certified kitchen or with a co-packer, start-up costs range from around $2,500 to $5,000. But the cost really depends on what you're making and how it's packaged. Punk Rawk Labs calculated down to the penny that it needed to raise $10,000 on Kickstarter to get its "living cuisine" operation off the ground. The money paid for food-manufacturing equipment, packaging and ingredients, software and office equipment, insurance, and a few months of employee salaries.

For a launch in which you're aiming to get onto retail shelves, many entrepreneurs name $75,000 as the minimum cost for getting your product ready for market and getting national visibility. And you'll eventually want to pay yourself. You will need about $1 million in sales to be able to take home a $75,000 annual salary, according to specialty food business consultant Deb Mazzaferro.

UNDERSTAND THE IMPORTANCE OF STRUCTURE

A solid business foundation sets the stage for a sustainable business. Imagine the foundation of a house, the pedestal supporting a heavy and complex structure. Should a force of nature blow, drench, or shake your house, you'll want the foundation to be able to withstand it. The same goes for your business. This humdrum yet oh-so-important foundation will let you serve your customers well (especially when times get busy). To build your business foundation, you'll start with 1) your systems to organize and track your people and money, 2) your support system (the people who help you with your business), and 3) your business structure and funding.

SET UP YOUR BACK-OFFICE SYSTEMS

Back-office systems keep a business orderly, operational, and organized. We're in a wonderful time, with almost too many free apps and online data-storage options at our disposal, without the hassles of installing and managing software. Do yourself a favor and set up a few easy-to-use systems as well as business software sooner rather than later. Unlike the old days of small business, you can easily spend less than $1,000 per year on the systems that run your business basics, including e-mail marketing, e-commerce, and other online services. Google masterfully integrates calendar, mail, spreadsheets, documents, and everything else under the sun you'd want to plan and share. The Google Apps also tie in third-party online tools, for easy access to things such as expense-reporting and time-tracking apps (great for not only tracking your helpers' time but also your own).

Here's a breakdown of the most basic system setup you'll need to get you going:

- **QUICKBOOKS**, for tracking inventory and managing finances.

- **A SPREADSHEET PROGRAM**, such as Excel, for just about everything, including your schedules and plans, and as an entry-level expense-tracking system. Online spreadsheets allow multiple people to edit at once and give you access anywhere, including on your smartphone.

- **A CALENDAR SYSTEM**, preferably shareable, where you can manage your time and production schedules and set reminders for tasks and deadlines. The calendar can also be consumer facing: For example, you can set up a Google calendar with your event schedule to embed on your website, and customers can subscribe to keep tabs on what you have coming up.

- **A FILE STORAGE SERVICE**, such as Dropbox, to back up your files on cloud-based servers that you can access anywhere (one less thing to worry about).

- **CONTACT MANAGEMENT TOOLS**, such as Salesforce, to help you manage relationships as they grow from "contact" to "customer."

- **A CUSTOMER-SUPPORT SYSTEM**, such as Get Satisfaction or Zendesk, becomes more important as you grow.

- **PHONES, FAX, AND VIDEO CHAT** (such as Skype). Between a cell phone and voice over Internet protocol (VOIP) phone service such as Skype, Google Voice, and others, as well as multifunction printer/fax/copier devices that allow for easy use without a landline, there are plenty of affordable options for old-fashioned communication. The iPhone even has FaxBurner, a cool app that sends a fax from a doc or photo (i.e., a pic of a signed contract) that you upload from your phone.

- **FOOD-BUSINESS-SPECIFIC SOFTWARE** for managing production and inventory, such as NumberCruncher and LabelCalc.com for nutrition labels.

- **PAYMENT PROCESSING SYSTEM** such as Square or PayPal to take credit cards.

To avoid scatterbrain, a daily task app on your phone that syncs to the Internet (such as Google Tasks, Evernote, or Wrike) will help you focus on priorities. Using a tip from productivity consultant Jason Womack, I've been planning each 15-minute increment of my day in a Google spreadsheet, along with recording the reality of what panned out. This technique quickly brings to light wasted time and gives you a nice daily journal.

TAKE 5:
TIPS FOR SYSTEMS THAT WORK

Systems give you the freedom to focus on the food. Set yourself up for success by:

1. Using whatever works for you. Good old-fashioned notebooks could serve your daily organization needs.

2. Paying someone to help set up your systems if you find yourself procrastinating.

3. Planning a regular backup of all your documents and data on an external drive and in the cloud.

4. Finding mobile-friendly apps to help you manage your business if you'll be out and about frequently.

5. Requiring data import and export, so your systems can "speak" to one another, and you can get your data out of the system— for example, by importing PayPal payment records into Quickbooks.

BUILD YOUR SUPPORT SYSTEM:
COMMUNE, CONTRACT, AND HIRE

The Small Business Administration consistently reports much higher failure rates among solo businesses versus those with one or more partners. Yet entrepreneurs often make the mistake of doing it all themselves or waiting too long to hire help. Tight control can sometimes lead to perfection. It can also stifle your vision. Naturally, a solo act leads to overwork. If you find yourself insisting you simply must go it alone, ponder the source of that idea. Is it really serving you and your success or holding you back?

Share and Bond with Fellow Food Entrepreneurs

In our connected world you can easily overcome the challenges of being "single." The people you choose to work with can make or break your business and make daily life a delight . . . or full of misery. Build a mutual support team, whether local or virtual, to collaborate in areas such as resources and supplies, ingredients, attending markets and events, mutual venting and celebrating, sales opportunities . . . and whenever else you wish you had a partner.

Look into local food-entrepreneur support and social groups such as the Texas-based Better Bites of Austin. Los Angeles has the Fine Foods Group, which runs frequent, useful food-business workshops and an online forum. Local Food Lab in Palo Alto, California, takes a Silicon Valley–esque approach to helping entrepreneurs form their business ideas and get started, from products to services. FoodLab Detroit describes itself as a "network of triple bottom-line food entrepreneurs in the Detroit Area," and has an e-mail list for collaboration. In Kansas City, Kansas, chef Mark Alan's KC Food Artisans encourages entrepreneurs to collaborate in buying, making, and even potentially selling through a shared storefront. Can't find a local group? Start one. That's how these groups got off the ground!

Along with the in-person events, look for niche communities online. Two guys I know became besties (or do guys not refer to themselves that way?) after meeting on an online barbecue-geek forum. Clay Gordon hosts discussions among thousands of chocolate professionals on TheChocolateLife.com. And I've been known to troll CoffeeGeek.com. The list goes on and on.

General entrepreneurship Meetup groups can also be a great source of folks you might form into a mastermind group, an idea to which many of the world's most successful people attribute their success. It's simple. A group of six to eight likeminded entrepreneurs get together every couple of weeks to share their goals, solve their challenges, and just plain old be accountable for getting stuff done.

Seminars from Zingerman's ZingTrain as well as at the Fancy Food Show and the Natural Product Expos also get you in a room with others who are working through similar business challenges. Communing tends to energize your own efforts. And validate your struggles.

Tap In to Experts

A trusted advisor can complement the expertise or experience you lack, which can be very useful, especially while planning. Advisory boards made up of such experts tend to be informal in the early stages. Tap in to your audaciousness and approach people you might be in awe of, even if they seem too famous and too busy for little old you. And when they do say yes, set expectations for how much time you think you'll need. Compensation might be lunch, your food products, or some amount of money. Some may request equity, in which case you need to formalize an agreement of expectations with a lawyer. Advisor involvement may ebb and flow over the years, based on your needs and their schedule. Over time, you might formalize an advisory board.

Explore Consultants and Coaches

Beyond your advisors, a nudge or kick in the pants may propel your momentum. Enter the coach. Or consultant. But which should you hire? Consultant Deb Mazzaferro offers both services to specialty food sales executives, and she explained the difference between the two.

In short, coaches give you clarity. Business coaches work one-on-one to increase your knowledge and understanding of the specialty food business, develop customized strategies for growth and profitability, and ensure you are focusing on the things that will make a difference, including motivating you to discover what you want and to pursue it. If you're not clear about your vision, a coach can help you reveal what deep down you may have already known.

On the flip side, consultants bring you expertise. A consultant works with you and your team to examine all the opportunities, then taps into his or her expertise to recommend a path that will help you reach your distinctive goals. Investing in this expertise is especially valuable when it comes to understanding pricing, cost of goods sold (COGS), distribution, adding new product lines beyond your area of expertise, and other make-or-break aspects of your business. Ask a couple of consultants very specific questions to compare their experience, pricing, and fit with your personality. Also, look to the SBA's Small Business Development Centers for referrals to seasoned consultants.

During what will likely be a free-of-charge introductory meeting (by phone or in person), listen deeply, without defensiveness, to feedback. The best consultants and coaches choose which clients to take on. If you really want a consultant, and she says she's not available, dig a little deeper to find out if it's her or you.

Attract a Great Team: Who and How

Want to do it all? Stop. Rather than flame out like an artisan s'more, take stock of what you do best and what makes you happy. Then find partners who complement you, whether a co-packer, a sales team (see "Good Idea: Hire a Sales Rep," page 150), or a production helper. Liz Gutman and Jen King spent many sleepless nights and long days making and selling their modern-retro Liddabit Sweets candy in Brooklyn, New York. "When you're used to doing everything yourself, it seems impossible to trust that someone else can do it," reflects Liz. "Kind of like the first ding on your new car, though—once that happens, the pressure's kind of off, and you learn how to deal with it in a constructive way." In Oakland, California, I-li Chang metaphorically dinged her car at a Yelp event where she was sampling her Vice Chocolate. A college student asked to be her intern. The student had limited pastry-making experience—granted, at Alice Waters' Chez Panisse restaurant—but I-li took a chance. With the added help, I-li soon added a second farmers' market after being limited for many years to one market.

When bringing on partners, be sure you share common values and vision. That's how Karin Campion was able to build Sonoma Syrup with the help of co-packers and a team that works remotely. "Everyone on the Sonoma Syrup team is positive and hardworking, and has a can-do attitude," says Karin. "We share the same passion, which gives us the synergy. Things just flow and beautiful stuff comes to you." Seattle's Skillet Street Food is a good example of partners bringing complementary skills to the table. Chef Josh Henderson sticks with the food, while his business partner, Greg Petrillo, tackles sales and day-to-day operations. By aligning their work with the company vision, the duo gets good stuff done with a lean operation. And remember that great Punk

Rawk Labs partnership story too. (See "Inside Scoop: Punk Rawk Labs Connects the Dots for Success," page 34.)

Here's a short summary of the people you'll likely be involved with early on. I cannot emphasize this enough: No matter how cool, competent, and helpful someone may seem, get references. Think twice about anyone who gets the least bit miffed at your requesting them.

Who You'll Need	Probable Relationship	Quick Tips
Business advisors	Contract	Some can guide you from solidifying your idea through launch. Others can help you fill in your weak spots.
Food production	Contract/vendors	You can contract out parts of your production to makers or packagers, or use a co-packer who handles everything.
Food testing/ labeling	Contract/vendors	A company that works mainly with new food entrepreneurs may be more sensitive to your limited budget.
Food sales	Contract or hire	Passion can substitute for experience, but most of all you need a "closer" who loves to make sales.
Packaging designer	Contract/vendor	Look for someone who has small-food-company experience.
Brand designer	Contract/vendor	Your packaging designer can also serve as your brand designer.
Marketing writer	Contract/vendor	This person can do all of your marketing writing, or just fill in piecemeal.
Photographer/ videographer	Contract/vendor/intern	A good portfolio is worth a thousand words.
Developers	Contract/vendors	These folks provide coding and website maintenance, to whatever degree you need help.
PR/social media	Contract/vendor/intern	Your arrangement could be one-time, campaign-based, or ongoing.

Who You'll Need	Probable Relationship	Quick Tips
Lawyer	Vendor	Legal fees add up quickly; look for solo players, rather than large firms, for lower fees.
Financial consultant	Contract/vendor	Find a food-business expert to project funding needs and set you up for ongoing management.
Insurance broker	Vendor	Be sure your broker understands the food-product business to avoid over-paying or underinsuring.
Jack- or Jill-of-all-trades	Contract or hire	Your right-hand person should complement you and *want* to do the work you need him or her to do (as opposed to wanting to do the work you plan to do yourself).

Pick the Right Vendors

Vendors are people. People mean relationships. Relationships need clear communication, understanding one another's goals and limitations, knowing what you want, negotiating effectively, and knowing when to compromise or concede.

Embark on Your Hunt

Like any talent search, you'll use similar steps to land on the perfect candidates for technical experts, creatives, and even interns who you might find at local universities.

Shortcut your search by reaching out to food companies whose brand, websites, and products you envy. Many food entrepreneurs negotiate a lower rate for services, and they're often happy to pass along referrals.

If need be, hit the Internet. Put your dot-connecting skills into high gear. TheDieline.com is a great place to find designers and discover some amazing food-packaging examples. That's how Yael Miller came to my attention. I contacted her, learned how she went about branding Olli Salumeria and a marshmallow company, and discovered the "vanity bar codes" her firm had created to add a bit of fun to UPC codes. To find local designers, an online search never hurts, especially when you start with a great design example. I'd admired Drake Brewing's beautiful website and Googled "Drake Brewing website design portfolio." Designer Molly McCoy's website popped up, and we had a nice chat. Same with Alyssa Warnock, whom I found after my obsession with bakery chain La Boulange's brand got the best of my curiosity. Turned out her husband, Todd Berardi, founded Hiball, the energy drink company.

If you come up empty-handed when searching for help in your area, look for creative and technical talent, and even virtual assistants, through online freelance marketplaces such as oDesk/Elance, Fiverr, Behance (especially for design), Guru, and 99designs. For writing, I'd stick to workers in the United States, because of the innate cultural knowledge that Americans share. Many of these sites have satisfaction agreements and let you collaborate through an e-mail system on the site, in case of disputes later. Cautionary tales: Ratings do not always reflect future performance. People get busy. Customers with lower standards give higher ratings. Put on your research hat to dig deep before hiring people and assigning them jobs.

Vet the Vendors

Screening vendors can be exhausting. You might feel guilty or rude asking so many questions. Don't worry. Good people understand that you're on a budget. They get that you need to make the right decision—as do they, if they agree to work with you.

Use your intuition as to whether a vendor's style clicks with your own. That doesn't mean that he needs to be palsy-walsy with you, just that he needs to be responsive, respectful, and helpful. Oh, and take any flattery with a grain of salt. Prospective vendors may love your food. Or they may just want your business. All vendors should offer:

- A willingness to educate you on some level.

- References and a solid track record on similar projects. Some may say they keep their client list confidential, which may be valid. Think of other ways to dig into the vendor's reputation for quality. Beware of folks who sound too good to be true and don't have a track record to back up their enthusiasm. (But do not discount vendors with a great client roster but a lame website: Remember, good cobblers have no shoes.)

- A detailed project estimate and price quote.

- A realistic timeline. Small business owners often take work even when they're overbooked (just as you'll be tempted to do).

- A willingness to sign a nondisclosure agreement (NDA). You may not always need an NDA, especially if you're already selling in the marketplace. If you feel more comfortable having vendors sign NDAs, know that some might not want to sign. You'll have to decide if that's OK.

Here are some more pointers on what to look for in vendors. Branding, packaging, and other creative vendors should be able to:

- Show you a portfolio of designs for food products, which have unique challenges and requirements.

- Point to a track record of getting brands into your target stores (or other equivalent successes).

Web companies should:

- Give smart feedback on your website strategy and ask about your long-term plans.

- Suggest various approaches, prioritizing what you need first and what you can defer till later, if the vendor's quote is way over your budget.

- Pick a system that can expand to add new features later.

- Estimate up-front and ongoing costs.

- Offer to train you to make updates yourself or explain how to use the system yourself (and how to go about doing so).

Attract the Right Hires

Although in the beginning you may rely more on vendors, the time will come to hire your own employees. For every hire or intern, strive to find—and train—the type of person you as a customer would want to interact with. There's a simple secret to defining a company culture that will attract the right people: an incredible customer experience. You want to create meaning in work, inspire loyalty, and motivate employees, who in turn will feel self-actualized (remember Maslow's hierarchy, on page 57?) and want to provide equally transcendent experiences to customers. On a more cautionary note, Whole Foods cofounder John Mackey explains in *Conscious Capitalism*: "It's much harder today to remedy hiring mistakes than it used to be, so companies should invest a great deal of time and effort to make sure they hire people . . . who believe in the purpose of the business and resonate with its values and cores."

Commit to treating your staff with respect and inspiring them to feel instrumental to your success, as part of your promise that your business will improve people's lives. The employees at Numi Organic Tea's headquarters in Oakland, California, enjoy a happy, casual culture. Cofounder Ahmed Rahim explains that when you form a business with clear values and an empowered company culture based on those values, you will attract people who will be in it for the long haul.

Numi practices open-book financing, which allows employees to see how their work impacts the business. At the privately owned Clif Bar & Company, employees own 20 percent of the company, which also has an open-book policy so that employees can review financials. At Zingerman's, yet another open-book company, the career part of its website lays the philosophy out straight: "Above and beyond all else, working at Zingerman's means making a serious commitment to learning about great food and great service; to helping to create an exceptional workplace."

Job descriptions say a lot about a company culture too. Jeni's Splendid Ice Creams recruits "ideal, positive-minded, and energetic Ice Cream Ambassadors (also known as scoop shop employees) able to provide consistent, world-class service to every single customer, and exhibit passion for the community, a willingness to clean (a lot), and stamina (to serve people in long lines)." Now compare that to an ad I happened upon on Craigslist: "Able to withstand repetitive work (i.e., rolling and cutting out cookies, scooping hundreds of cookies at a time). Must be able to lift up to fifty pounds. Must be able to stand for long periods of time. Come to work in a timely fashion." Which company would you rather work for?

Shortcut your staff or intern search with GoodFoodJobs.com, a "gastro-job search" website and newsletter with thousands of Good Food–minded job seekers. No job is too odd. Positions listed range from internships to full-time jobs, from cheesemongers to chocolate sales reps. You'll be hard-pressed to find a more efficient way to reach Good Food fans who want to be your employees. Plus, the founders are really cool, genuine gals.

TAKE 5:
TIPS FOR HIRING STAFF

Before bringing on employees, revisit your vision and mission to reflect on how a team fits into your company. After all, you might remember you wanted a "virtual" team, unfettered with W2 employees! When you do decide to hire:

1. Ask for references, follow up on them, and dig for dirt online. For staff who will work on financials or make deliveries, do a background check—it's a cheap, fast, and simple measure to avoid possible financial catastrophe.

2. Interview professionally. No matter how you click, ask those tough questions to gauge character, such as, "How will you feel coming in at 2 A.M. in the dead of winter to start baking?" or "Won't the farmers' market be horrible when it's raining?" Trust your instincts if responses seem faked.

3. Be sure any hire is aligned with your values, mission, and culture—and fully enthused.

4. Triple check that you can afford the employee's salary and insurance. Does your area offer incentives for employing locals?

5. Seek out people with complementary skills and strengths, whether hires or partners. Mini Me's you click with are fun, but a team to manage what you can't or don't want to do is priceless.

GOOD IDEA:
GET WORKERS' COMPENSATION INSURANCE ASAP

Workers compensation insurance is state-mandated and covers medical costs and lost wages when an employee is injured on the job. New York insurance broker Susan Combs says entrepreneurs often delay workers' comp to save a few dollars—but the potential fines are not worth the "savings." She suggests setting up workers' comp even before you hire employees.

Rooibee Red Tea first approached Foodzie in 2009 as a tiny start-up launching a new kind of bottled, certified organic iced tea. With an impressive background and connections in the beverage industry, founder Jeff Stum was soon ready for growth.

He presented his concept at an event at which angel investors were seeking to invest in new food start-ups. Through this event, he met Heather Howell, who was ready to leave the corporate life for an entrepreneurial endeavor. The two took time to get acquainted, making sure Jeff was ready to turn over the reins. Heather came on board as CEO (or rather, CTeaO), agreeing to forgo a salary for a year and a half. With a woman on his team, Jeff was able to get Rooibee Red Tea certified by the Women's Business Enterprise National Council (WBENC). The certification not only made the company exempt from the annual $250,000 slotting fees supermarkets often charge food manufacturers for shelf placement, it also increased the company's appeal to large organizations, such as Walmart, that seek out minority- and women-owned suppliers. Plus, as a nonindustry insider, Heather brought fresh thinking to the company. She may have been new, but she also saw no limits as to how far the company could go.

The Rooibee team approached the Fisher College of Business at Ohio State University and presented Rooibee Red Tea to an MBA class. Four young women and two men set off for six months, researching, writing, and ultimately presenting their findings— at no cost to the company. They concluded that the brand most appealed to 18- to 34-year-old women, primarily young moms who grew up with Whole Foods and its field-to-fork values. Along with this insight, Heather says, "With students, you end up with these amazing ambassadors you can mentor in the future."

Jeff contracted a co-packer who happened to hail from South Africa, home of rooibos tea, who now brews the tea, bottles it, packs it, and inventories it. Heather explains, "We prefer the experts manage production because of all the complexities complying with FDA regulations." The company sources its own USDA-certified organic sugar and lemons.

Jeff and Heather agreed to do everything regionally, "from social media to our PR to our bottling, caps, and labeling," says Heather. "When you think about giving back—every dollar is going back into my community." A "Kentucky Proud" logo emblazons the bottles. They donate product to many local causes and events, also great for exposure. "Louisville has wrapped their arms around our brand for many reasons and because we give back."

Because few women lead the charge in manufacturing, Heather's role adds marketing value, not to mention that she fits the target customer profile.

From the time Heather joined the company in 2010, sales grew 140 percent. In the first five months of 2012, its sales equaled all of the 2011 sales, primarily through nationwide exposure through distributors UNFI, KeHE, and others. Retailers known for health and wellness, such as health food stores and supplement and vitamin stores, were the first to adopt the line, placing it mainly in their refrigerated grab-and-go sections.

Rooibee Red Tea takes care to select investors who care about and understand consumer products. The team first raised $1 million and, based on its success, set out to raise $1.5 million more, all with the goal of creating a nationwide brand. The company's Kentucky location has its advantages, with a bevy of beverage companies in the region as well as what Heather describes as "world-class water." "It's a secret sauce. I will do everything I can to keep our bottling here," she says, a good reminder that simple H_2O can add to a winning mix.

DECIDE ON YOUR BUSINESS STRUCTURE

Wait as long as possible to formalize your business structure. Believe it or not, that advice comes from a lawyer—one who has seen many food entrepreneurs fritter away cash on legal fees only to realize the business wasn't viable. Before formalizing, solidify your plan, who is involved, where you're located, and any financing you're raising. In short, know your company is a go.

As you make progress, the right formation will come to light. For example, Valley Girl Foodstuffs, maker of healthful school snacks, opted to set up as a for-profit company. The underlying goal? To train at-risk youths how to run a business. The company collaborates with a nonprofit organization that provides skill-based programming for the disadvantaged teens of Sonoma Valley. Founder Anea Botton strategically chose a for-profit model to show her young workers that they are perfectly capable at succeeding in a commercial business.

There are many ways to structure a business, all with different implications for growth possibilities, issuing stock, tax benefits, and paperwork load. Here's a snapshot:

- **SOLE PROPRIETOR.** By default, you are a "sole proprietor." This means you can declare any profits and losses on your personal tax return. You'll be personally responsible for any claims or lawsuits. Liability insurance covering food problems (not liability for your premises) generally costs less than $1,000 per year. If you get a higher quote, keep looking. Insurance brokers less experienced in food might not understand the nuances and thus might quote you for the wrong type of insurance.

- **LIMITED LIABILITY COMPANY (LLC).** The IRS notes that "LLCs are popular because, similar to a corporation, owners have limited personal liability for the debts and actions of the LLC." A single person can form an LLC. Investigate the best time of year to form an LLC, as you may save on fees and taxes by forming earlier in the year.

- **LOW-PROFIT LIMITED LIABILITY (L3C).** A relatively new type of business entity, L3C ventures are commonly thought of as enterprises that serve a so-called triple-bottom line: people, planet, and profits. Organized much like an LLC, the L3C has as its primary purpose achieving a socially beneficial objective, with profit as a secondary goal.

- **CORPORATIONS.** Individual owners might look into forming an S corporation rather than an LLC. This is a corporation that elects to pass corporate income, losses, deductions, and credit through to their shareholders for federal tax purposes. If you plan to bring on investors and issue shares, a corporation or S corporation may be the right option. Making money and wanting to pursue a social mission are not mutually exclusive. Some states offer a "Benefit" corporation option (not to be confused with the non-profit BCorp), for companies layering social good over the base corporate structure. I'd keep it simple and wait to "add on" the paperwork that comes with managing another layer of legal structure.

- PARTNERSHIP. The IRS defines partnerships as the relationship existing between two or more persons who join to carry on a trade or business. Each person contributes money, property, labor, or skill, and expects to share in the profits and losses of the business.

- NONPROFIT. You might choose to organize as a 501(c)(3) nonprofit if your food business exists for an underlying charitable reason. Homeboy Industries, a nonprofit in Los Angeles, trains former gang members to work in food service establishments, through its Homegirl Cafe & Catering.

- COOPERATIVE. A co-op is a business organization owned and operated by a group of individuals for their mutual benefit. Along with sharing profits, you share decision-making and often roles. Olive Loew took this idea even further with her savory biscotti company. Saint & Olive combines a for-profit, worker-owned cooperative model and a nonprofit model to support a skills-training program that helps women reenter the workforce after incarceration.

When you're ready to figure out which legal form is right for you, consult a lawyer, tax advisor, the Internal Revenue Service website, or small business how-to books.

INSIDE SCOOP:
RUNA GUAYUSA ORGANIZES TO MAXIMIZE GOOD

If you're one for world travel and social change, let this innovative company structure stretch your vision to new possibilities: Runa Guayusa makes a naturally energizing tea-like drink called guayusa. The company's mission is to help small, indigenous farming families in the Ecuadorian Amazon rainforest. It does so with a unique hybrid organizational structure that achieves integrity, strength, and flexibility to accomplish a triple bottom-line mission.

Two for-profit companies manage the supply chain and sales core of Runa's business. Runatarpuna Exportadora S.A. in Ecuador

CONTINUE ▶

buys fresh guayusa leaves from farmers, processes them, and exports containers of leaves to the second company, Runa LLC, which packages, markets, and sells retail guayusa products in the United States.

Runa Foundation USA, based in Brooklyn, New York, and its counterpart in Ecuador, Fundación Runa, serve as the nonprofit branch. These nonprofit foundations tap into the network and economic impact of Runa's commercial structure to train and support local farmers for community and environmental good. This three-part structure helps the company deliver on its commitment to helping Ecuador's people and the environment while earning profits to support the efforts. Helping farmers and writing off travel, while making Good Food: definitely a great business.

FUND YOUR FOOD COMPANY

Companies live or die based on financing and cash flow—money flowing in and out. Your promise to be good and to do good means keeping your business healthy, especially when hiring employees and contracting vendors such as co-packers. You're not the only one affected if things go south, as a small co-packer learned the hard way. He trusted an undercapitalized entrepreneur, manufactured a pallet load of pasta sauce, and didn't get paid. The co-packer now tells people, "If you can afford to produce only one manufacturing run, you can't afford to be in business." As you're selling the first product batch, you need funds to produce the next run before your money comes in from the first batch. As a useful rule of thumb, he concludes, "If you're overly concerned with $1,000 to cover variable costs, you shouldn't get into this."

To start your search for outside funding, set aside any fears of rejection or not being able to repay your debt. Also commit to avoiding those horror stories of credit cards maxed out (at exorbitant interest rates), houses mortgaged (seriously risky), and savings drained (not the best choice). (Those millionaire entrepreneurs who got started charging tens of thousands on credit cards are the exceptions.) Strive to lock down funding early, before you really need it. Waiting till you're desperate not only redirects your energy but (as with dating) may cause you to make bad choices.

How much will you need? In addition to equipment, rent, permits, vendor fees, and ingredients, your potential insurance costs may include health, property, business interruption, liability, workers comp, and commercial auto if you're doing deliveries or selling from a truck. Get clarity on your short- and long-term needs by reviewing your plans with a consultant, the Small Business Administration, a lawyer, or a financially savvy friend.

Personal Funding: Chipping In (Yourself, Friends, Family, Crowdfunding)

The more people lend to or invest in you, the more the money costs you in terms of interest, or loss of control, or giving up a piece of the company in return. This is why so many entrepreneurs start out with funding from a nest egg, day job, or sugar daddy/mama while starting slowly and keeping expenses low. When choosing this so-called "bootstrapping" approach, be sure your metaphorical straps are long enough to sustain you until sales cover your costs. In the early days of the Sticky Toffee Pudding Company, Tracy Claros had a vision to build a great business without borrowing or spending very much money. She soon discovered that the more slowly she built sales, the more she was missing her opportunity to earn a living. Meanwhile, her personal resources waned, just as she was learning that doubling her sales did not mean doubling her cash flow.

Investing your own funds invests you in your success like nothing else can. You might see your cash outlay as similar to investing in an MBA program, only with a lot more potential. Set aside an amount of money you're willing to lose—not your family home—and then use it for your business. I once decided to invest (and risk) $15,000 in a project. Pre-determining the investment put me in control and inspired resourceful thinking (i.e., lots of advisors and partners) to meet my goals within the budget.

These days, you have a world of microinvestors to appeal to for funding. Crowdfunding websites such as Kickstarter and Indiegogo let fans easily fund projects that can add up to thousands of dollars. The money is yours to keep, with no repayment, although you will need to shell out thank-you gifts to your funders, such as product samples, mentions on your website, or other goodies. The Potomac Chocolate team raised $2,505, well over their $1,650 goal, on Kickstarter. This cash funded some small-scale equipment and enough cocoa beans for product development. The campaign also got the company's name out there and built up a following for the fledgling chocolate company, which began garnering awards in its first year. For successful crowdfunding, you need a community following, willingness to reach out to a broad social network, dedication to keeping the campaign alive (with perhaps an intern to manage it), and a really fabulous video and thank-you gifts. Managing such campaigns to success takes time. If you're short on time, consider hiring an intern or social media expert to help you; any stipend can come from your campaign's proceeds.

Turning to friends and family is a time-honored first step when looking for an investment or loan. Any potential funders should understand your plans, how and when their investment will be returned, and their level of involvement (including silently, if that's what you or they prefer). Punk Rawk Labs had no clue how quickly its living foods business would take off. Along with a Kickstarter campaign, founder Alissa Barthel connected with an unlikely investor: a company whose vice president she had played violin with in the school orchestra. Says Alissa, "They own part of Punk Rawk Labs but are not involved in operations." How's that for making beautiful music?

Make sure to set up a formal agreement to cover the legalities, if you're taking a loan or an investment, and any related terms. Approach family investments like a pre-nup. Consider going so far as hiring a consultant who specializes in family business. Be careful to avoid losing something even more important than your business: your relationships.

Direct public offerings (DPOs) present another funding option, in which a company sells shares to the public. As author Amy Cortese explains in her book *Locavesting*, the expenses to set up a DPO can range from a few thousand to tens of thousands of dollars. Yet this funding option can fill a significant gap for companies looking to raise from tens of thousands up to several million dollars from ordinary investors. Natural mac-and-cheese maker Annie's Homegrown chose to fund the company by promoting its DPO on product boxes before eventually joining the stock market. That's homegrown!

Loans: Payback Time

With a loan, you must eventually pay back the money in an agreed-upon time frame. Since the 2008 financial crash, bank lending has been hit or miss, one reason why loans from individuals, called peer-to-peer lending, has flourished. Investors get the satisfaction of helping people and an interest rate far higher than banks pay. New models for individuals to finance Good Food businesses, such as

Credibles.org, are cropping up all the time. Credibles essentially lets fans prepay for food to fund a company's development. On websites such as LendingClub.com, Prosper.com, and Kabbage.com, you can state the amount of money you want to borrow and terms such as the loan's term length. Investors minimize risk with insight into the borrower's creditworthiness. Naturally, high-risk borrowers pay higher interest rates.

Look into the Whole Foods' Local Producer Loan Program, which the company started largely to help meat and vegetable producers expand their businesses. Whole Foods loaned several million dollars within a few years of starting the program, ranging from $1,000 to $100,000, with a very reasonable interest rate (in the ballpark of bank loan rates). After receiving a Whole Foods loan, Julie Nirvelli rapidly expanded her White Girl Salsa from Denver, Colorado, into the entire Southwest region. Julie chose to grant Whole Foods a temporary exclusive, which was not required, for the chance to get extra marketing support in each region. Smart move. "I think our relationship is stronger because of the exclusive, and that there was plenty of opportunity to grow within Whole Foods. For Texas-based Whole Foods to take on a nonlocal salsa is quite a statement," Julie says.

When considering bank loans, community banks might be a smart place to start. They may have more flexibility and more commitment to the local economy. At least that's what Beverly and Douglas Takizawa learned when seeking funding for their Savory Creations concentrated-broth company. They had first funded via friends and family, building up a credit history and customer base before approaching the national bank where they had been customers for 30 years. To Beverly's shock, the bank declined their loan request. Next, they went to a local community bank. This bank extended a line of credit and helped them with an SBA loan.

Earlier you read about Tessemae's All Natural's fast-growth story (see "Inside Scoop: Tessemae's All Natural Becomes an Accidental Manufacturer," page 45). When Greg Vetter decided to approach a local Annapolis bank for a loan to fund Tessemae's growth, he had already proved a market by selling at Whole Foods. With all his ducks and his paperwork in a row, Greg submitted his application. Not only was the bank impressed by the projections he had an accountant prepare, Greg happened to have several salad dressing fans on the loan-review team. The bank granted him a $200,000 line of credit.

Look into loans before maxing out your credit cards for a better chance of qualifying. Artisaneur I-li Chang learned this the hard way. She drained her own savings and credit to get Vice Chocolates going, thinking she was doing the right thing—until, ironically, the SBA declined a loan due to her debt load.

Investors: Giving a Piece of the Pie (Angels, Venture Capital)

Many beloved large food companies got started with funding from angel investors. Angels might be individuals or small investment companies who give you a few thousand to a million dollars outright or in return for a share of the company, called "equity." Investors want a nice return, but they may be more patient, forgiving, and involved in your business. They may also be hands-on, wanting to give input or advice. Or they may be silent, uninvolved in the daily operations.

Sonoma Syrup kicked off with Karin Campion's own funds in addition to a loan from an angel investor, a best friend, whom she repaid quickly. The investor, who now sits on the board and is her chief advisor, supported the company from Day One. The company can now take whatever path Campion likes rather than basing its future on investor desires.

Fifty investors backed Justin's Nut Butter, whose story you read on page 63. Management nightmare? On the contrary. Many investors can mean a built-in support system and crowd of evangelists who will be sure to spread the word. "I have a responsibility to get the investors a good return," Justin Gold told me in 2011. "Whatever I choose to do— pay them back and keep going or sell Justin's Nut Butters—all depends on where I am as an individual." In 2013, a venture firm took a minority stake in Justin's Nut Butter, raising $47 million to power the company's growth. Boulder's *Daily Camera* reports Justin as saying: "There's no exit in sight. It was an opportunity for us to grow more strategically."

As you see, when you're ready for a major cash infusion, venture capital firms can provide fast growth in return for equity, meaning a piece of your company. You can't do enough due diligence when seeking funding, as the team at Mary's Gone Crackers learned. As the gluten-free craze propelled sales, Mary's Gone Crackers sought outside investment to supplement early friends-and-family investments. The team then raised money from a venture capital group to keep production at pace with sales. They soon needed more funding, only to discover the terms the venture capitalists offered had become what Mary Waldner calls "very onerous." So, the Mary's Gone Crackers team focused on profitability, turned the company around within a few months, and blocked the VC's path to control. "It took a huge amount of effort to thrive and meant a big chunk of our energy was spent on surviving," says Mary. In 2013, Japanese rice-cracker company Kameda, USA acquired a majority stake in Mary's Gone Crackers, vastly expanding the company's reach to a new world of gluten-free eaters.

To find ethically minded (yet also money-minded) investors, tap into the Slow Money movement. Similar to the Slow Food ethos, Slow Money principles state: "We must learn to invest as if food, farms, and fertility mattered. We must connect investors to the places where they live, creating vital relationships and new sources of capital for small food enterprises." With a mission like that, the organization might shortcut your search for "good" money.

TAKE 5:
TIPS FOR GOOD FUND-RAISING

Determine a funding strategy that fits with your style, growth plans, and vision. This will help you avoid being attracted by shiny money offers that may derail you in the long run.

(1) Don't have a product yet? Make a lifelike prototype at a reasonable cost through companies such as VirtualPackaging.com.

(2) Potential investors will want to go over your financials with a fine-toothed comb. Before agreeing to "open the kimono" and show them everything, first ask exactly what they will want to see—all sales records, from all customers? Then decide what's okay with you or if they're asking for too much.

(3) Wait to seek major investment capital until you've built value in your company and have grown revenues. Otherwise, investors are buying in at a bargain-basement price.

(4) Clearly understand if and when your investors expect an exit strategy, in which they will cash out. Be sure your investors align with your vision of a sustainable Good Food business.

(5) Get a short, polished business plan together and demonstrate your ability to make the plan come to fruition.

INSIDE SCOOP:
SCHOOLHOUSE KITCHEN LEARNS THE HARD WAY ABOUT STRUCTURING A BUSINESS

Patsy Smith debuted her first all-natural SchoolHouse Kitchen product in 2005, the highly regarded SweetSmoothHot Mustard, then went on to create eleven more all-natural products across four categories. Numerous magazines, and its mission-based beneficiaries, praised the company. Yet two years later, SchoolHouse Kitchen was still being run primarily by passion, as opposed to hard business. Patsy's daughter Wendy Wheeler Smith jumped on board to help. "Originally there was no business plan or thought process into the future, as far as an expandable line," says Wendy. "Mom knew I had no experience in the food business, but we thought we'd just go for it." They grew and needed even more people. She reflects, "The plan was to hire people who were better at certain things than I was, like operations. Then I could have focused on the things I did really well such as sales, marketing, and strategy. But this is what sometimes happens when you learn on the job and perhaps too slowly. You lose a window of opportunity or burn out."

The more they grew, the more their larger wholesale accounts demanded of the company. Margins kept getting squeezed. Wendy says, "We simply didn't realize, at the beginning, how much was needed for things like trade marketing, distributor fees, and other costs along the supply chain." In 2012, the team made a hard decision to close SchoolHouse Kitchen and move on to new adventures.

GREAT BUSINESS ACTION PLAN

☐ Set up your back-office systems to get and stay organized.

☐ Think about which business structure fits with your mission once you're solid that the business is a go. Refer to your vision to guide your company structure and support systems.

☐ Consider who might make a good business partner or collaborator, then look into possibilities.

☐ Check out SBA.gov's Hire and Retain Employees section.

☐ Identify and prioritize the staff you'll need, and then get creative: Ask local producers if any star staff need more part-time work. Look to MBA programs, cooking schools, local social service programs, LinkedIn, and retirees through the local SBDC office. Post on GoodFoodJobs.com.

☐ Look into workers' compensation insurance.

☐ See if and how you might qualify for Small Business Administration certifications (women-owned, minority-owned, or veteran-owned businesses), which could make you eligible for certain loans and other support.

☐ Set funding goals or budgets, even if you're self-financing.

☐ Understand expectations and roles clearly, including how any investors may be involved in your business. Get every single agreement in writing, no matter how yucky or uncool it seems.

ON *GOODFOODGREATBUSINESS.COM*

Get a quick start with articles and links to resources
to start building your foundation.

SO YOU REALLY WANT TO START A FOOD BUSINESS?

BURNING QUESTION: IS IT THAT COMPLICATED?

Yes and no. When you're planning to make it big, yes. For local-only sellers, maybe. When starting small, you can pretty easily get licensed, find a place to make your food, and calculate the costs to figure out if you'll make enough profit to sustain your endeavor. Despite all you've read, your business may take off suddenly, as did People's Pops when three friends in New York ran a one-day experiment. The pops, made with sustainable herbs and fruits, quickly got set up with an ongoing spot at the New Amsterdam Market, distribution at local shops, and their very own shop at Manhattan's Chelsea Market.

FROM PIE IN THE SKY TO REALITY

Unless you've been in a mad rush to exhibit at the Fancy Food Show or launch at another highly visible event, your actual "launch" will likely be gradual. Your Web presence will go live. You'll start selling at a market. Orders will trickle in. In the words of one who has been in the trenches: Temper your passion and ego, and have patience.

You'll grow into your new identity. One entrepreneur likened his new business to a new girlfriend. "I was afraid to tell people about it, thinking it would end, so what's the point. Once I reached out, help rolled in. I discovered that friends, family, and the community wanted to be there for me." Mary Waldner described practically crying every time she walked into the Mary's Gone Crackers factory her first year. Years later, she can't imagine it any other way.

Your life and business joys will ebb and flow. "It is easy to get down on yourself when things don't go as planned," reflects Nuts About Granola's Sarah Lanphier, a wise one in her early 20s. "Progress comes from the little accomplishments. I love sitting down at the end of the year and looking back at all the little achievements that contributed to a successful year for Nuts About Granola. Things could be better, but it could be worse. We aren't a huge company, but we have a loyal following of customers, are able to support ourselves, and don't have a lot of debt. The company has allowed me to pursue the things I love, educate others about the causes I fight for, and has made me a better, stronger, more independent woman."

You'll learn, make mistakes, then adapt or call it quits. "I'm not telling you everything, as I don't want to discourage you," one exhausted yet intrepid Business Builder shared as she worked to roll out a second product line. "When people tell me they want to start a food business, I just want to grab them by their collar and yell, 'Are you out of your @*#& mind?'"

As you connect the dots between your passions, your community, and what you want, reality might surpass all of your dreams. Feel Alissa Barthel's joy when updating her Punk Rawk Labs supporters after a successful Kickstarter campaign: "I vacillate between being overwhelmed by the impossible and being inspired by the impossible. It feels like I'm pushing a giant boulder up a mountain, but I am continually lifted up by all the beautiful people out there. It's crazy. I just keep hearing from stores saying that their customers are demanding my product! I was so ready to give up today—on a lot of days. You are making a difference to me. And I am so thankful."

Even if you don't run your business forever, you'll likely look back and enjoy having lived your dream, like Maite Zubia. She handed over the reins of her *alfajores* cookie business to a partner when her visa expired and she had to leave the United States. "I was lucky enough to invest in the best thing you can really invest in: people, good people . . . It is about creating with my hands, something that I know for sure will make someone else happy. The sweetness behind each Maitelates will make people happy forever, and that, that will always make me smile."

INSIDE SCOOP:
SQUAREBAR CHARTS A GOOD FOOD BUSINESS PLAYBOOK

A Berkeley Vegan Earth Day celebration lured me into a building where tables of raw, animal-cruelty-free, vegan foods lined the walls. In the midst of this earthy scene, Squarebar's slick branding caught my eye. Sarah Gordon explained how a recent shift to an allergen-free diet left her with few food options. And so she and her then-boyfriend, now-husband, Andrew were inspired to build a snack-bar company, despite having no experience in the food business.

In a year and a half, they developed a line of chocolate-covered, high-protein, organic snack bars that now sell in stores nationwide. Here's how they went about it:

1. **Self-funded.** Both saved money from their jobs to self-fund their start-up. Sarah smartly kept her day job, while Andrew moved to part-time consulting.

2. **Experimented.** They formulated the bars at home, using non-GMO, organic, whole-food ingredients.

3. **Learned.** They took new entrepreneur seminars at the Fancy Food Show, turned to the Internet for advice about anything and everything, and got tips from a fellow snack-bar company. Outreach to peer food entrepreneurs was vital for their progress, as well as a source of new friendships. Natural-products guru Bob Burke offered them tips as well.

4. **Turned to food experts.** They found a co-packer whose food scientist helped them tweak the formula, ensuring that Squarebar kept the recipe rights. Squarebar products are non-GMO verified, which will increase their appeal to buyers in countries that ban GMO foods.

5. **Mastered costs and pricing.** They tracked every little cost, knowing that expenses add up *very* quickly. They learned to overbudget 20 to 30 percent and base prices on today's costs, rather than a suggested retail price or pricing for economies of scale they don't yet have. Their pricing model considers the profit margins of a distributor to ensure a seamless transition if or when they go that route.

6. **Crowdfunded.** They set up a Kickstarter campaign, after reaching out to a Kickstarter entrepreneur for advice. They promoted the campaign on Facebook and Twitter. Grandma spread the word throughout the family. The Non-GMO Project promoted their campaign to its many thousands of supporters. The $13,000 or so raised exceeded expectations—and the duo didn't have to give up any company equity or ownership.

CONTINUE ▶

(7) **Launched.** They built a website and got a booth at the Natural Products Expo West. A coveted Daily Candy article soon followed after a writer discovered them on Kickstarter.

(8) **Promoted with demos.** At San Francisco's Rainbow Grocery, they sold 17 cases in four hours of demos, establishing the bars as a customer darling. Demoing also gave them first-hand feedback.

(9) **Connected.** They tapped into social media, helped by an intern.

SKETCH OUT YOUR BUSINESS PLAN

You have just absorbed a lot of information. *A lot.* So, what's the plan? Better sooner than later, put your fingers to keyboard or pen to the pro-verbial cocktail napkin—a technique I love, thanks to Dan Roam's *The Back of the Napkin*. No matter how preliminary your plans, get them out of your head to clear your mind and make progress.

Start with an App or a One-Page Plan

App-loving readers rejoice! The team behind the wildly popular *Business Model Generation* book has created a companion Web-based app: Strategyzer, geared for brainstorming, collaboration, and testing ideas. When you're ready to put that plan on paper, a one-page blue-print is a happy medium between the napkin approach and a full twenty-page plan. Jim Horan wrote the book *The One-Page Business Plan* to help entrepreneurs simplify and focus their business goals. For example, when Jim met Clarine Hardesty at one of her cookie demos, she was arms-deep starting up her bakery Clarine's Florentines. She had everything—except a written plan defining her path to growth and how she would get there. In twenty-nine sentences, Jim and Clarine crafted her plan using his one-page technique. She refers to and updates the plan often because it's short, simple, and focused.

So how do you do it? Well, luckily you've already done half the work while reading this book:

- VISION. Boil it down from the vision you outlined (see "Write Your Vision Statement: Where Do You Want to Go with This?" page 46).

- MISSION. Your company's mission says what it does and for whom (see "State Your Mission: Why Are You Doing This?" page 38).

- **OBJECTIVES.** What specific business results will you aim for, and how will you measure them? Make these big-picture S.M.A.R.T. Goals (see "Set S.M.A.R.T. Goals," page 25, for a goal-setting refresher).

- **STRATEGIES.** How will you build this business, and what will make it successful over time? Include strategies for your 5 Staples mix (see "Learn the '5 Staples' for a Good Food Marketing Mix," page 20): product, promotion, places (distribution), pricing, and promise.

- **ACTION PLANS.** What specific work needs to be done during the next year to implement your objectives and strategies? In the spirit of a one-pager, keep the plans brief—just one sentence. I recommend then writing one-page plans (which I call strategy briefs) for each activity, such as marketing, sales, and production, that you outlined in the action plan.

Once you have your one-pager written up, keep it in front of you. Stick it to your fridge. Shoot a photo of it with your phone so you always have it accessible. It will keep you on track.

Graduate to a Big, Formal Plan

After your one-page plan is solid (and in sync with reality) you might want to write a more formal business plan. You'll need to have this when seeking funding. A detailed business plan forces you to do the detailed research, find that market niche, and create a product that people will buy. Typical business plans include:

- **EXECUTIVE SUMMARY.** The summary is the first and most important thing people read. This is a snapshot of your company—who you are, what you do, for whom, and why. Make it one or two pages at most. The summary should make the reader—whether a lender or potential partner—want to learn more about your business and believe that you are capable of running it.

- **COMPANY OVERVIEW.** Include your vision, business goals, and objectives; your mission statement; a brief history of the business; the key team; and your legal business structure.

- **MARKET DEFINITION, COMPETITION, AND YOUR NICHE.** This section puts your company into perspective within the larger realm of the industry and your customers' options. For this section, you'll detail your customer profile(s) and the critical needs of your perceived or existing market; you should discuss the competition and how you fill a need that it does not, and anything else that makes you stand apart.

- **DESCRIPTION OF PRODUCTS AND SERVICES.** These are your foods, classes, catering, and whatever else you're selling. Get specific about what makes your offerings different from the competition, such as any certifications, like fair trade certified and certified organic; trademarks, patents, and research and development, if applicable; value proposition; any distribution partners such as retailers; and any future products or extensions planned.

- **MARKETING AND SALES STRATEGY.** Your planned channels of sales and distribution, including online; and your marketing strategies and tactics.

- **ORGANIZATION AND MANAGEMENT.** The legal structure of your business (sole proprietorship, partnership, LLC, etc.), and information on operations (facilities, suppliers, and capability, and the necessary or special licenses and/or permits required).

- **FINANCIAL MANAGEMENT.** When raising funds, new businesses should also include required funds, costs, and projected income and cash flow. I recommend you work with a consultant for this, unless you're a financial whiz.

Your Plan Can and Will Change

Formal business plans can wither once you get into day-to-day realities. Edit your plan often. It's your road map, not a doorstop.

Unexpected success quickly surpassed Alissa Barthel's modest vision, as she explained on the Punk Rawk Labs website: "The Kickstarter money was to move into a larger kitchen so that I could meet the growing demand for my product. I moved into that kitchen shortly after the campaign ended. But as luck would have it, we grew out of that kitchen almost immediately. The demand for our [nut milk] cheese has been nothing short of miraculous. They have been selling like crazy. All over the country. I've never seen anything like this. As such, we had to regroup and come up with a larger plan. And we did." Alissa had to be open-minded and nimble to change her course quickly for continued success.

GOOD IDEA:
MAKE YOUR GOOD FOOD CHECKLIST

What better way to test your business plan than to answer the questions some very popular shops ask when a food manufacturer approaches them? Learn from this checklist, compiled from criteria the Pasta Shop in Oakland, California; Bi-Rite Market in San Francisco; and Zingerman's in Ann Arbor, Michigan, generously shared:

- Who are you?
- Why are you running this business?
- What are your values?
- How passionate are you about Good Food?
- What is appealing about the product? Is it tasty?
- Is this something that I'd feed my kids?
- What is the story behind the product?
- What are the ingredients? Are there any genetically modified ingredients? If so, why?
- Would our guests want this food?
- How will you treat our staff?
- How do you run the company?
- Where are you located?
- Who else sells your products?

Note how these questions relate pretty closely to the Good Food Award criteria for entry ("tasty, authentic, and responsible") mentioned on page 14.

RETHINKING? RE-IMAGINE THE IDEA OF GOOD FOOD

You picked up this book with an idea to create some food products. Then came the onslaught of 101 realities. Maybe you're feeling less inspired than you once were . . . or your tasting party didn't go quite as planned. Perhaps long-time blocks to your potential are holding you back. Or perhaps you still want to start a great business, just not food products. The good news is that products are just one small way to express your passion. For example, say you've had thoughts of starting a fair-trade coffee roastery and café to quench your coffee lust and desire to help farmers. Yet for some reason, the idea isn't working out. Connect the dots and you'll discover there are many ways to slice a Good Food business:

- Coffee kiosk within a store

- Coffee cart for special events and conferences

- Mobile coffee truck

- Coffee-of-the-month club

- Green coffee-bean importer

- Packaged coffee importer

- Coffee educator or event organizer

- Wholesale roaster, supplying locally to businesses

- Review coffee for print, a blog, or even as an online video show

- Barista, pumping out the perfect cups

- Fair-trade coffee advocate, spreading good far and wide

- Buy a town and dedicate it solely to coffee business

That last idea may sound more ludicrous than audacious. But a Vietnamese importer really did buy 10-acre Buford, Wyoming (for less than most San Francisco Bay Area house prices), with intentions for creating a Vietnamese coffee hub. Let ideas like these kick off a brainstorm of your own. Think of the revenue potential of each business idea, the skill set you'd use, and how the day-to-day work would fulfill you and fit with your ideal lifestyle.

TIME TO CONNECT THE DOTS

Look back and you'll see a common thread in many of the real-life stories so many fabulous companies shared: Inklings, instincts, and casual remarks combined with hard work and resilience lead to some of the best, most successful food businesses. While working on the final edit of this book, I read the story of Tate's Bake Shop, how Kathleen King created a multimillion-dollar baking business starting in 1980, partnered with the wrong people, and then got out and rebuilt an even more successful business from scratch. She is a poster child for living the American food-entrepreneurship dream, overcoming everyone's worst nightmare.

I hope what you've read in *Good Food, Great Business* both inspires you and arms you with the street smarts to connect the dots and make your dream a reality on your own terms. You've got one life to live. Make it good!

Please spread the word about this book and share the wisdom of so many who contributed their knowledge, hopes, dreams, and tales. I'm honored that you read this far and can't wait to connect!

FOOD BUSINESS GLOSSARY

accounts. Business customers.

allergens. A substance that causes allergic reactions.

artisan. Traditionally refers to skilled food crafters making products using mainly manual processes, rather than machines.

artisaneur. Coined in this book, an artisan-entrepreneur making Good Food at home or in a rented kitchen.

barcode. *See* UPC.

batch process recipe. A detailed procedure for a single product issued by a recognized process authority that includes formulation, critical control points, processing steps, storage, distribution, and selling conditions and restrictions. The exact steps and formula for producing a recipe in a production quantity, used to guide a contract manufacturer (co-packer) or production person. Also called *schedule process recipe*.

BOGO. An abbreviation for *buy one, get one*; the second item is usually free. A sales-promotion technique.

Branded Program. A USDA initiative to help U.S. food manufacturers using domestic ingredients to export products to international markets.

business builder. Coined in this book, an entrepreneur who manufactures food through a co-packer to allow for focus on the business.

case pack. A (usually) cardboard carton containing multiple units, such as a pack of eight or twelve, usually either for wholesale or sold with a bulk discount to a consumer.

certified organic. Products meeting standards set by the USDA National Organic Program may label their products as "USDA certified organic."

community builder. A term used in this book to describe an entrepreneur who sets up a production kitchen/manufacturing facility with an eye toward local expansion.

co-packer/contract manufacturer. A food processor that companies can hire to produce their foods.

cost of goods sold. Abbreviated as *COGS*. An accounting term referring to costs of the products a business has sold during a particular period.

cottage food laws. Laws some states have that allow people to make certain low-risk foods in their own home kitchens and then sell them on a small scale to the public, usually locally.

cross-contamination. A basic and critical food sanitation concept, referring to undesirable and potentially harmful elements creeping into food.

cross-merchandising. A display, demo, or product bundle involving products from diverse categories or multiple companies. At the farmers' market, sampling your jam along with one vendor's bread and another's cheese cross-merchandises the other two products.

cross-promotion. An ad or other marketing campaign involving products from diverse categories or multiple companies. Your jam photos may include crackers from a certain producer. Promoting brand-name ingredients is also cross-promotion.

CSA. Abbreviation for *community supported agriculture*. A share of produce sold directly from a farm to a consumer, usually in a box, for a fee that includes weekly delivery or pickup.

direct sales. Selling and shipping to a buyer without a middle party. Selling on third-party online marketplaces where you drop ship products is considered direct.

distributor. A company that purchases products at a distributor price (less than wholesale), then warehouses, sells, and delivers products to wholesale buyers.

drop ship. When you fulfill and ship orders you have received through a third-party catalog or website.

DSD. Abbreviation for *direct-to-store delivery*. Selling and delivering directly to stores rather than through a distributor.

e-commerce. Selling product on the Internet, whether on your own website or third-party websites.

endcap. The coveted, highly visible product display at the end of a store aisle.

export. Selling to markets outside the United States.

fair trade. An organized social movement and market-based approach that aims to help producers in developing countries earn better prices under better trading conditions while practicing sustainability. Products using the Fair Trade USA label must be certified by FairTradeUSA.org.

flexible pouches. Resealable stand-up thick poly bags, an affordable, popular way to package snacks.

food broker. Freelance sales reps who sell multiple product lines into target wholesale accounts. Some specialize in segments such as natural foods, convenience stores, or food service.

food technologist. A trained food science professional.

GF. Abbreviation for *gluten-free*. Avoiding all foods containing wheat, barley, rye, and hybrids like triticale. Visit CeliacDiseaseCenter.org.

GMO. Abbreviation for *genetically modified organisms*. Per the Non-GMO Project, GMOs are organisms that have been created through the gene-splicing techniques of biotechnology, also called *genetic engineering*.

GMP. Abbreviation for *good manufacturing processes*. The FDA specifies GMPs as the minimum sanitary and processing requirements for producing safe and wholesome foods. GMPs detail the methods, equipment, facilities, and controls for producing processed food. The FDA references GMPs when conducting inspections.

Good Food. Refers to sustainably produced, all natural, GMO-free, minimally processed delicious food products.

goodwill. In the context of business, goodwill quantifies the value of your reputation from an accounting perspective. Any goodwill your business creates with customers and the community translates into monetary value, such as if you sell your business.

grab-and-go. Food portioned in sizes that a consumer might buy on impulse to eat on the run.

gross. Revenue, or income, before subtracting costs.

HACCP. Abbreviation for *Hazard Analysis and Critical Control Points*, usually pronounced "HASS-ip." A management system in which food safety is addressed through the analysis and control of biological, chemical, and physical hazards from raw material production, procurement, handling, manufacturing, distribution, and consumption of the finished product. See FDA.gov for more information.

inventory turnover. A measure of the number of times inventory is sold or used in a time period, such as a year. The equation for inventory turnover equals the cost of goods sold divided by the average inventory. Also called *turn.*

liability insurance. Insurance to cover damages resulting from product problems that cause harm, such as a nutshell that breaks a customer's tooth.

markup. Increase in product price above the purchase price or cost.

master case. Large carton holding multiple cases of product (e.g., holding twenty-four cases or displays, each packed with eight units).

mobile payment. Processing credit card purchases through a mobile phone, very handy at events or farmers' markets.

MSRP. Abbreviation for *manufacturer's suggested retail price*. The price at which you believe customers will buy.

natural. Foods that are minimally processed and do not contain any hormones, antibiotics, sweeteners, food colors, or flavorings that were not originally in the food. The lack of official definition means that the term is often misused.

net. Income after subtracting costs.

non-GMO. Free of genetically modified organisms. Visit Nongmoproject.org.

nutrition label. The panel stating ingredients, nutrition facts, and other FDA-regulated information.

open book. When employees and stakeholders can view an organization's "books," or finances, versus the business norm of only allowing management to view financial data.

overhead. The ongoing cost of doing business that usually stays the same monthly, such as employee salaries, rent, and taxes.

P&L. Abbreviation for *profit and loss*. Financial statements outlining revenue and expenses.

pallet. A wooden or sometimes plastic platform that can be stacked and shrink-wrapped with master cases, which a forklift can load and unload.

planogram. Used at retail, this diagram of fixtures and products shows what and where retail products are displayed on store shelves.

POP display. Abbreviation for *point of purchase*. Any in-store product-marketing materials, such as displays and posters, often located at the checkout area.

private label. When one company manufactures a food for stores to market under their own brand names. Visit PLMA.com.

process authority. The person or organization that scientifically establishes thermal processes for low-acid canned foods or processing requirements for acidified foods.

QR code. Abbreviation for *quick response* code. A matrix of black images encoded with text, URL, or other data readable by dedicated QR code readers and smartphones.

retail price. The price that end consumers pay for your product.

sales representative. An employee or contractor who sells your products to various target customers either on commission or salary. Also called *rep*. *Also see* food broker.

sell sheet. A data sheet or brochure with your product line, SKU numbers, descriptions, prices, minimum quantity to qualify for wholesale prices, how to buy, and other relevant information for the wholesale buyer. Also called a *line sheet*.

set. Selection of products within a particular category at a retail store.

shipper. A shipping carton that doubles as a self-sustaining floor display unit.

SKU. Abbreviation for *stock-keeping unit*, or any distinct product you sell that might have its own bar code, or UPC code.

social media. Online services such as Twitter, Facebook, and Pinterest that connect people for easy information sharing.

Specialty Food Association. A business trade association established in 1952 supporting the specialty food industry. Visit SpecialtyFood.com.

specialty foods and beverages. A term coined by the Specialty Food Association for foods with distinct quality, innovation, and style in their category, with originality, authenticity, ethnic or cultural origin, specific processing, ingredients, limited supply, distinctive use, extraordinary packaging, or specific channel of distribution or sales.

trademark. Text or design that is registered and owned by a company, as assigned by the United States Patent and Trademark Office (USPTO).

turn rate. How quickly products sell, or "turn over," within a certain period.

unit. The package or form in which a product is offered for sale, such as one bottle or one six-pack.

UPC. Abbreviation for *universal product code*. Unique product identification codes used for inventory management and ordering.

USP. Abbreviation for *Unique Selling Proposition*, the value only you offer your customer.

USPTO. Abbreviation for *U.S. Patent and Trademark Office*. Visit USPTO.gov for how-tos.

value-added products. Products that command a higher price than the agricultural commodities they were made from. Think oranges into marmalade, beef into jerky, nuts into nut butter.

variable costs. Costs that change depending on your business activities and production, such as utility costs and temporary labor.

vertical integration. Manufacturing everything in one place rather than sourcing externally, perhaps even producing or growing much of what goes into a product.

warehouse. A place to stuff stuff. You may have a warehouse (or a co-packer may have one) to store your products, or you may pay a third-party warehousing company.

wholesale. Selling (or buying) for resale to other customers.

wholesale minimum. The minimum quantity you require buyers to order to get the wholesale price. You can set the minimum anywhere you like; it can be as low as one case.

wholesale price. What a wholesale buyer pays to allow for a profitable retail price.

word-of-mouth marketing. Extremely effective marketing by personal recommendations (provided the word of mouth is positive).

10 EASY FIRST STEPS AND FURTHER READING

TODAY'S THE DAY TO GET STARTED

1 Hop over to GoodFoodGreatBusiness.com for links to resources mentioned in the book and the latest updates.

2 Sign up for the SpecialtyFood.com and NewHope360.com daily e-mails, awesome food-news sources.

3 Sign up for any newsletters specific to your type of food (such as Candy Industry).

4 Plan trips to a Fancy Food Show (visit SpecialtyFood.com) and/or NewHope360 Natural Products Expo West and Expo East (visit NewHope360.com).

5 See what's winning Sofi awards at www.specialtyfood.com/sofi.

6 Visit the Small Business Administration's helpful SBA.gov site whether you're new to business or experienced.

7 Find out if you have a local Small Business Development Center (SBDC) and, if so, find out how it can help.

8 Plan how you'll capture information you gather when researching on the go (in a notebook or on your phone or tablet?) and at home (spreadsheet, sticky notes on a board, notebook, etc.).

9 Get out to markets and/or hop online to see who's doing what and where you'll fit in.

10 Say hello to me at susie@goodfoodgreatbusiness.com or share what you're cooking up on the Good Food Great Business Facebook page.

BOOKS FOR BUDDING ENTREPRENEURS

Alper, Noah, with Thomas Fields-Meyer. *Business Mensch: Timeless Wisdom for Today's Entrepreneur*. Berkeley: Wolfeboro Press, 2009.

Anderson, Chris. *The Long Tail: Why the Future of Business Is Selling Less of More*. New York: Hyperion, 2006.

Burke, Bob, and Rick McKelvey. *Natural Products Field Manual*. Andover: Natural Products Consulting Institute, Updated Ongoing; www.naturalconsulting.com/fieldmanual.

Burlingham, Bo. *Small Giants: Companies That Choose to Be Great Instead of Big*. New York: Portfolio, 2006.

Collins, Jim. *Built to Last: Successful Habits of Visionary Companies*. New York: Harper Business, 2004.

———. *Good to Great: Why Some Companies Make the Leap . . . and Others Don't*. New York: William Collins, 2001.

Conley, Chip. *Peak: How Great Companies Get Their Mojo from Maslow*. San Francisco: Jossey-Bass, 2007.

Cortese, Amy. *Locavesting: The Revolution in Local Investing and How to Profit from It*. Hoboken: John Wiley & Sons, 2011.

Ferriss, Timothy. *The 4-Hour Work Week: Escape 9-5, Live Anywhere, and Join the New Rich*. New York: Harmony, 2009.

Gerber, Michael E. *The E-Myth Revisited: Why Most Small Businesses Don't Work and What to Do About It*. New York: HarperCollins, 1995.

Hall, Stephen F. *From Kitchen to Market: Selling Your Gourmet Food Specialty*. Chicago: Upstart/Dearborn Financial Publishing, 2008.

Hill, Napoleon. *Think and Grow Rich: Your Key to Financial Wealth and Power*. New York: Ballantine Books, 1987.

Horan, Jim. *The One-Page Business Plan*. Berkeley: The One Page Business Plan Company, 2004.

Karbo, Karen. *Julia Child Rules: Lessons on Savoring Life*. Guilford: skirt!, 2013.

Kawasaki, Guy. *Art of the Start: The Time-Tested, Battle-Hardened Guide for Anyone Starting Anything*. New York: Portfolio, 2009.

Mackey, John. *Conscious Capitalism: Liberating the Heroic Spirit of Business*. Boston: Harvard Business School Publishing Corporation, 2013.

McGraw, Philip. *Life Strategies: Doing What Works, Doing What Matters*. New York: Hyperion Books, 1999.

Mcmillen, Tedde. *Million Dollar Cup of Tea.* El Monte: Wbusiness Books, 2009.

Osterwalder, Alexander, and Yves Pigneur, with 470 contributors. *Business Model Generation: A Handbook for Visionaries, Game Changers, and Challengers.* Hoboken: John Wiley & Sons, 2010.

Pollan, Michael. *The Omnivore's Dilemma: A Natural History of Four Meals.* New York: Penguin Press, 2006.

Roam, Dan. *The Back of the Napkin.* New York: Portfolio Trade, 2013.

Schwartz, Barry. *The Paradox of Choice: Why More Is Less.* New York: Harper Perennial, 2005.

Sher, Barbara. *Wishcraft.* New York: Ballantine Books, 2003.

Tasch, Woody. *Inquiries into the Nature of Slow Money.* White River Junction: Chelsea Green Publishing, 2010.

Ü, Elizabeth. *Raising Dough: The Complete Guide to Financing a Socially Responsible Food Business.* White River Junction: Chelsea Green Publishing, 2013.

Underhill, Paco. *What Women Want: The Global Marketplace Turns Female-Friendly.* New York: Simon and Schuster, 2010.

———. *Why We Buy: The Science of Shopping.* New York: Simon and Schuster, 1999.

Weinzweig, Ari. *A Lapsed Anarchist's Approach to Building a Great Business.* Ann Arbor: Zingerman's Press, 2010.

ACKNOWLEDGMENTS
AND MANY THANKS

What made this book equally special and challenging is the sheer volume, variety, and expertise packed into just a few pages. It took a village!

CONTRIBUTING GOOD FOOD ENTREPRENEURS

Layers of knowledge weave through the book, along with detailed stories on these fine folks who make everything from candy to condiments, frozen to raw. Find links to these good folks at GoodFood GreatBusiness.com.

Food companies of all sizes, categories, and locales shared their do's and don'ts, including: Lotus Foods, Alive & Radiant, Oren's Kitchen, YouBar, Effie's Homemade, Peeled Snacks, Lisa's Cookie Shop, Villa Cappelli, Clif Bar & Company, Saffron Road, Mother-in-Law's Kimchi, Simply Nic's, Clarine's Florentines, Nory Candy, Maitelates Alfajores, Numi Organic Tea, P.O.P. Candy, Nuts About Granola, Cake Chicago, The Girl & the Fig, Square Bar, Stonewall Kitchen, Dave's Gourmet, Little Pots & Pans, Saint & Olive, June Taylor Jams, Two Degrees Foods, Punk Rawk Labs, Askinosie Chocolate, Attune Foods, Rooibee Red Tea, Squarebar, Liddabit Sweets, Mary's Gone Crackers, Cooperstown Cookies, Hiball, Mendocino Sea Salt & Seasoning, Paleo People, Vibrant Flavors, Love & Hummus Co., Tasty Bakery, Slather Brand Sauces, Skillet Street Food, Nuts Plus Nuts, Taza Chocolate, Sticky Toffee Pudding Co., Equal Exchange, White Girl Salsa, Das Foods, Happy Girl Kitchen, Black Dinah Chocolatier, Mast Brothers Chocolate, Stone-Buhr Flour, Runa, Peas of Mind, Savory Creations, Droga Confections, Justin's Nut Butter, Mama Baretta, Ocho Candy, Tessemae's All Natural, Sweet Revolution, Poco Dolce, Rustic Bakery, Lusty Monk Mustard, Red Boat Fish Sauce, Terra Verde Farms, Back to the Roots, Amella Caramels, Schoolhouse Kitchen, 18 Rabbits, and more.

RETAILERS, BROKERS, AND DISTRIBUTORS

Zingerman's Community of Businesses: Ari Weinzweig, Brad Hedeman, Maggie Bayless; Bi-Rite Market: Sam Mogannam; The Pasta Shop at Market Hall: Linda Sikorsky; many Whole Foods Market team members; Chelsea Market Baskets: David Porat; Fromagination: Ken Monteleone;

The Epicurean Connection: Sheana Davis; Waterfall Beverages: Douglas Kuehn; Buyer's Best Friend/Joyce Guan; the Foodzie team (acquired by Joyus); and the many kind unnamed sources.

CONTRIBUTING FOOD BUSINESS CONSULTANTS

Deb Mazzaferro, Bob Burke, Jeff Landsman, Anni Minuzzo, Rob Leichman, John Maggiore, Jeff Santos, Jim Horan, and Clay Gordon.

CONTRIBUTING BUSINESS SERVICE PROVIDERS

Specialty Food Association: Ron Tanner and team; Eat My Words: Alexandra Watkins; Miller Creative: Yael Miller; Alyssa Warnock Design; Rowland Heming, packaging designer; Haven Bourque, PR consultant; Amy Sherman, author and blogger; Susan Combs, insurance broker; Susan Whipple, career coach; Laiko Bahrs, culinary consultant.

FOOD FRIENDS, FAMILY, AND COLLEAGUES

Thanks to Laiko Bahrs, Frieda DeLackner, Annelies Zijderveld, Robert Bergstrom, Brett Fisher, Heather Dean, Oren the jam maker, Jane Smith and family, Vanessa Barrington, Arnon Oren, and David Browne. My old Foodzie team: Rob and Emily LaFave, Christina Olson, Nik Bauman, and Nic Rosenberg. Buyer's Best Friend's Adam Sah and Joyce Guan. My expert proofreader sisters, Jeanne and Robin. Food-testing victims and reality checkers Patty, Madi, and Matthew. And my loving and supportive mom, Lillian, and dad, Bob. Thanks to the Hub Berkeley community (especially Jeff the caramel evangelist) and BAM group, whose feedback on the Nutless Professor set me on the right trajectory.

BOOK TEAM: A MUST-READ CONNECT-THE-DOTS STORY

At the judging for the Good Food Awards, chocolate and cookbook maven Alice Medrich suggested that I contact Dianne Jacob for help with my book proposal, when it was just a twinkle in my eye. The proposal went on the back burner until I saw Chronicle Books at the Fancy Food Show and proposed writing the book, then and there at the booth, with no pre-meditation. (Mind you, I grew up shy. Thanks to Toastmasters and improv classes, I can kind of pitch on the fly.)

We connected the dots—it was the right time and place—and suddenly editor Amy Treadwell was tasked with wrangling the immense amount of knowledge I wanted to share into this small book. The project ebbed, flowed, and put my relationships to the test . . . writing about such a fast-changing business (despite the "slow food") is nearly on a par with starting a food business. I've suggested you need to ask for help. I finally did the same. I expected the writing consultant to emerge from the local food-writing community, but then an e-newsletter from perfumer Mandy Aftel caught my eye: Mandy had just landed a book deal. I quickly hit "reply," asking if she knew an editorial consultant. She suggested a freelance resource agency, which connected me immediately with Naomi Luck. Naomi had edited *The Story of Your Life*, a self-help book that Mandy had written years earlier—fabulous reading to manage the "parts" people play in your life. I hired Naomi. She kicked ass. Then I remembered Alice Medrich had given me a copy of *The Story of Your Life*. That's a not-so-unusual story of what my life's like—and why I'm dedicated to helping people connect the dots to make synchronicity happen.

INDEX

A

Advertising, 189

Advisors, 210, 212

AIDAE marketing cycle, 169–70

Allergens, 95

Allstar Organics, 108

Amazon, 136

Amella Caramels, 74, 187–88

Analytics, 203

Angel investors, 226–27

Arora, Nikhil, 180

"Artisaneur" model of production, 41, 44, 117–19

Askinosie, Shawn, 49

Askinosie Chocolate, 49

Awards, 202–3

B

Back-office systems, 206–8

Back to the Roots Mushroom Kits, 180–81

Baretta, Debra, 32–33

Barthel, Alissa, 34–35, 224, 232, 236

Bergstrom, Robert, 151

Bi-Rite Market, 103, 237

Blogs, 176, 182–83

BOLA Granola, 21–23

Brand equity, 74

Branding. See also Logos; Names
authentic stories and, 81–83
components of, 73
do-it-yourself, 73
importance of, 73
packaging and, 88

pricing and, 74
strategy for, 75–76
taglines and, 78–80, 81

Breaking even, 163

Brochures, 181

Brown, Janet, 108

"Business Builder" model of production, 42, 44, 121–28

Business plans
changing, 236
necessity of, 53
sketching out, 234–35
testing, 237
writing formal, 235–36

Business structure
deciding on, 219–22
importance of, 206

Buyer's Best Friend, 136, 145, 148, 188, 199, 202

Buzz, creating, 169

C

Campion, Karin, 42, 158, 211, 226

Case packs, 90

Cash flow, 199–200, 222

Certifications, 96, 104–6

Channel conflict, 167

Chargebacks, 163, 199

Clif Bar, 42, 166–67, 216

Coaches, 210–11

"Community Builder" model of production, 42–43, 44, 117–19

Competitions, small-business, 228

Competitors
co-operating with, 59
discovering, 59–60
hidden, 59
researching, 76–77

tasting party comparing your product to, 70–71

"Connecting the dots," 24–25, 31–33, 238–39

Consultants, 210–11

Content marketing, 179

Contract manufacturers. See Co-packers

Cooperatives, 221

Co-packers
acting as, for other companies, 43, 44
benefits of working with, 121
contracts with, 127–28
definition of, 42
discussions with potential, 125–27
downsides of working with, 121–22
ingredient sourcing and, 106, 128
packaging and, 89, 125
searching for, 124–25
training, 125

Corporations, 220–21

Costco, 43, 54, 153–54, 195

Cost of goods sold, 163

Costs
retailer's total product, 165
shipping, 166
start-up, 206
variable vs. fixed, 163

Craft shows, 140–41

Credit cards, 174, 208, 222

Crochet, Michelle, 74–75

Crowdfunding, 223–24

CSA (Community Supported Agriculture), 139, 142

Customers
communicating with, 193
demographics of, 54
engaging, 170, 193
issues with, 193–94
needs of, 57–59
picturing, 53–57
psychographics of, 54

D

Davis, Kelly, 140, 146–47
Davis, Kris, 147
Dean & DeLuca, 22, 87, 136
Decision-making, 30–31
Discounts, 186–187
Display cases, 89–90
Distributors, 143–44, 154–56
Doerr, Christine, 115–16
Domain names, 172–73
Donations, 164, 196
Dorf, Josh, 49
DPOs (direct public offerings), 224
Droga Confections, 74–75
Drop-shipping, 142

E

Effie's Homemade, 125, 196, 198
80-20 Rule, 31, 70
E-mail, 174, 179–80, 186
Employees, 215–17
Engagement, 170, 193
Entrepreneurs
motivations of, 15–19
readiness to be, 14
sharing and bonding with fellow, 209–10
Equipment, 119

Etsy, 136
Experts, 210
Exporting, 156–58

F

Facebook. See Social media
Fair Trade, 105
Fancy Food Show, 15, 107, 200, 205, 210, 233
FAQs, 175, 176
Farmers' markets, 137–39, 142
FDA
Good Manufacturing Practices (GMP), 114
labeling requirements, 94–95
registering with, 119, 128
Fears, overcoming, 33–34
Festivals, 140–41, 142
Financial consultants, 213
First steps, 10 easy, 245
"5 Staples" concept, 20–23
Flores, Rachel, 16, 80, 140
Food brokers, 147–49
Fox, Betsy, 151
Free fills, 90, 167
Funding, 222–28

G

Gifts, 140, 198
Gluten-free products, 95, 104–5
GMOs (genetically modified organisms), 15, 106
Goals
combining, 27
lofty, 38
prioritizing, 27
S.M.A.R.T., 25–26
Gold, Justin, 18–19, 63–65, 75, 157, 226

Good Food
definition of, 14–15
re-imagining idea of, 237–38
Good Food Awards, 14, 202, 205, 237
Good Manufacturing Practices (GMP), 114
Gordon, Sarah, 232–34
Gross margins, 163
Growth, path to, 134
Guiding principles, 50–51, 82
Gutman, Liz, 19, 184, 211

H

HACCP (Hazard Analysis and Critical Control Points) plan, 114
Hägerström, Anastasia, 87
Harris, Josh, 119–20
Hiball, 93, 214
Hiring, 215–17
Home-based businesses, 16, 41–42
Howell, Heather, 218–19

I

Ingredients
calculating product yield from, 167
certifications and, 104–6
growing, 108
listing, on label, 94–95
managing costs of, 108–10
sourcing, 102–3, 106–8, 128
unacceptable, 103
Insurance
brokers, 213
liability, 220
types of, 222–23
workers' compensation, 217

International sales, 156–58

Interns, 215, 216

Investors, 224, 226–27

J

Jacobsen, Marty, 108

Justin's Nut Butter, 18, 19, 63–65, 75, 157, 158, 226

K

KATZ Farm, 185, 186

Kiamilev, Emir and Elena, 74, 187–88

Kickstarter. *See* Crowdfunding

King, Jen, 19, 211

King, Jonathan, 40–41, 138

Kosher certification, 105–6

Kucirek, Scott, 68

L

Labeling requirements, 94–95

La Mar, Bob and Lora, 16, 82

Landing pages, 186

Lanphier, Sarah, 231

Lawyers, 213

Lee, Ken, 49–50

LeValley, Carol, 119–20

Levine, Caryl, 49–50

Liability insurance, 220

Liddabit Sweets, 18, 19, 184, 211

Little Bee Pops, 169, 182

Litwin, Jill, 106, 122–24, 127

LLCs (limited liability companies), 220

Loans, 224–26

Location
renting vs. owning, 118–19
selecting, 112, 117–18

Logos
branding strategy and, 76
designing, 81
testing, 80

Loss leaders, 164

Lotus Foods, 50

Love & Hummus Co., 83, 174

L3Cs (low-profit limited liability companies), 220

Lusty Monk, 140, 146–47

M

Magazines, 184, 189

Maitelates Alfajores, 135, 232

Mama Baretta, 32–33

Mantras, 39

Marketing
advertising, 189
bloggers and, 182–83
cause-related, 179–80
content, 179
cycle, 169–70
goals, 170, 171
national press mentions, 184
online, 172–80, 185–86
planning strategy for, 170–72
press releases, 183–84
printed materials, 181–82
promotions, 186–87
public relations, 183
target audience for, 171

Market research, 27–30

Markets, selling at, 137–39

Markoff, Katrina, 176

Mary's Gone Crackers, 39, 60, 107, 161, 226–27, 231

Master cases, 90

Mendocino Sea Salt & Seasoning, 16, 82

Miller, Michele, 21–23

Mission statements, 38–40

Money. *See* Cash flow; Costs; Funding; Profits

N

Names
choosing, 77–80
hierarchy of, 78
testing, 80
trademarking, 81

Natural Products Expo West and Expo East, 107, 200, 205, 210

Neo Cocoa, 115–16

Newsletters, 179

Nirvelli, Julie, 174, 225

Nondisclosure agreements (NDAs), 127, 215

Non-GMO Project, 106

Nonprofits
as business structure, 221
as partners, 115

Nutritional analysis, 94, 130

Nuts About Granola, 39, 103, 115, 186, 231–32

O

Ocho Candy, 17–18, 68–69

Order forms, 182

Orders
fulfilling, 197–98
repeat, 199

Oren, Arnon, 115

Oren's Kitchen, 115

Organic certification, 104

Overhead, 163

P

Packaging
filling and, 89

importance of, 86–87
information on, 88, 93–97
innovative, 16–17
minimum production runs for, 89–90
prices for, 99
producing, 98–99
prototypes of, 97, 98
purposes of, 88
ready-made vs. customized, 88
starting to think about, 86
sustainability and, 91–93
testing, 97–98
types of, 92–93
Parties
  as distribution option, 140, 142
  tasting, 70–71
Partners
  bringing on, 211–12
  as business structure, 221
  nonprofits as, 115
Part-time businesses, 24
Peas of Mind, 106, 122–24, 127
Permits, 114
Pham, Cuong, 150–51
Photos, 177, 212
Pinterest, 173, 176, 177
Poco Dolce Confections, 91
P.O.P. Candy, 16, 80, 88, 140–41
Press kits, 175
Press releases, 183–84
Price lists, 182
Prices
  brand equity and, 74
  delivered, 166
  incorrect, 20, 160
  sales projections and, 160–61
  setting, 161–68

value and, 162
  wholesale, 166
Privacy policy, 176
Private labels, 43
Production. *See also* Co-packers
  choosing method of, 116–18, 121–28
  equipment for, 119
  licensed, safe, and sanitary, 114–15
  location for, 112, 117–19
  models of, 41–44
  nutrient profiles and, 130
  product testing and, 129
  rules of thumb for, 112–13
  scaling recipes for, 113–14
Product line
  defining, 69–70
  depth and breadth of, 60–63, 113
  expanding, 167
  pricing within, 167
Product strategies, forming, 60–63, 65–68, 69–70
Product testing, 129
Product yield, calculating, 167
Profits
  definition of, 163
  donating percentage of, 164
  guiding principles and, 50
Promise, 21, 50
Promotions, 185–87
Public relations, 183, 212
Punk Rawk Labs, 34–35, 178, 182, 206, 211–12, 224, 232, 236

Q
QR (Quick Response) codes, 96

R
Radio, 184
Recipes
  family, 15–16
  scaling, for production, 113–14
Red Boat Fish Sauce, 17, 32, 150–51
Research, 27–30
Retailers
  pricing by, 165–66
  selling to, 143, 144–46
Reverse-flowchart technique, 27, 31
Ring, Denis, 68–69
Rooibee Red Tea, 90, 200, 218–19
Runa Guayusa, 221–22
Rustic Bakery, 119–20

S
Sabel, Hugh and Sandi, 141
Sales
  direct-to-consumer, 134, 135–42
  through distributors, 143–44, 154–56
  donating percentage of, 164
  expenses, 163
  international, 156–58
  online, 135–37, 141, 174
  projecting, 160–61
  to retailers, 143, 144–46
  to supermarket chains, 152–54
  tracking, 204
Sales reps, 150
Samples, 194–96
Savory Creations, 42–43, 62–63, 225
Schoolhouse Kitchen, 228
Search engines, 176, 178
Sell sheets, 181

Service culture, cultivating, 193–94

Service marks, 81

Shelf life, 88, 130

Shiloh Farms, 115

Shipping, 166, 197–98

SKU (stock-keeping unit), 95–96

Sky, Donna, 83, 174

Slogans, 39, 79

Slow Money movement, 227

S.M.A.R.T. goals, 25–26

Smith, Patsy, 228

Smith, Wendy Wheeler, 228

Snyder, Liz, 169

Social media, 96, 172, 179, 185, 212

Sofi Award, 202

Software, 206–8

Sole proprietors, 220

Sonoma Syrup, 42, 107, 158, 211, 226

Sound bites, 184

Specialty foods
definition of, 15
perils and paradoxes of, 19–20

Squarebar, 232–34

Start-up costs, 206

Stone-Buhr Flour Company, 49

Stonewall Kitchen, 40–41, 61, 138, 143, 144

Stories, writing authentic, 81–83

Stott, Jim, 40–41, 138

Stum, Jeff, 218–19

Supermarket chains, 152–54

Support system, 209–17

Sustainability, 50, 91–93

Sweet Revolution, 87

T

Taglines, 39, 78–80, 81

Takizawa, Beverly and Douglas, 62, 225

Tasting boxes, 136

Tasting parties, 70–71

Terra Verde Farms, 141

Tessemae's All Natural, 45, 144, 225

Testimonials, 175

Time management, 203

Trademarks, 81

Trader Joe's, 43, 53, 106, 154

Trade shows, 107, 200–202

Traditions, preserving, 17

TV, 184

Twitter. *See* Social media

Two Degrees Foods, 39, 82, 164, 180

U

Unique selling proposition (USP), 67

UPCs (Universal Product Codes), 95–96

V

Value propositions, 67–69

Velez, Alex, 180

Vendors, choosing, 213–15

Vetter, Greg, 45, 144, 225

Video, 177, 212

Vision, achieving your, 40–41

Vision statements, 46–48

Vosges Haut-Chocolat, 19, 79, 176

W

Waiste, Bill, 16, 80, 140

Waldner, Mary, 107, 161, 227, 231

Warnock, Alyssa, 93, 214

Websites
analytics for, 203
contact information on, 175, 178
content for, 175–76
creating, 173–74, 215
domain name for, 172–73
landing pages, 186
with online stores, 137, 141, 174
search engine optimization for, 178
testing, 176, 179
tips for, 176–77

Weddings, 140, 142

White Girl Salsa, 174, 225

Whole Foods, 43, 45, 53, 103, 106, 123, 143, 144, 147, 149, 152–53, 180, 194, 215, 218, 225

Wholesale
cash flow and, 199–200
definition of, 142
through distributors, 143–44, 154–56
meeting buyers at trade shows, 200–202
pricing, 166
to retailers, 143, 144–46
to supermarket chains, 152–54
tips for, 198–99
typical path for, 143–44

Wiley, Kathy, 91

Workers' compensation insurance, 217

Y

YouTube, 173, 177, 191

Z

Zingerman's, 46, 51, 135, 136, 152, 165, 210, 216, 237

Zubia, Maite, 135, 232

Susie Wyshak is a Good Food business strategist and one-woman think tank based in Oakland, California. She has sourced artisan food for several online market-places, planned (and scrapped) her own snack-food business, led the Confections category for the Good Food Awards, and worked on the Fair Trade cocoa program, and wrote her MBA thesis on Consumer Attitudes Toward Giving Chocolate as a Gift. Meet Susie and connect the dots at GoodFoodGreatBusiness.com

||||||||||||||||||||||||||||||||||||||||||||||||||||||||||||

Chronicle Books publishes distinctive books and gifts. From award-winning children's titles, bestselling cookbooks, and eclectic pop culture to acclaimed works of art and design, stationery, and journals, we craft publishing that's instantly recognizable for its spirit and creativity. Enjoy our publishing and become part of our community at www.chroniclebooks.com.